Praise for *Experiencing Chronic Pain in Society*

Lous Heshusius' first book, *Inside Chronic Pain*, became a life line to me and my wife and family and a vital anchor to educate people all around us. I have been waiting with great anticipation for her follow up. And it is even better! It describes the way I am forced to live, and the people I try to communicate with in great detail and accuracy. An eye opener for all who live with pain AND for everyone who deals with us in one way or another.

    Tobias Smit, person living with chronic pain

This powerful book shows that besides more effective medical interventions we also urgently need a more thorough understanding of the lived experience of chronic pain – what factors beyond the biological contribute to suffering and how suffering is often compounded by those who desire to help -- doctors, researchers, insurance companies, even self help groups. *Experiencing Chronic Pain in Society* should be read by everyone touched by pain, which whether we'd like it or not, includes every single one of us.

    David Biro, MD PhD
    Author of *The Language of Pain*

Writing with gusto and reality, Heshusius lays out a societal model that poses the question: Who holds the power to define and represent the invisible condition of chronic pain? Clinicians, researchers, insurers-- all impose their professional frames onto the chronic pain experience. Heshusius elegantly argues that such impositions often trivialize and function as disease factors by themselves. It's terrific to hear the voice of one who not only lives with pain but is able to tease apart the complexity of the experience. Her insights inform how professionals and others might become part of the solution. This provocative thesis really asks the question of anyone in contact with those living with chronic pain: To what extent is your input a disease factor?

    Coralie Wales, PhD President
    Chronic Pain Australia

This is a remarkable and important book within the field of chronic pain! Heshusius writes incisively and convincingly about an important missing piece in our understanding of chronic pain: the constituting role that societal factors play in chronic pain. Politicians, researchers and clinicians need to read this book and reflect seriously on the reasons why this is still a missing piece in the 'puzzle of pain.'

     Lennard Voogt, PhD
     University of Applied Sciences, Rotterdam
     Author of *De Ervaringswereld van Patienten met*
     Chronische Pijn (The Life World of Patients with Chronic Pain)

I have lived with constant pain since 1996 when my beloved horse tripped and rolled over me. Reading Lous' books has made me feel less lonely. She lets me know that my thoughts are not "strange" or "abnormal." Her books have taken me off the path to suicide. I will continue to carry my burden of pain but I now know that I am not alone.

     Liesl Fulton, person living with pain

As a family physician I "fell" into pain management after a hard working man who had lost his job due to a workplace injury, began to cry in my office... Lous Heshusius first book *Inside Chronic Pain* became a must read for all my students and pain patients. This time, Heshusius proposes a societal model that lays out a wide range of societal forces impacting chronic pain: From patronizing self help messages to disbelief by healthcare professionals and researchers, from stigma to suicide, and more. Read this powerful book if you want to understand chronic pain.

     Ruth E. Dubin MD, PhD
     Co-Chair Project ECHO Ontario chronic pain

Experiencing Chronic Pain
in
Society

Lous Heshusius

Book design by Graphics by Erick, San Luis Obispo, CA

To order additional copies of this book contact:
Amazon Corporation
www.Amazon.com

Author contact information:
Lous Heshusius
2000 Oak Way
Arroyo Grande, CA 93420
lheshus@me.com

For all living beings who cannot escape chronic pain

You have failed in the most base and human of ways–you have not imagined the lives of others

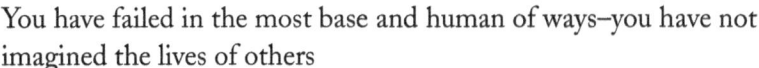

Protagonist, Michael Cunningham, *By Nightfall*

Contents

Preface and acknowledgments

There was a moment while doing research for "Inside Chronic Pain," my memoir about living with pain since a 1996 near fatal car accident, that I saw the need for the present book in a flash. It happened when reading the transcript of the 2003 broadcast "The Culture of Pain" in the series IDEAS by the Canadian Broadcast Corporation. In this broadcast, a physician –I'll call him Doctor D– is asked how his pain patient is doing. His patient, who lives with severe pain since a major accident, has just told us that she has lost everything in her life – her career, her partner, her social life, her active lifestyle, her sense of self. Responding to the question as to how his patient is doing, Doctor D says:

> Relatively well. But I think that we have to consult her psychiatric physician… and maybe try a new anti-depressant because she's really depressed. Every time I see her after sitting for a while she is crying. It's really incredible because it starts with a smile, and (then) she just breaks down… (p.16).

His patient going from smiling to suddenly crying presented Doctor D with a paradox. A puzzle. Smiling and crying don't go together.

For me there was no paradox. No contradiction. I had gone from smiling to crying, without knowing that would happen, so many times myself. There wasn't a framework in Dr. D's head that could contain *both* crying and smiling. There was in mine: my life, too, was in chaos. As with Doctor D's patient, everything had been lost. My emotions were upside down. Little things could trigger emotional outbursts. And big things, in my numb moments, could pass by me without noticing them. Severe ongoing pain had crumbled the rational framework by which I had lived.

This does *not* mean that I was irrational. Or hysterical. I need to be clear about this, lest the psychiatrically inclined reader will assign to me a personality disorder of some kind or another. In fact, my behavior was perfectly normal: given relentless daily severe pain, the inability of the medical world to help, the ignorance on the part of others, the willful denial by insurance companies, the loss of career and social life – anyone would react as Doctor D's patient did, and as I did.

More than once have I seen a person living with chronic pain going from smiling to crying, and I think: she must be overloaded; she can't bear the pain anymore; perhaps she has a letter from her insurance in her purse, still unread, for she fears her claim is denied again; perhaps she has trouble keeping her job as her employer has refused to accommodate her; perhaps her marriage is falling apart because of her pain; perhaps she can't tolerate the side effects of drugs and the thought of being prescribed still another kind of pill scares her; perhaps her best friend has not called for weeks and she feels a loneliness so deep that it smothers her; perhaps she has just felt a sharp increase in pain sensation; perhaps her teenage children play their music loud which makes her headaches worse, perhaps... perhaps... Perhaps several of these things went through Dr. D's patient's mind as her smile changed into tears. Perhaps the thought of death was swirling around in her head...

I wanted to say to Dr. D: Go and live with your patient for a week. Be a fly on the wall, day and night, witnessing everything as a good anthropologist would, and you will find the sudden shift from smiling to crying completely understandable. You will understand it is not a symptom of a personality disorder, or a mood disorder, requiring yet another pill. For you would be witnessing the chaos we live with, the many unbelievable challenges of all kinds, and you will understand why the crying is always already going on underneath the smile.

Reading this doctor's reaction made me realize that he had only an extremely narrow set of parameters available within which to make sense of his patient's behavior and a narrow range of options how to approach her pain problems. We needed far more complex models, I thought, so Doctor D would have had a wide array of possible explanations in his head as to why his patient went from smiling to sudden crying and would not have thought it was "incredible." He would have already been tuned in to the realities of her life that directly impact pain, prepared to carefully listen, ask helpful questions, give sensible advice, send her to someone who could help her with her practical problems and provide guidance as to how to handle the societal forces impacting her pain. He might even have become an advocate in the wider society trying to counter the ignorance of employers, lawyers, insurers, and of society at large. Instead, the explanatory models for chronic pain he had available to him made him send her back to a psychiatrist for still another pill.

There was another moment that reinforced the need I perceived for the present book which happened during a class I took in self help pain management. At the beginning of the first class, we went around the circle, introducing ourselves and responding to the question of what chronic pain meant to us. People mentioned the isolation resulting from their pain; the fact that no one understood them; their friends had fallen by the wayside; their marriage was falling apart; they grieved over losing their job. They spoke of descending into poverty.

Yet, the activities we engaged in, and the information in the workbook, dealt exclusively with our bodies and with a range of psychological processes. Whenever we brought up our many problems caused by societal ignorance or institutional maltreatments, our stories were ignored and the conversation was refocused on our feelings, and on the need to distract ourselves and to replace our "negative" thoughts with positive ones. I started to realize I was witnessing what I have come to think of as the over-psychologizing of chronic pain: the pushing away of those contexts in our lives that often increase our pain while attributing all problems solely to our psyche. Thus, while the world around us often makes my pain worse and stands in the way of getting better, sitting in that circle we were only allowed to address what were seen to be our individual thoughts and emotions presumably severed from the actual contexts that brought them about.

All my reflections and analysis in this book, as in my memoir, are based in actual experience, situated in specific time and place. Initially, I thought the many horrible things that happened to me, including in my interactions with the world of medicine, were unique to my experience. But based on the feedback to my memoir, I now know that my story is the typical story. The following statements are among the feedback I have received: "Now I know I belong somewhere." "You have written my story." "Thank you for writing our story." "I felt a jot of recognition at every turn." "I identify with everything you write." "I feel not so alone anymore." "Finally someone has put my pain into words." "I just wanted to say a million thank yous for putting into words what I could not." "I cried throughout the book." "Now I know that the experiences I have gone through are not isolated to my own chronic pain struggle." "This is astonishingly accurate." "Thank you for giving those of us who struggle a voice." "My picture could have been on the front of the book."

"The stories are so, so familiar." "I feel as if the writer is telling my story along with every chronic pain patient out there." "I feel better for knowing that someone else can identify with my experiences." "Between my mother and me we have experienced everything you write." "Every page … reflect yet another turn in the road I've already traveled. It was oddly comforting to know that someone else has spent nights living from one minute to the next…" A pain specialist wrote me that he had heard numerous stories like mine. Had his patients had the motivation and ability to write, he said, they would have written a similar story. Major research reports, such as the 2011 report by the Institute of Medicine, "Relieving pain in America: A Blueprint for Transforming, Prevention, Care, Education, and Research," further underline the commonality of my experiences. Hence, I have approached the writing of this book from a collective voice, often using "we" instead of "I."

I have cherished the many contacts I have developed with others who live with pain. Their experiences and understandings show up throughout this work. I want to particularly thank Leslie Broun, Tobias Smit, and Liesl Fulton for our in-depth talks about what it means to live with pain and for their feedback to several chapters. For the impact their writings on the lived experience of chronic pain have had on me, I thank Professors Arthur Frank and Lennard Voogt, Dr. David Biro and Dr. Coralie Wales. I am grateful to Dr. James Henry for our many fruitful conversations over the years about issues addressed in this book. I thank Alain Vincent for his helpful feedback on my "bashing" of the pharmaceutical industry.

I look forward to responses that highlight shared experiences and that fill in what I may have missed given the complexity of a societal model of chronic pain.

L.H.

HOW WE TALK –AND DON'T TALK– ABOUT CHRONIC PAIN

THE CASE FOR A SOCIETAL MODEL

1   *Models of chronic pain – lives lived in chronic pain*

> All readers and creators of narratives reserve the right to resist narrative, to recast cultural stories so that they suit our preferences or to reject stories we find inadequate.
>
> Daniel Carr, John Loeser & David Morris (Eds.)
> *Narrative, Pain, and Suffering*

The purpose of this book is straightforward: to point to the need for a broader narrative within which to understand the experience of chronic pain and the societal conditions that stand in the way of more effective solutions. A broader framework needs to be grounded in the actual experiences of the person living with pain, experiences both personal and social.

I have lived with daily pain for over 20 years, six of those years with severe pain day and night.[1] I still suffer from severe pain for stretches of time almost every day, particularly in the early morning hours. I have widely traveled the mazes of pain medicine and pain management–getting lost, lost and lost again–and I have become deeply concerned with what is *not* addressed within the parameters of existing models of pain management. After years of seeing doctors, specialists, therapists, and more doctors, specialists, and therapists, and having attended pain management programs and read self help books, I feel a great deal of my pain experience takes place in the enormous gaps that exist between what existing models of chronic pain and approaches to pain management offer on the one hand, and how the bodily pain I live with is impacted by social and societal forces on the other hand. Existing models do not incorporate these social and societal forces which often constitute disease factors as powerful as what is attributed to me as "an individual" (that is, to tissue damage, thoughts, emotions, or brain functions).[2]

Within the context of this book, I use the word "model" to refer to a formalized framework constructed to understand what can (1) help to relieve pain; (2) make chronic pain worse; or (3) stand in the way of accessing pain relief.

Of course, I –and the millions like me– continue to hope for a medical or pharmaceutical breakthrough. But no such breakthrough is imminent, although its coming is often implied. As David Morris aptly notes, chronic pain patients may be seriously deceived to think that relief is just around the corner.[3] "The promise of an imminent cure, continually deferred, in some ways makes a difficult situation even more difficult," says Morris. Exactly.

Given this state of affairs, it becomes imperative to look into as many closets as possible, and examine all societal forces that stand in the way of accessing pain relief as well as those that directly make our pain worse by agitating an already wound-up hypersensitive nervous system, pushing it beyond a pain threshold. Such forces must be considered actual disease factors. Existing models that explain chronic pain focus on various aspects of the individual in pain. They do not explicitly address these societal disease factors. In the literature on chronic pain in general, societal forces that contribute to chronic pain, if noted at all, are rarely examined. Further, as I will show in later chapters, they are avoided altogether in self help programs which are characteristically based on 'positive psychology' and on models of individual responsibility. By keeping silent about the day-to-day societal forces that push a given person in pain over pain thresholds, these forces are inadvertently strengthened and empowered.

In referring to chronic pain as, in part, a societal process, I am not referring to cultural and historical accounts of the meanings of pain, which David Morris and Elaine Scarry have done so brilliantly.[4] Nor am I referring to the values and calculations the conservative and liberal political parties bring to bear on deciding whose pain is real and whose is fraudulent, who deserves treatment and who doesn't, political processes extensively chronicled by Keith Wailoo.[5] Nor am I referring to advocacy work. Pain advocacy is very important, offering support, information, giving a voice to people in pain, working with legislators, offering social networking, suggesting pain management strategies. But it does not offer formal models to help us understand the chronic pain experience in this society.

In this book I am referring to social and societal forces, attitudes, institutions, and incidents operating daily "on the ground," directly impacting our individual lives in pain of each and everyone of us. To pain-related encounters that happen every day in the concreteness of our lives and which stand in the way of pain relief and all too often make the actual pain worse. Of course, these every day experiences, at various levels and in various ways, tie into the web of cultural and political patterns that have provided a range of contradictory views on who has standing to judge and to speak for and about pain.[6] As Wailoo notes, people living with pain carry the burden of being "props" in the political theatre.

Chronic pain is a real-life-sensitive disease to a degree very few other diseases are. Cancer, AIDS, diabetes, heart disease, while they may be linked to social and societal conditions in how they came about, do not get worse or better by the hour, even by the minute, depending on social and societal forces as chronic pain often does. Other major diseases and their trajectories have a certain stability to them. There is a more or less known course of the disease, a prognosis, a treatment, all of which are largely independent of daily and hourly circumstances. But for those suffering from chronic pain, the circumstances of the day, of the hour, for some of us even of the moment (noise, a doctor who is callous, music played too loud) can worsen the actual pain, which, from the perspective of the lived experience, is the disease.

Acute pain on the other hand is not real life sensitive, it simply is (though it may well be caused by real life incidents). It has a cause, and in most cases can be eliminated by addressing the cause. Acute pain lands us in the doctor's office. Chronic pain keeps us in the midst of society where many pain-related forces directly impact our pain. Chronic pain can only be understood as it plays itself out in the full swing of life.

I have come to see that explanatory models of chronic pain and approaches in pain management must strive to be congruent with the day-to-day lived experience of those living with pain. To the extent they are not, they will miss major opportunities to positively affect our lives. For when models of chronic pain are not congruent with the day-to-day realities and truths of our lives, the research they stimulate will have limited relevance, and the well documented incongruence that characterizes a good deal of the physician-pain patient relationship as well as formal pain management programs will continue.

Although I am an academic, writing this book has not been an academic exercise. Nor is it a critique of the details of every model. Nor is my purpose to propose improvements for each model though I do hope existing models will improve, in part by becoming more willing to open up to the social and societal realities and truths of our lives. This book came about because of a body and a soul damaged by pain which have to live in the world nevertheless and which are greatly impacted by that world. I am not just a "self" in pain as existing models would have it. I live in a self/other world, the forces of which impact the pain at every turn. I need research to address that. I need doctors to understand that.

Chronic pain is so complex, so complicated, multi-layered, embodied yet hidden, unpredictable, involving every level of life, from cell to society, and so costly in every way imaginable, that nothing should be excluded in considering what influences it and what stands in the way of pain relief. Having lived for over 20 years (that is, 7325 days) with severe pain almost every day, I am taken aback when I read the title of a book or web site that says "Pain Explained" or "Explain Pain." If pain can be "explained," then why do I and millions of others still live with severe pain regardless an array of treatments based on these explanations? Whose pain is "explained"?

As we will see, existing models propose a direct relationship between their explanation of pain and particular treatments. If the model's explanation of pain would be correct, the treatments based on it should work. Yet, existing models have not rendered effective and lasting pain relief for the majority of us. To state that pain has been "explained" deceives society and physicians alike and lulls us all into a complacency that only serves to maintain the status quo. Couldn't one of the problems be the notion of "explaining" itself?

"Explaining" typically points to the assumption of linear and causal relations between variables, an assumption central to standard research methodology. As such it refers to the statistical ability of researchers to say: Variable "A" leads directly to variable "B." "Variable" is defined by Wikipedia as "a logical set of attributes." It distinctly does not refer to the lived experience. For there to be a "variable," the lived experience first has to be stripped from its immediate, concrete, embodied experience so it can be defined into measurable factors. This is a process of abstraction and quantification referred to as operationalization. Essentially, something that is not directly measurable is defined as a factor that is measurable. In this way of thinking about knowledge, the resulting variables can then be statistically manipulated into explanatory frameworks that can lead to formalized models.

Acute pain can often be so explained. There typically is a detectable cause, a direct relationship between two or more variables which can be deemed accurate when the treatment applied accordingly takes the pain away. But what if chronic pain cannot be so explained because of its non-linear, complex, real-life-sensitive nature? What if the forces that interact with each other to produce chronic pain, or to keep it going, are too complex to be represented by linear relations? What if chronic pain is a process of both physical pain and of living-in-the-world, a process that needs to be both witnessed and examined for all its social, political, and societal dynamics? A process that, pain being invisible and unmeasurable, requires empathetic listening and imagination on the part of others?

Existing models

When using the phrase "existing models" I am referring to the three major conceptual models in pain medicine. The *biomedical* model, familiar to every one, its 'cultural story' based on the adoption of Cartesian body/mind dualism. Its parameters focus on the body in pain and what a healthcare professional can do about it. The psychosocial model which, in contrast, focuses on certain psychological features –thoughts, emotions, perceptions, behaviors– that people in chronic pain are said to exhibit and, presumably, also on the "social" aspects of a patient life (I will argue that the social aspects default to the psychological). Then, more recently, there are what I think of as brain models, models that focus on how the brain and central nervous system are actively involved in the generation, modification, or the blocking of chronic pain, which can lead to brain modulating practices that may help lower pain intensity. Various sub-models stay within the broader parameters of these three models.[7] The parameters of each of these models restrict who can be held responsible for pain relief.

Figure 1 shows a simple representation of these models:

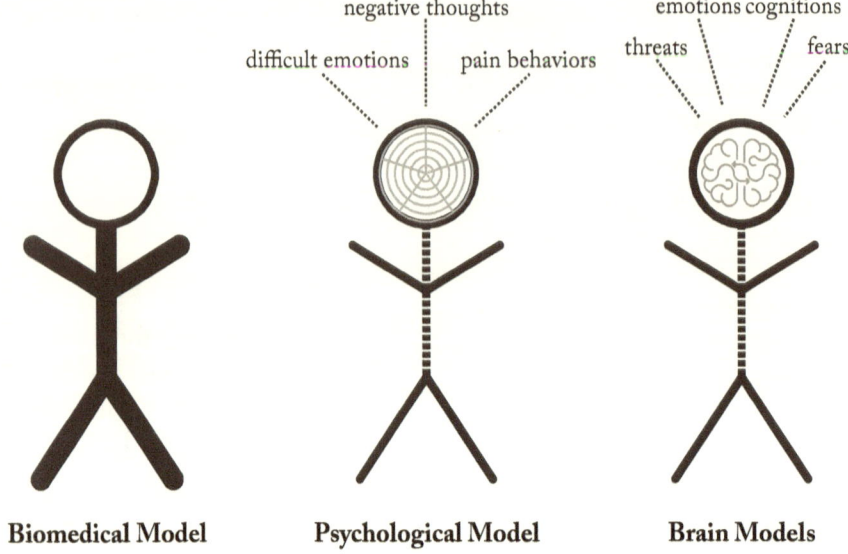

Biomedical Model   Psychological Model   Brain Models

Figure 1: Existing models of chronic pain

Biomedical model

The parameters of the biomedical model are straightforward: grounded in the body/mind dualism of the Cartesian heritage, the parameters are drawn tightly around the body in pain. And when we hear our physician say, as one of mine did, "We are out of options" when traditional body oriented interventions he had carried out had not worked (nerve blocks, a rhizolysis, injections with chemicals), we have literally bumped into the model's parameters beyond which it cannot go. When the surgeon of a pain patient I met suggested operation number 23 for a back problem she had for years, one must wonder, as a colleague of mine remarked, what he was thinking. Something like, "Well, let's see. Twenty two operations have done no good. Let's try number 23." The surgeon is recycling the only model he knows. The model does not point him elsewhere. He has bumped into its parameters.

The biomedical model holds that pain can be traced to a pathological cause. Pain is a response to tissue damage. With acute pain, tissue damage can often be found. If it cannot, then the power of the model ends. Alternative body-focused approaches are tried (massage, acupuncture, chiropractic treatments) and if these do not help either, there is nowhere else to go but to the other side of the Cartesian dualism: the psyche. Hence, when the body refuses to heal, the default setting is to be sent to a psychologist or a psychiatrist.

Psycho(social) model

The parameters of the psychosocial model are not what the label says they are. After 20 years of seeing physicians, therapists, reading in pain management, and attending pain management programs, I have had to conclude that I never can find the "social" in the "psychosocial." I finally figured out that the "social" refers to us talking to professionals about the adversarial social and societal forces that stand in the way of pain relief. But rather than exploring ways to solve the actual problems we encounter, we are routinely redirected to *our* feelings and emotions about these problems. What often originates in the social/societal spheres and unduly –and very often unjustly– agitates our already hyper-sensitized nervous system (a core characteristic of chronic pain), thus increasing pain, ends up being translated as our psychological problems.

Thus we are told how to "manage" our anger and frustration, no matter these emotions are often a direct outcome of social, societal and medical ignorance, incompetence, injustice, and even willful neglect. It all becomes our weakness, even our pathology. "Difficult emotions" or "negative thoughts" (as they are typically referred to in pain management programs) hang strangely and abstractly in the air, emptied of their context. We are supposed to deal with them as if they exist outside of the social and societal contexts within which they emerged. When a pain-related social or societal problem was brought up in the pain management programs I attended, the response by those in charge invariably was: "How do you feel about that?" Or, "How do you deal with your anger about that?" The "real" problem was seen to be our emotions and our frustrations, severed from the context that gave rise to them. The context itself was not up for discussion or analysis. The "social" of the "psychosocial" model falls by the wayside.

The psychosocial model then defaults to the psychological. It functions within the same oppositional body/mind dualism as does the biomedical model. Once the focus shifts away from the body, there is no other option to turn to than the territory of the mind and the psyche. The responsibility for pain relief in the psycho(social) model, as in the biomedical model, lies with the healthcare professional and the person living with pain. Actual, concrete social and societal forces that adversely make our disease worse are not held responsible in this model either.

I was glad to see someone else raise the "where-is-the-social-in-the-psychosocial-model" question. The Health Skills Weblog, asks, "How 'social' is your biopsychosocial model?"[8] The answer is, "little if any." Qualitative studies of the delivery of healthcare by twenty five clinicians in the United Kingdom showed that although they said they adhered to the biopsychosocial model, they essentially used only cognitive/behavioral based management strategies. "The majority of interventions were biomedical or psychological – the social got left behind." Given my own experiences, and those of many pain patients I have come to know, it is clear this also holds for pain management in North America. In essence, we do not have a psychosocial model. Instead, we have only a psychological model.

Brain models

The discovery of the modulating powers of the brain has introduced complexity and non-linearity into the understanding of the brain's role in chronic pain. Risking oversimplification, let me offer a brief description of the Gate Control theory and the Neuromatrix theory that placed the inaccuracies of previous input-output models, which assume linear cause and effect relations, into focus. The Gate Control theory as developed by Ronald Melzack and Patrick Wall proposed how central nervous mechanisms –nerve "gates" in the spinal cord– modulate noxious sensory input (by either blocking it, altering it, or allowing it to travel on) before it evokes pain perception. This theory integrates upstream processes with downstream modulation from the brain, according to a person's mood, environment, past experience, and context.[9]

The Neuromatrix theory as further developed by Melzack sees the brain as a self-organizing and self-generating organ, involving neural networks which integrate multiple inputs to produce the output pattern that evokes pain.[8] This is made possible by the brain's learning capacity, or its plasticity, as the brain creates changes in the brain itself, which accounts for the generation of longer lasting pain activity. The "multiple inputs" include sensory inputs, cognitive events and interpretations of the situation, emotional inputs, and the body's stress regulation systems.

Many readers will understand the fine points of these brain models far better than I do. The reason for noting them here is to say, that from the perspective of living with chronic pain in the midst of society, the same problem exists as in the earlier models: referring to stressful emotional and cognitive states that can increase pain in the absence of making explicit their groundedness in actual social and societal situations that gave rise to them in the first place, make these emotional and cognitive states appear as things by themselves – dislodged from their contexts. The fact that they might have been generated because a letter from the insurance arrived with unjust news, or because the employer, not understanding chronic pain, did not want to make the needed scheduling adjustment, leading to job loss, or a doctor behaved ignorantly and callously, or any of the other pain-related societal problems, none of that seems to matter. The adversarial forces that give rise to these stressful thoughts and emotions are, again, transferred onto the psyche of the person in pain, to be dealt with psychologically. While the brain models have cast a more complex lens on our brains-in-pain, they do not speak either to concrete actual social and societal forces that impact our pain states.

Melzack does refer to the "hassles of every day life," that influence cortisol release which in turn can contribute to pain and fatigue.[11] I believe Melzack is referring to the common daily hassles all people have to deal with, not specifically to the unjust social and societal hassles people living with chronic pain encounter because of their chronic pain. The stress regulation system with its complex, delicately balanced interactions, Melzack states, is an integral part of the "multiple contributions" that give rise to chronic pain.[12] But what, exactly, are the "multiple contributions" that give rise to chronic pain?

Melzack would surely have to consider our terrible experiences with insurers, with disbelieving employers, with the lack of access to professional pain care, or with descending into poverty, as major "stresses" and "hassles" specific to the chronic pain experience and increasing the actual pain. But no such social and societal stresses are noted. The model stops with the psychology of the individual. That makes sense of course as Melzack is a psychologist. It was not his professional task to also engage ethnography and social analysis to extend his theories to the social and societal particulars of our real lives in pain.

However, someone needs to go there, needs to go beyond "the individual," beyond the psyche, to pain-related societal stresses. To not do so reduces these societal stresses, that initially have nothing to do with our psychology – to our psychology. *We* become the problem. No longer the insurance company. The employer. The doctor. Society. This is misdirected responsibility. It points to the need for a truly interdisciplinary approach to chronic pain – an interdisciplinarity that includes fields of research that directly address the actual specific social and societal forces that amplify pain states. Doing so was not the purpose of the Gate Control theory nor of the Neuromatrix theory. Hence my comments are not a critique of these theories. But they do point to the limits of the theories' parameters and show what has not yet been addressed and which must be addressed if the chronic pain experience is to be understood.

Brain models are picked up eagerly by pain educators. One can find psychologists, counselors and pain educators on YouTube "explaining" in a few minutes, how the brain is responsible for chronic pain. The worst over-reach by those popularizing neuroscience surely must be a short video using cartoons, called, "Understanding Pain: What to do about it in less than five minutes." It 'explains' the-brain-in-pain, indeed in less than five minutes, telling us that the brain is fully responsible for our chronic pain, but not to worry, you can reverse it![13] You can retrain your brain. How you do that is told in a few words: by watching how your thoughts and emotions affect your brain; learning ways to reduce stress; watch your diet and life style (stop smoking and drinking); examine your psychological background (for worri-some times in your life that supposedly could have brought on chronic pain); and exercise. These activities are strikingly alike to those routinely suggested by the default psychological model. They are now merely repackaged with the word "neuro-plasticity" added to them.

This video immediately appeared on several pain web sites: anoth-er quick, easy "tool" for the pain management "toolkit." It doesn't seem to matter that the story of the brain is highly over-simplified. In these popular-ized versions of the "brain story," chronic pain, an utterly complex societal, political, medical, psychological, physiological and neurological problem is, once again, magically transferred to the individual, who supposedly bears full responsibility to properly influence her/his brain to control pain.

A critique of the popularization of brain plasticity –the simplistic rep-resentations, the unfounded promises– is offered by Sally Satel and Scott Lilienfeld, in "Brainwashed: The Seductive Appeal of Mindless Neurosci-ence," who discuss in detail the premature applications of neuro-imaging and the grandiose claims made in its name.[14] Neuroscience is a science, they say, barely out of its infancy. Within pain management, Scott Fishman, Chief of Pain Medicine at the University of California, Davis, comments, "Function-al imaging provides a two-dimensional snapshot of a three-dimensional or four-dimensional event…"[15] Says Melanie Thermstrom, "The brain has more than a hundred billion neurons. All functional imaging can tell us now is that a few hundred million of them become more active at certain times."[16]

The cartoonish video on what to do about chronic pain in less than five minutes, picked up by too many pain management web sites, is a prime example of just how outrageous the over simplification of the intricate and dynamic complexity between chronic pain, the conditions of our lives, and the brain can get. It trivializes our lives in pain. It obscures, rather than clarifies, the multiple factors impacting chronic pain.

The social and societal web of pain: Concrete starting points, new responsibilities

In all three major models then, in the biomedical model, the psychological model, and the brain models, self and world are kept separate. Yet, as chronic pain plays itself out in our lives, "self" and "world" are never separate. As everyone living with pain knows, chronic pain is sustained involving both self and world in complex ways.

A societal model would of course not replace existing models. But it changes the starting point. In existing models, the starting –and ending– point is always the individual. In a societal model, a web of configurations is the starting point. Of course, individuals in pain continue to be a crucial thread in this web, but simultaneously –not just in addition to– so are societal forces that impact pain.

The reader may say to me: But if you had not had your accident, you would not be in pain! Of course you are the starting point!

My pain, in some very important ways, did not start with me. When I crashed my car, I crashed my car into a society that is ignorant about chronic pain, an ignorance that awaits us around every corner. An ignorance that has disastrous consequences for our chances for improvement.

I crashed my car into a society, and, importantly, into a science, where only seeing and measuring equate believing. Pain being invisible and not measurable, we are frequently seen –also by too many physicians and researchers – as attention seekers, exaggerators, malingerers, drug seekers, catastrophizers, out for 'secondary gain,' hostile, and whatever else. People with measurable diseases are not thought of in these ways. We, on the other hand, are continually put in a position where we need to try to prove that we are not any of those things, that we have the pain we say we have. But pain not having an external referent, proving we have "it" is not in the realm of the possible. Hence, researchers, clinicians, insurers, and society at large, can –and do– pin negative labels on us to "explain" the invisible, and we have no defense, no defense at all in the language of visible "data." The fundamental and profound devaluation of the invisible in the world of science excludes any deep understanding of chronic pain when science is seen as the only way by which knowledge about our lives can be claimed.

I crashed into a society in which insurers pretend chronic pain is not real and get away with it by using outdated theories. How is that still possible? A society that allots less than one half of 1% of all health funding to pain. How is that still possible?

I crashed my car into a medical world that is extraordinarily ill-prepared for us (compared to its knowledge of and interest in other diseases) and for many is not even accessible. A medical world in which most of us get help far too little and far too late, which is disastrous for the development of chronic pain. Many doctors' ignorance about chronic pain is a disease factor for us, and the question is, why society allows this ignorance which it never would allow in relation to cancer, or heart disease, or diabetes. After I moved to my current residency, I tried out a new general practitioner who rather nonchalantly said: "Oh, we don't know what to do with chronic pain. What refill do you need?" Can you just imagine a doctor saying, "Oh, I am not really interested in cancer. Just take some vitamins." Or, "You are exaggerating or catastrophizing your heart disease." Or, "There is no organic reason for your cancer… no more claims allowed" – the letter I received from my car insurance, as have millions of other pain sufferers.

I crashed my car into a society in which all the decks were *already* stacked against my recovery. A society set up to ignore chronic pain. While all diseases may well be influenced by societal forces, I make a case here that these forces are the most damaging and adversarial when it comes to chronic pain. My poor recovery was already foreshadowed by them. Pain's invisibility and its unmeasurability makes it a disease easily ignored and denied, and thus easily distorted by political and societal forces. The web into which those who end up in chronic pain fall has already been laid out for everyone. This begs for a societal model of chronic pain. Then, the starting point for action can be anywhere: with any aspect particularly relevant to a given person. Chronic pain becomes a complex and multilevel societal problem rather than a problem individuals "have." A societal model will not cure chronic pain. But it will increase the seriousness by which chronic pain is approached, encouraging conditions that are favorable to our healing. It will not let forces that contribute to chronic pain off the hook. It can even facilitate the effectiveness of existing models.

Forces that contribute to chronic pain, or stand in the way of pain relief, and which are not examined, exert immense unacknowledged power over our lives.

Concentric models: Self and world still separate

Proponents of concentric models move toward greater complexity by combining existing models and by at least gesturing toward the shaping influence of "the environment" or "the social." However, the inclusion of "the environment" or of "the social" occurs at the level of abstraction. That is, no specific forces are examined for their power over chronic pain. What are the forces in "the environment" or "the social" that directly impact chronic pain states? That is the question. As is, the concentric models too are empty of actual social context.

John Loeser, for instance, offers "four components that are necessary and sufficient to describe the phenomenon of pain."[17] The components are drawn in the form of circles which are separated by solid lines. The smallest circle around which the others are drawn represents "nociception," to which the layer called "pain" is added. Then the circle of "suffering" is added, to be followed by "pain behaviors." These four layers pertain only to the individual, and given the solid lines that separate the circles, they are imaged as additive, discrete phenomena.

But Loeser offers a second figure in which similar aspects are presented ("somatic tissues" "peripheral nerve," "spinal cord," "brain," "behavior") and in which the aspect of the "environment" is added.[18] Here, these aspects are no longer separated by solid lines and "interaction" between components is represented with arrows going from one level to the other and back.

My interest was perked by the addition of the "environment." Loeser, however, doesn't really go there. He pushes the edge of the psychological model, reaching toward the social/societal/environmental but does not describe and examine what the factors in the "environment" that interact with pain actually are, what can be done about them, and who is responsible for their adverse effects on chronic pain. It occurred to me, that had Loeser been also an ethnographer or an anthropologist in addition to being a neurosurgeon, he may well have carefully observed, described, and critiqued the specific "environmental" forces he now refers to only in the abstract.

Similarly, Loeser and Melzack note that "environmental" factors "can contribute to the intensity and persistence of the pain," but they do not provide any discussion of what the pain contributing environmental factors may be either.[19] The discussion stays at the abstract level. And nothing is easier to ignore than the abstract.

Biologist and neuroscientist Francisco Varela summarizes the importance of the concrete.

> "Rationalistic," "Cartesian," "objectivist": these are some terms used to characterize the dominant tradition of recent times… (but) I find that the best expression to use for our tradition is abstract: nothing characterizes better the units of knowledge that have been deemed most "natural." It is this tendency to find our way toward the rarefied atmosphere of the general and the formal, the logical and the well defined, the represented and the foreseen, which characterize our Western world.[20]

Varela notes that within the "loose federation of sciences" dealing with knowledge and cognition, the conviction is slowly growing that this picture is "upside down," and a major shift in perspective on knowledge is on its way. A perspective at the center of which is the conviction that

> …the proper units of knowledge are primarily concrete, embodied, incorporated, lived; that knowledge is about situatedness; and that the uniqueness of knowledge, its historicity and context is not a "noise" concealing an abstract configuration in its true essence. The concrete is not a step toward something else: it is both where we are and how we get to where we will be.

I am convinced that Varela's perspective on knowledge is fundamental to any effort to improve chronic pain research, clinical practice, and professional support groups and is at the core of a societal model of chronic pain.

A societal model

Figure 2 offers an image of what a complex, dynamic, non-linear model that includes concrete societal forces that impact pain might look like. In developing this figure, it soon became apparent that, in general, I could draw a connecting line (indicating mutual reinforcement, co-emergence, and interdependence) from each societal factor to every other. But not all factors will play a role in any individual life. Hence the connecting lines in Figure 2

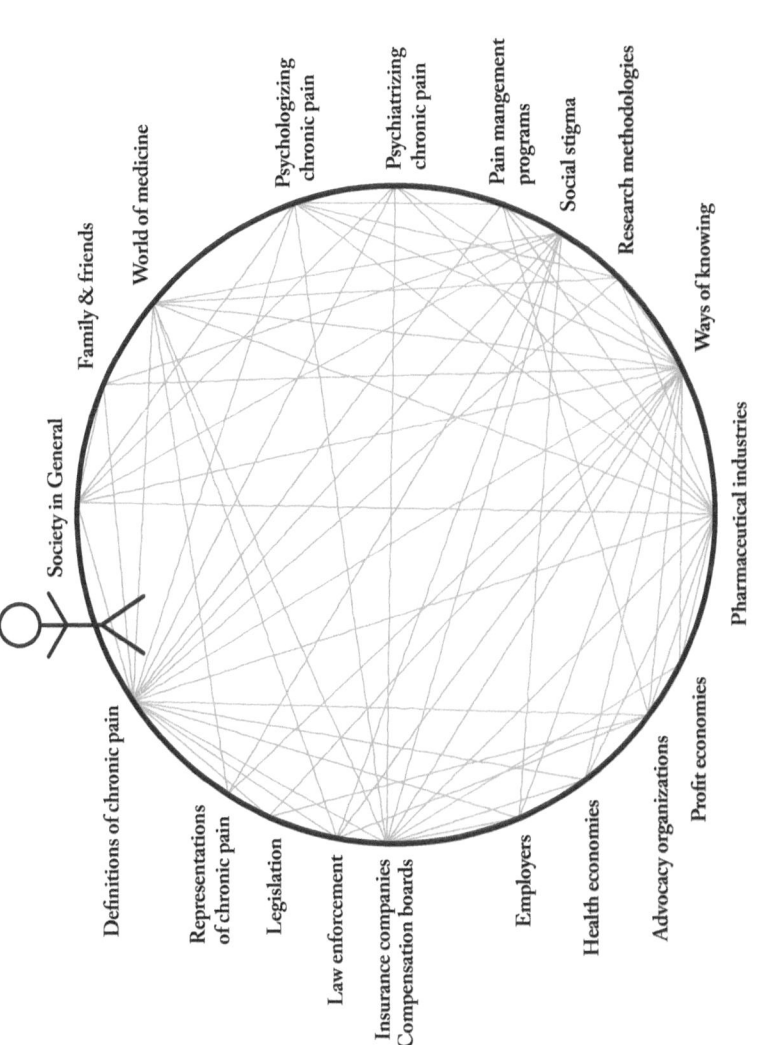

Figure 2: A societal model of chronic pain.

present an image of the web-like reality of possible connections, not an exact representation. Figure 2 then identifies actual specific societal forces, without claiming to be comprehensive (additional ones can be added), that impact the experience of chronic pain. It provides an image of the interdependence of these forces where one force would not exist, or come into being, without the presence of another.

For instance, there was a reason why, when I was sent to a psychiatrist, he fired a set of standard questions, not related to my life in pain, at me, read from a sheet of paper, rather than having an in-depth talk about my pained life as I had anticipated. And why I was immediately prescribed Prozac, without even being asked if I wanted it. The tight mutually reinforcing connections between today's psychiatry as psycho-pharmacology, the aggressive marketing practices of the pharmaceutical industries, and insurance companies that pay for quick diagnosis and drug prescription, but not for in-depth talk are obvious. They co-emerge. They reinforce each other. For me, it made for a highly unsatisfactory visit and did nothing for my life in pain. I never went back.

Regarding health economies, I was offered an open neck surgery, no guarantees, risky, it could have increased my pain permanently, 5 days in the hospital, thousands of dollars, and all would have been paid for. No one would have questioned the surgeon. But prolotherapy (repeated injections with dextrose into weakened ligaments), for a total of $3,500, which in fact was safe and took a chunk of my pain away, was not. It was not "mainstream" I was told. Who decides that? On what grounds? On whom does society bestow benefits here? How is it that a procedure with the possibility for permanently increasing pain is paid for, but the likely possibility for pain relief without any harm is not? What configurations of social, societal, and political forces are in play here? Who benefits from these rules? Who doesn't?

The effort in Figure 2 then is to replace (1) the abstract nature of generic references to "the social" or "the environment," with concrete contexts, (2) the assumed separateness of influencing factors, with their co-emergence, and (3) the individual in pain as the only point of focus, with the web of social and societal forces that impact pain.

Thus, while the features of existing models are maintained, Figure 2 sketches a more open ended, flexible, more complex and a more dynamic image of the co-emergent forces that impact lives in pain. As noted, existing models and concentric models default to a model of individual responsibility.

Only the healthcare provider and the person living with pain are held responsible. A societal model calls everyone to the table.

Political?

Some have told me that what I want to happen is political. Pain belongs to the scientific realms of medicine, psychology, and psychiatry. Everything else is political.

If one insists on casting the conversation in political terms, history of science shows that the decision to borrow the scientific method from the hard sciences and apply its dictates to the study of human behavior, was in itself a value-move, even a political move as it dealt with power relations. The social sciences became a "science," it was claimed, because of the use of a borrowed method. This denied the humanities an equal voice. It denied the epistemology of the lived experience a primary voice. The humanities and the voice of experience became mere decorations of sorts. Interesting perhaps, but not scientific, as they do not, it was decided, involve rigorous methodology, and thus they are not seen as capable of rendering formal knowledge claims.[21] Our voices and the truth of experience were formally silenced. In chronic pain research this has led to many strange, narrowly conceived, and plainly incorrect knowledge claims about our lives. This does not mean that science is "only" a story, or "only" a cultural phenomenon, as some postmodern thinkers would have it. Science is a big story.

But it does mean that, when it comes to the study of human behavior, it is not the only nor the best story we have. As Francisco Varela, Evan Thompson, and Eleanor Rosch pointedly comment,

> We often forget just who is asking (the) question and how it is asked. By not including ourselves in the reflection, we pursue only a partial reflection, and our question becomes disembodied; it attempts to express, in the words of the philosopher Thomas Nagel, a "view from nowhere." It is ironic that it is just this attempt to have a disembodied view from nowhere that leads to having a view from a very specific, theoretically confined, preconceptually entrapped somewhere.[22]

Theoretical physicist Werner Heisenberg's often quoted words come to mind, "We have to remember that what we observe is not nature itself but nature exposed to our method of questioning."

Further, to the charge that what I want is political, I say, "Let's not deceive ourselves." The structure and focus in pain research and care is already political. The neglect of chronic pain in the world of medicine and in the world of research funding, the denial of its reality by many insurers, by employers, and by society at large, the domination of the pharmaceutical industries in pain research and management – all of that is politically shaped. Who benefits from all this? Who decides, and on what basis, what is and what is not taught in medical school? Which medical disciplines reign? To whom does the available money go and why? How is it that insurance companies will pay thousands of dollars to a surgeon even if he or she messes up our back or neck (which happens not infrequently) with no questions asked? But "alternatives" that help are "not mainstream." Why are they called "alternatives" in the first place? Who decides, and on what basis, what is and what is not "mainstream"? Why is it that psychology and psychiatry are relied on so heavily in pain research, but not anthropology and ethnography? None of these questions reflect an innocent state of affairs. The status quo that does not ask these troubling kinds of questions is entrenched by privilege: the very privilege that is at stake in the posing of these questions.

Elaine Scarry points to perhaps the deepest reason why ways of understanding and treating pain are so readily impacted by political forces.

> Given the verbal signs we have for pain are so unstable and cannot portray a certainty of understanding, they can be intentionally enlisted for the opposite purposes, invoked not to coax pain into visibility but to push it further into invisibility… The relative ease or difficulty with which any given phenomenon can be *verbally represented* also influences the ease or difficulty with which that phenomenon comes to be *politically represented*.[23]

Or misrepresented. And therefore mis-treated. Anything I say to anyone, can push me further into invisibility because my words never accurately reflect the pain. It is not within the realm of the possible for my words to be accurate. You have to be around a person living with serious pain for a while, before you might understand the meanings of the tone in which feeble words are said, the dullness in the eye, the certainty of the pain hidden in the hesitancy of words. Before you understand that chronic pain, internalized and silenced, can hurt as much as pain that is acute and recognizable.

It is tautological to observe, says Scarry, that given any two phenomena the one that is most visible will receive more attention. Something so nearly impossible to express, she says, will not receive the attention in the presence of almost any other phenomena in the same environment. The difficulty of articulating physical pain, she says, permits political complications of the most serious kind.[24]

That explains, in part, why research for pain gets less than 1% of available funding for health care. Other diseases, being visible and measurable, will receive far more attention. It explains why others tell us: "Oh, but you look good!" It explains why we so readily lose our insurance fights: there is no "organic" (i.e. visible) damage, hence we can't have pain. It explains why in the absence of visible tissue damage too many of us are sent to a psychiatrist. The psychiatric label we end up with pushes our bodily pain out of focus even further. Indeed, in all these cases, and more, our pain is politicized by pushing it "further into invisibility." If one wants to speak in terms of politics, there is already plenty of it to go around.

Critical voices

Others too have critiqued the existing models' exclusive focus on the individual and have noted the lack of congruency between theories of chronic pain and the lived experience of chronic pain. For instance, John Quintner, Milton Cohen, David Buchanan, James Katz, and Owen Williamson, engaging a slightly different argument than mine, lament the dis-connect between theory and experience.[25] Ruth Dubin, a family physician, traces the concrete events in the life trajectory of six of her pain patients and concludes that "physicians, insurers, lawyers and employers may be contributing to patients' pain and disability by adopting a disbelieving and confrontational approach."[26] Her patients encountered major financial losses, huge struggles with insurers, employers, lawyers, relationship breakups, all making their pain worse. Dubin argues for an expanded understanding of the pain experience through input from the humanities and social science, because, she says, the medico-legal models lead to a destructive path for too many patients.

Amanda Nielson, a research officer in the School of Health and Rehabilitation Science at The University of Queensland, concludes that the "promise" of the biopsychosocial model has not materialized.[27] Nielsen cannot find the "social" in the psychosocial model either. The social dimension, she says, cannot be addressed at an individual cognitive level – as the psychosocial model does. Precisely my objection. It needs to be articulated instead, Nielsen says, at a policy and practice level to ameliorate the social suffering that increases pain. Nielsen speaks of "structural discrimination" that leads to stigma and to the mutually interacting institutional practices that lead to the disbelief and marginalization of people in pain encounter. These social practices, she says, result in stereotypes of "malingering", in actual job losses and income, often because of unavailability of alternative or adjusted employment options, to loss of status which is tightly linked to job loss, and to separation from many social spheres.

Coralie Wales, president of the Chronic Pain Australia advocacy organization, further documents how the continued reliance on incorrect and outdated theories by insurers creates structures which effectively deny patients compensation for disabling pain – thereby impoverishing them and increasing their pain.[28]

Other critical voices are of course those of people living with pain. They can be found on pain web sites and in projects such as "Pain-Is-Not-Invisible" by Chronic Pain Australia, describing in precise, concrete terms, the many injustices done to us by pure neglect, ignorance, and disbelieve, increasing pain states.[29]

Understanding a disease as having, in part, its roots in societal forces is not a new proposal. Philip Coulter reminds us, lung cancer once understood as an individual problem, is now placed in a complex societal matrix, an outcome of the complex interdependencies between such forces as farm subsidy policies, the power of advertising, and teenage rebellion.[30] Obesity, once explained as an individual problem involving overeating or a metabolic condition, is now placed in an explanatory societal matrix of cheap, fattening food, lack of access to healthy food in poor neighborhoods, advertising junk food to children, corporate greed, manufacturers deliberately loading packaged food with addictive additives, and unhealthy school lunches. Physicians and researchers have been involved in articulating the significance of these societal matrices as disease factors.

Societal models of disease understand that the "self" does not end where we think it ends. The boundaries around the self are not nearly as solid as we have thought. Real life is characterized by intricately interwoven self/other phenomena, biologically, ecologically, socially, ethically, and even neurologically.[31] Lewis Thomas, former president of the Memorial Sloan-Kettering Cancer Center points out that the original root of "self" was *se* or *seu*, the pronoun of the third person, and most of the descendant words, except "self" itself, were constructed to allude to other somehow connected people."[32] Self and other are interdependent. The self in chronic pain is no exception.

2 Problematic definitions and cheerful representations

Pain is an unpleasant sensory and emotional experience associated with actual or potential tissue damage, or described in terms of such damage.

> The International Association for the Study of Pain[1]

Chronic pain is a thief. It breaks into your body and robs you blind. With lightening fingers, it can take away your livelihood, your marriage, your friends, your favorite pastimes and big chunks of your personality. Left unapprehended, it will steal your days and your nights until the world has collapsed into a cramped cell of suffering.

> Claudia Wallis [2]

Pain (is) the experience of discomfort.

> Vranceanu et al.[3]

Pain is a sensory and emotional experience shaped by a complex web of intra- and interpersonal dynamics arising from professional policies and practices and deeply rooted beliefs and assumptions about pain and addiction.

> Lynn Young[4]

Pain is an all-consuming internal experience that threatens to destroy everything except itself – family, friends, language, the world, one's thoughts, and ultimately even one's self.

> David Biro[5]

Pain is what the patient says it is.

> Scott Fishman[6]

Chronic pain is arbitrarily defined as pain that last longer than 3-6 months. But I define it as "Any pain that has really lost that purpose of being an alarm that is now only serving to produce suffering."

> Scott Fishman[7]

Chronic pain is pain that lasts long enough (after normal healing or for at least three months) or is intense enough, to affect a person's normal activities and well-being.

American Pain Foundation[8]

Chronic pain is defined as pain that persists longer than the temporal course of natural healing, associated with a particular type of injury or disease process.

Wikipedia

Chronic pain may push us toward an area of human life we know almost nothing about…It places people in utterly different worlds of feeling. It surrounds them with silence. In many ways the person in chronic pain might as well be standing on the moon.

David Morris[9]

Mild pain is still pain but it doesn't ruin your life, whereas severe pain hijacks your attention system. That's almost a definition of severe pain, that it commands all of a person's attention.

Temple Grandin and Catherine Johnson[10]

I have learned to distinguish between mere discomfort and pain that can't be tolerated…the deepest pain holds no meaning. It is not purifying. It is not ennobling. It does not make you a better human being. It just is.

Dana Jennings[11]

What is quite literally at stake in the body in pain is the making and unmaking of the world.

Elaine Scarry[12]

The way to begin learning about pain, then, is not to start by defining it – as if by sheer will we could forge it into something very clear and simple – but rather to explore the ways in which it tends to get away from us. We need not remove all possible uncertainties in order to think clearly. *What we end up thinking about with all its uncertainties removed, will certainly not be pain.* We can learn much by seeing where our ordinary language, with its inherent slipperiness, will take us. In this way, we will at least begin with the knowledge that meaning and pain do not belong to the class of clear and distinct ideas cherished by empiricist philosophers but rather constitute a summons to look further, to resist prefabricated definitions, *to examine the terrain for ourselves, and, most important, to proceed in a spirit of openness* (emphasis added).

David Morris[13]

I can tell you, that definition means nothing.

17 year old girl living with pain

On problematic definitions

The most quoted definition of chronic pain, in research but also in pain management, is probably the definition by the International Association for the Study of Pain (IASP): "Pain is an unpleasant sensory and emotional experience associated with actual or potential tissue damage, or described in terms of such damage." The first time I read it, I blinked my eyes: "What? Unpleasant? Are you kidding?" How am I to think of "unpleasant" when sharp, intense pain wakes me at 4 or 5 am? When I reach for pain pills, ice packs, stumbling out of bed, my brain still asleep, frozen by pain, hearing myself say: "Oh god, I cannot do this anymore." "Unpleasant?"

The IASP definition in particular illustrates the seemingly unbridgeable chasm between how professionals think and the actual experience of living with chronic pain. People in pain have written or told me how Claudia Wallis' description of chronic pain as "a thief," "took my breath away" as one person put it. We can surely assume that no person actually living with pain, has ever said how much they value the IASP definition.

The wide range of attempts at defining chronic pain, from the most reductionist to the broadest and most contextual view, is indicative of the lack of clarity that complicates the interpretation of research in a world where clear definitions are demanded for research results to be reliable. Basically, cancer is cancer, regardless of where it appears in the body. AIDS is AIDS. Largely, the basic definition of common visible diseases have a certain clarity and consistency for both the patient and the professional that cannot be found in the literature on chronic pain. Context-less reductionist definitions of chronic pain, while they may mean something for a researcher who focuses on a narrow aspect of chronic pain, mean little or nothing in terms of lives lived in pain. Further, they claim a clarity that narrows both research and clinical care.[14]

The 17 year old girl who said, "I can tell you, that definition means nothing," was referring to common reductionist definitions of chronic pain such as linking it to recurrent pain of three months duration. It is heart breaking to hear of her life:

> I can easily say that I'm not sure I've ever lived a pain free set of two days in my whole life. The maximum I can remember is barely twenty-four hours and within those moments in time, that marked my soul, I came to taste what normality is. I am not disfigured, nor do I have a life threatening illness, instead, I have chronic pain.[15]

"Unpleasant" – that means a little bit of pain here and there. Or, an ongoing low level of pain that is annoying, discomforting, but not life destroying. Not a thief. Not an all consuming interior experience. Not a hijacking system. The disconnect between chronic pain defined as "an unpleasant sensation" and the reality of hell that is a life lived in severe pain demands attention and exploration if definitions of chronic pain are to be relevant to human life.

IASP's minimal definition is informed by the lowest common denominator: one cannot go much lower than a "sensation." "Sensation" is the function of a "low-level biochemical and neurological event."[16] It is an "event." A temporary event. Acute pain is such an event. Laboratory inflicted pain is such an event. Chronic pain is not such an event.

Chronic pain is *a state of being* that stretches way beyond a sensation-and-related-emotion. It is a state of being that is intensely sensitive to and shaped by the conditions of life's circumstances. A state of being that is shaped by multiple facets of society – yet, its serious nature not understood and often denied by society.

One might argue that the IASP definition was not meant to reflect real life. It was meant for researchers and clinicians. There are at least two problems with this. First, it is used everywhere. I recently attended a session on chronic pain at the University of Victoria offered by their Continued Education Program for the general public and for people living with pain. The presenter *started* with the IASP definition. I wanted to raise my hand and asked if anyone in the audience thought they lived with an "unpleasant sensation." And second, if the definition was only meant to be of use by researchers and clinicians, that in itself would be a serious problem, for the definition casts an extremely narrow lens on the scope of research and clinical care.

A definition provided by a powerful organization, that focuses so squarely on a physiological sensation and an emotion evoked by it, further stands in the way of being open to research methodologies that address real lives. Ethnographic, anthropological, narrative, and other qualitative and phenomenological methodologies that address real life meanings and experiences can not be used to make knowledge claims about low level chemical and physiological sensations. These methodologies are rarely used in chronic pain research.

One can only imagine how research, clinical practice, self help programs, and funding priorities could change if chronic pain would be formally defined, let's say, as "A thief that robs you blind." Or, as "An all-consuming experience that destroys everything except itself." Or, as "The making and unmaking of the world." Had Doctor D, who we met in the preface, adhered to such a definition, what a different kind of conversation he would have had with his patient. How much more helpful and supportive he could have been.

The IASP definition contain this rider, "Many people report pain in the absence of tissue damage or any likely pathological cause; usually this happens for psychological reasons." As Milton Cohen and John Quintner stress, this view sets the stage to further solidify the assumed Cartesian mind/body split adopted by the biomedical model.[17] The IASP definition can easily be seen as portraying chronic pain as either a body-event of a nociceptive nature or as a mental event, strengthening the stereotypes too many in society have of us as being emotionally unstable, of being complainers and whiners.

Of course emotions are intricately involved in the chronic pain experience. How could they not be. But these emotions emerge from *having to live* with physical pain and with the range of social and societal consequences. Just adding "emotion" to "sensation" will not do in the light of pain's complex social and societal markers. Just adding "emotion" to "sensation" allows the fields of psychology and psychiatry to appropriate research on chronic pain to a degree where it no longer seems to matter that the person lives with bodily *pain*. The person in pain then easily becomes a psychological or psychiatric "case" as I will address in later chapters.

Perhaps those sitting at the table when deciding on the IASP definition, were not thinking about chronic pain. The definition makes more sense in relation to acute pain, or laboratory inflicted pain. But its wide use leads to bizarre dis-connects, such as seeing chronic pain as "devastating and disabling," yet defining it in the same article according to the IASP definition as an "unpleasant sensation."[18]

A great deal of pain research takes place in the laboratory, where subjects (often healthy volunteer college students) are subjected to a brief pain stimulus, which, because of ethical standards, cannot be severe, and cannot be inflicted 24/7, or for months or years. The subject can opt out any time. Compare *that* to lives lived in moderate or severe pain, month after month, year after year, in the midst of a largely dismissive and ignorant society. We cannot opt out. How, possibly, can the experimental results be generalized to our lives? Yet, that is done as a matter of methodological habit as "generalization" is seen as a keystone of experimental research.

A reductionist definition such as the IASP definition then can become completely non-representative of our lives. Within mainstream approaches to research, definitions have to lead to the specification of variables which must be defined as measurable units. The research enterprise hinges on how the researcher defines and plans to measure her or his variables. At the most basic level this means having to assign numbers to things and to relations between things. In other words, to count. The question then becomes, what can you count when faced with chronic pain? What gets lost when deeply qualitative phenomena are forced into countable units? And what sorts of questions can therefore *not* be asked? A "sensation" can be forced into some kind of measurement. Then it can be counted. But by so defining chronic pain we lose everything that matters in the struggle to improve our lives.

Definitions matter

As philosopher Ludwig Wittgenstein famously said, to imagine a language means to imagine a form of life. Those who have the power to define, have the power to shape a particular form of life, thereby ignoring or denying other forms of life. When scholars, researchers, and clinicians in the field of chronic pain work with constructs such as "unpleasant," "sensation," and "discomfort," it will be near impossible to imagine what living with persistent pain is like, which, one would assume, should be the basis for a research and clinical agenda for pain management. It allows for easy trivialization instead. With no visible symptoms, and no language-for-pain on hand, our disease is a form of life that stays hidden.

Last year I spoke to a group of people living with pain about my memoir of my life in pain. One person asked a pointed question: "How would you summarize your book in one sentence?" It took me a few seconds of gathering a mindful moment, and I said: "It is terrible to have to live with chronic pain." They all nodded their heads. I could not possibly, *ever,* have said: "I write about chronic pain as an unpleasant sensation and an unpleasant emotion." Will Rowe, former CEO of the former American Pain Foundation, notes that the starting sentence of my book, 'How do you put hell on paper?' is "the most important message for the world to hear about living chronic pain."[19] The IASP definition is in many ways an insult to people living with serious pain. Arthur Frank characterizes the problem of definition well:

> Pain and illness call for expanded metaphoric repertoires, and first-person narratives often tell regrettable tales of institutional medicine stultifying metaphorical capacity instead of nurturing it thus creating barriers to communication and self-understanding.[20]

Rather than reductionist definitions that have no meaning for the lived experience of chronic pain, we need expansive metaphors that can evoke meaningful communication.

As quoted at the start of this chapter, Lynne Young, a scholar of nursing, offers a definition of chronic pain as a "relational experience," and does not use the word "unpleasant." Her definition reflects the complexity of the nurse-pain patient relationship which include factors, such as "professional policies and practices," that directly impact a patient's pain and thus are, in fact, disease factors. Young's efforts to adjust the definition of chronic pain to the particular setting of nursing care raises the question: do we perhaps need a definition that differs for different settings? While woefully inadequate for an understanding of how chronic pain is impacted and experienced, the IASP definition may be just right for very specific kinds of research. Perhaps we need different definitions of chronic pain for different purposes and different contexts.

I agree with David Morris: To try to eliminate all uncertainties from a definition of chronic pain, just so it is clear, simple, and concise, leaves us with an empty shadow. It is best not to retract from the complexity of chronic pain. To keep "an open spirit," to try to imagine and to perceive what is at stake. Narrow definitions stand in the way of doing so. Hence, I refrain from even trying to propose a 'new' definition of chronic pain, simply because I do not think a definite, or even an adequate definition that fits all purposes is possible. However, if I were to try, words like "societal disease factors" would be in it. Perhaps even "the making and unmaking of the world."

Pain, as an outside-of-language experience, has no external referent unlike other internal states that require an object, such as love, fear, hate. One loves, hates, or fears *someone* or *something*. Their external referent is what gives words like "love" and "fear" their meaning. But pain doesn't take an object in the external world. As Scarry says, "Physical pain is exceptional in the whole fabric of the psychic, somatic, and perceptual states for being the only one that has no object."[21] Any attempt to define pain or understand pain runs into this problem. Paradoxically, that is precisely why words and defini-tions do matter: because they cannot grasp pain, because pain has no external referent, words and definitions that claim to speak to pain are self-referential. That is, they directly refer back to the investments and values of those who do the defining: there is no external check for accuracy. Those who have the power to define an experience that has no external referent create a world on their terms. Hence, definitions of chronic pain are consequential: they reflect on whose terms chronic pain comes to be understood – and how it fails to be understood.

"Chronic?" "Normal?" "Bad?" "Good?"

Focusing on specific meanings of words used to define chronic pain we run into further problems. Take "chronic." While "chronic" clearly refers to the duration of the pain, it has no consistent meaning. "Chronic" has been defined anywhere from "more than 24 hours" to six months, and to anything in between.[22] According to existing definitions, a "chronic pain patient" can have three headaches a month, or be in severe pain 24/7 for years undoubt-edly engaging, for better or worse, multiple aspects of society.[23] Two entirely different kinds of lives. Two entirely different maladies. Yet, in most publica-tions we are all lumped together. Thus, research findings such as that some people living with chronic pain self-report that they lead "happy and success-ful lives" in spite of their "chronic pain" hold no relevance.[24]

Others have called attention to the dualistic and binary ways of knowing in the study of chronic pain. Cronje and Williamson note that most of the IAPS' pain categories are defined in terms of a reference standard of "normal" pain.[25] "Normal," the authors note, "is nowhere operationally defined in the IASP Pain Terminology." Cronje and Williamson argue that this ambiguous use of the construct of "normal" against which various pain states are evalu-ated, tacitly serves to differentiate what individual clinicians decide is "legit-imate" normal pain, or what is "malingering" and drug seeking kind-of-pain *without* there being any consistent or valid basis for doing so.

Cronje and Williams point out that an "unspoken operational defini-tion" of the word "normal" throughout the IASP Pain Terminology refers to "what is expected." What is expected for pain is to heal and go away. If it doesn't, it becomes suspect when there is no apparent medical cause for pain's continuation. Or, I like to add, when the patient is poor, a minority, an un-attractive-woman-who-needs-attention, or a low-level-worker-who-is-out-for-secondary gain. Thus, when our pain does not behave "as expected," it can easily be seen as abnormal, a judgment which, as Cronje and Williamson also note, easily slides into the realm of moral judgment, and, as I will note in a later chapter, into psychiatric appropriation and the realm of societal stigmatization.

Definitions and pain levels

"Severe pain means suffering. Period. They aren't two different things," say Temple Grandin and Catherine Johnson.[26] This is so, they say, because when in severe pain the frontal lobes integrate sensory pathways so totally with frontal emotional pathways of suffering that we can't perceive any separation at all. Then, the suffering that comes with pain is not optional, as many in pain management who psychologize pain claim it is. "In serious pain," says Scarry, "the claims of the body utterly nullify the claims of the world."[27]

Severe pain itself *is* an interfering pattern that invades the brain. The young French philosopher Simone Weil, who herself suffered from severe constant headaches, wrote, "Physical pain, and that alone, has the power to chain down our thoughts."[28] The power of severe pain to overtake everything (attention, thought, function) is rarely noted by pain management professionals, but has been articulated by those living with pain, and by scholars, philosophers, and artists.

To truly separate severe pain from suffering, note Grandin and Johnson, we first would need to have a leucotomy done: have the connections between the frontal lobes and the rest of the brain cut. An operation only a bit less invasive than a lobotomy, and one with terrible side effects. But a couple of days after the operation patients who have been disabled by pain are up and about. Though the pain is still there in the same way, patients don't care about their pain anymore. It can be handled with an aspirin. The pain now feels like "discomfort" they say – the way too many self help books portray chronic pain. The way too many in society think of chronic pain. "Mild pain is still pain but it doesn't ruin your life," Grandin and Johnson observe, "whereas severe pain hijacks your attention system. That's almost a definition of severe pain, that it commands all of a person's attention."[29]

The reader may say: You are opening up a box of worms suggesting that severe chronic pain should be considered a malady of its own. Who would decide whether a person suffers from "discomfort," or from "light" or "severe" chronic pain? On what basis is such a decision made? Wouldn't you be creating unnecessary distinctions?

To that I would say: the box of worms is already open. These distinctions are alive and well – reflected in the thousands of severe chronic pain sufferers who are imprisoned in their own homes, excluded from society, insufficiently served by the world of pain management, and unable to get the strong medicine they need. Too many physicians rather not treat those with severe pain problems.[30] Self help pain management strategies are characteristically woefully inadequate for those living with severe pain, often trivializing their lives, as I will show in a later chapter. Severe pain sufferers experience intense isolation, and become, as Marni Jackson so poignantly states, "a stain" to others who do not understand the nature and effects of severe pain states.[31] Plenty of worms already crawling around.

A societal model of chronic pain is particularly needed for those with severe pain problems who are now falling through the cracks of various systems. Those who live with light pain, can typically find help from medications, from activities offered by pain management programs. They do not readily lose their jobs, their relationships. They do not end their lives over light pain. They can "get on" with their lives.

Those living with severe pain cannot get on with their lives. They all too often *end* their lives. Societal institutions and regulations invariably come into play in nearly every case involving severe chronic pain: insurance companies, employers, social services, government regulations regarding opioid prescription, support from family and friends or lack thereof, systems dealing with financial needs. If we take the opposite sides of any pain scale, and look at what the pain experience actually does to a life, we see two very different sets of consequences. Yet, as is, we are mostly all lumped together under "chronic pain."

Those who lead lives in severe pain surely should be approached with a different attitude, a more serious kind of attention, with more resources, and with a deeper and more sustained empathy and willingness on the part of healthcare professionals and of society at large to listen and be responsive.

And when professionals write about chronic pain, when still another toolkit or web site on pain is created, what must be asked is this: Is what we say relevant to those who suffer from severe pain? Is the five minute video "Understanding pain: What to do about it in less than five minutes," featuring cartoon figures, appropriate to present to those living with suicidal pain?"[32] Could what we want to offer trivialize lives lived in severe pain?

Should different advice be offered for those in severe pain? What might that be?

Of course a certain percentage of people in pain experience the entire range of pain intensities. Estimates of how many live with severe pain, among the millions who "qualify" to be counted as living with chronic pain, vary between 30% and 80%. This wide range – so wide it is almost meaningless – is a sign of both how little we know about the lived experience of chronic pain and how inexactly we think about what we think we do know.

On cheerful representations

Early on in my search for information, I came upon the web site of the Canadian Pain Coalition. As the web site opens, you see eight people of various ages, nicely dressed, healthy looking, straight postures, looking competent, ready to go to work, ready to take on the world. They could have been models for The Gap or for Tommy Hilfiger. They all look so healthy, and so *normal*. Perhaps, I thought, I had accidentally clicked on a web site for a community college or an employment agency. But no. These people were presumably suffering from chronic pain.

My instinctive reaction was: "They have no clue. This is not about me." I was in suicidal pain at that time. Essentially home bound. I exited the web site. Perhaps I missed out on some good information. But the image of myself as a healthy, competent, attractive looking worker or student turned me off. I felt I was asked to participate in the silencing of my difficult life.

Ever since, I have come across visual representations of many more very happy people living with chronic pain whose pictures are on brochures for self management programs, on web sites, and in pain management self help books. The web site of Chronic Pain Australia even had a young beautiful woman flying through the air, holding on to long scarf-like pieces of colorful material, flying up and away. Another young radiantly smiling woman, in a field of grass, had her arms up high, freshly picked wild flowers in her hands. I contacted the organization and objected.

I don't make it a practice to contact web sites to complain about illustrations, but I did with this organization, because it states serious objectives (including the prevention of suicide), and offers good information. I thought it worthwhile to put out the effort. The person I contacted was aware of the problem. Some of their board members had also objected. But their sponsor, I was told, had demanded the pictures would be cheerful. Thankfully, the images have been replaced.

And then there are the cartoons. I have already referred to the video, "Understand pain and what to do about it in less than five minutes." A short fast moving video (ironically, it moves so fast that it literally triggers my headaches and I have to look away) in which a hand draws cartoons that explain how the brain is responsible for our pain. Another example is the "Pain Toolkit," a program of basic approaches to pain management. Nearly every description of the twelve "tools" discussed is illustrated with funny cartoons.[33] On the "Pain Tool Kit Calendar 2011," a smiling cartoon figure even wishes us "A happy pain self management New Year!" I think of the hundreds of people worldwide, living with severe pain, who ended their lives in 2011. "Typically, the people you are dealing with," says pain specialist Edward Covington, who directs the chronic pain program at the Cleveland Clinic,

> are people who have spent the last three, four, five years of their lives on the recliner, watching television, dark room, no socializing, no work, no hobbies no family life, no sex life. Their lives have literally stopped.[34]

Another pain specialist, Colin Fernandes, has this to say after he has seen his patients all day: "I was left wondering which is worse: informing people that they are going to die, or that they are likely to spend the rest of their lives in pain."[35] Cartoons.

Further, there is the "Explain Pain" book by David Butler and Lorimer Moseley, scholars working in pain science and brain science respectively, a book that seems popular among a number of therapists who work with people living with chronic pain. It addresses chronic pain in terms of brain function. The explanations are illustrated with large, well drawn, colorful, funny cartoons. Many of them. On nearly all of the 100+ pages. Even the book cover features a very large supposedly funny cartoon.

Imagine a book that explains what cancer, AIDS, or obesity, or any other major health problem does to the body, illustrated with many funny colorful cartoons on every page. Just imagine the reception of such a book.

I think what the authors of "Explain Pain" took seriously was the brain, not the experience of chronic pain. Brain functions are amazing. And had the book been exclusively about brain functions (not tied to any major illness) then the cartoons would have been fine. But the book was about us. About the many people who live horribly difficult lives. Who end their lives more often than those with almost any other illness. Cartoons.

I have been intensely puzzled by all this cheerfulness that adds insult to injury: I could not have ever conceived of writing a self help book or developing a web site for chronic pain that featured healthy, happy, competent, attractive looking people or using cartoons to represent us. It wouldn't have occurred to me that that was an option. What goes on in the mind of those who do? There is a chilling parallel between society's attitudes (that our pain can't be that bad, so just cheer up) and the cheerful representations of us in so many of these pain management materials.

Thankfully, there are of course web sites and projects on chronic pain that portray us realistically. For instance, the image that accompanies an excellent narrative project on chronic pain called "Pain-Is-Not-Invisible," by Chronic Pain Australia, shows the face of a woman who looks straight at the camera in a sober fashion. One can read various things into how she looks at you, but cheerfulness and happiness is not among them. The IOM report "Relieving Pain in America" likewise shows sober faces. The program "Pain-Safe" of the former American Pain Foundation showed nine people living with pain, standing close together, all looking sober, some looking tired, no one happily smiling – a seriousness that suits our lives.[36] Four medical professionals shown in the same frame, all smile. That does not bother me. I want my healthcare professionals to be friendly people. In fact, I thought the difference in the faces of the people in pain and of their healthcare professionals was a poignant sign of how well the APF understood our difficult lives.

It is telling, that people in acute pain are always portrayed realistically: "Ouch!" Faces are contorted. Postures are doubled over. Books on migraines will have realistic pictures. One would not imagine a person in acute pain being portrayed as cheerful and happily smiling. They are incompatible states. Yet, when pain becomes chronic, cheerfulness often characterizes representations of us, signaling, however sub-consciously, that our pain can't be that bad.

Cheerfulness aligns with the upbeat advice we frequently receive from the many pain management programs and self help books influenced by "positive psychology." It may further be that chronic pain's invisibility makes pain management professionals feel helpless, and a cheerful approach covers up such helplessness. Cheerful representations represent a mindset that is too eager to help and therefore, by the very force of such eagerness, does not know how to witness, how to listen. Yet, witnessing and listening are prerequisites to developing the insights needed to provide real help.

A disease so mysterious to others, so invisible, so easy to deny – how it is represented, how it is pictured, how is it talked about, can make a major difference in how others construct its seriousness, and those others include insurers and employers: the happier we are portrayed, the easier it is to deny us claims and not feel burdened doing so.

The matter of representation is not unrelated to the problem of definition: when definitions are narrowed to an "unpleasant sensation," stripped from the difficult and complex conditions lives in pain encounter, it becomes easy to use pictures of cheerful individuals: there is not much of a contradiction. After all, pain is just a "sensation." But if embodied, realistic definitions of lives lived in pain were commonly used, pictures of happy, smiling, competent looking people would no longer work. Not to think of cartoons.

One might respond to my observations that many web sites about major illnesses show happy faces. In the case of cancer, heart diseases, or other major illnesses which *are* visible – society *knows* these diseases. Everyone knows they *are* real diseases. It doesn't matter whether a person who is portrayed as having the disease smiles or not. If the person looks depressed, everyone will understand. If the person smiles, the smile cannot erase that knowledge. Many people will in fact think: what a courageous person! She has cancer but is still smiling! No one will think: "Oh, she is smiling. She can't have cancer. It can't be bad." Which is what goes on in the minds of many when they see people suffering from chronic pain portrayed as happy, healthy, and smiling.

The false messages implied in the cheerful representation of chronic pain trivialize those who live with severe pain, have lost their jobs, their relationships, their lives. They foster the unfair notion that if only we do the activities in the workbook, the activities on the web site, we too could be happy and active. Cheerful images imply the message that people living with pain who are not happy, are weak. They prey on the cultural dictate to have to be happy at all cost – including the high cost of pretending. The question that needs to be asked is, For whose benefit are we portrayed as happy, competent, and upbeat individuals? My comments here do not represent an exhaustive review of web sites and pain management books. I've seen and experienced enough of both however, to object to this strong trend that incorrectly represents us to the world, reinforcing misleading social stereotypes.

Representation: efforts in language and beyond

How to represent that which lies outside of language *and* what is not desirable? By definition, an internal state of being lies outside of language.

That is not a problem when the internal state is desirable. Love. Joy. Happiness. People will readily imagine what is left unsaid by words. But who wants to imagine what living with serious daily pain is like?

Acute pain is a different matter altogether. "Ouch!" everyone understands. A contorted face, a doubled over posture, everyone understands. It is therefore easy to understand the validity and urgency of the pain, and get the person to a doctor.

When pain turns chronic, however, it turns inward. You can moan and say "Ouch!" only for so long. *Then*, the problem of representation begins.

When no clear definition can be formulated by assertive language, we start groping for metaphors. And even metaphors are not entirely satisfactory:

> In the realm of inner experience we have never developed a language relevant to the data. We constantly use metaphors from the see-touch realm as if the data of our inner experience were the same as that of our eyes and touch organs. The reason is, of course, that there are no rules of correspondence, no opportunities for measurements, for quantification of the ordinary kind in this domain.[37]

Lawrence LeShan and Henry Margenau's words made me think of the McGill questionnaire. Most of the seventy some descriptors (stabbing, stinging, beating, cutting, flickering, throbbing, lacerating, scalding, pounding, crushing, pressing, pinching, blinding, and so forth) are metaphors taken from the see-touch realm in an attempt to describe pain – acute or chronic. I have filled out this questionnaire a number of times but never felt it told anything about my pained life. I wonder whether a doctor, after years of hearing these words so many times, still feels something like a shock: "Wow, *stabbing* pain, that is like a knife going into you! That must be serious!" Or, having heard the word "stabbing" now hundreds of times, it has lost its descriptive power.

Given that the diagnostic value of the McGill questionnaire does not lie so much in the validity of any single one of the descriptors, but rather in the clusters they form, the dulling of each individual metaphor over time, may not be so much of a problem. But one must nevertheless wonder if it is possible for the chronic pain patient to make the nuanced distinctions among the many descriptors. And frankly, if I had to fill out the McGill questionnaire again tomorrow, I myself would feel bored with it having been asked to do so several times. "Here we go again," I would think and I probably would just mark a few things, quickly, and shrug my shoulders, because I would feel

I could not get it "right" anyway, as I have actually never been stabbed, nor burned, pounded, crushed or lacerated. The nuances of the many choices would escape me.

As physician David Biro points out: metaphors age.[38] They become part of the literal discourse. They need to be periodically renewed. "Like antibiotics," says Biro "they develop resistance, which deprives them of their descriptive and suggestive powers." Biro draws new metaphors for pain from novels and stories, and while we cannot be expected to write and speak like Joyce or Tolstoy, he says, the new metaphors taken from great writers give a glimpse of "the range of the possible" about how language can show us pain.

Then there are the pain narratives, or as Arthur Frank refers to them, "reports" which, on a moral level, he says, are "acts of witness, telling truths that are too often silenced because they speak of what any sane person would rather ignore among life's possible outcomes."[39] Having written such a report, Frank is correct, that my instinct for writing it was to provide a report on lives lived in pain, as there are so few of them, and to function as a witness in a society that turns its head the other way. I wrote to say: No, look here. Look at us. We are part of humanity. Further, says Frank, such narratives offer coherence for others who are ill or in pain that defies expression, and they offer a second language that can express what medicine ignores. An important question here is, will physicians actually take the time to read these narratives and learn from them? While there are many illness narratives about other major diseases, there aren't many about chronic pain. A telling sign of both how neglected chronic pain is, and how difficult it is to write about.

Beyond language there is art. Biro refers to the Mexican artist Frida Kahlo, who at fifteen was involved in a terrible bus accident in which she was literally impaled and which fractured her spinal column, her collarbone, and several ribs.[40] Over her life time, Kahlo produced a harrowing series of paintings that externalize the internal experience of pain perhaps more acutely than any verbal representation of pain could.

You do not have to be a painter to paint pain. The "Pain Exhibit," a beautiful on line visual art exhibit by people who live with chronic pain, represents chronic pain in a wide array of aspects, physical, emotional, and even social.[41] The "Pain Exhibit" was started by Mark Collin, who couldn't find a way to tell his doctor about his pain, and decided to create a piece of artwork to show him.[42] He then wrote to pain doctors around the world to solicit examples of art from pain patients. Some of them chill down my spine. The exhibit represents chronic pain to society in ways almost impossible to do in words.

Expression inevitably leads to knowledge and community, says Biro.[43] Expression is therapeutic for the sufferer but it is also crucial to create awareness in society. Borrowing Elaine Scarry's words, expressing pain is "a necessary prelude to the collective task of diminishing pain."[44] Scarry was referring to verbal expression. Given pain's hidden life, we need as many forms of expression as we can muster. For without expressing chronic pain –often, fully, everywhere, realistically, artistically– society is allowed to keep its eyes averted.

The courage to represent

In September 2011, I received a phone call from "Postmedia News," a Canadian company that owns many Canadian newspapers and on line publications. They were working on a four part series about chronic pain. Might they interview me? The interviewer, Sharon Kirkey, had read my book and she had read it well. She asked great questions. We talked for an hour and a half. During the interview I told her how upset I was by the happy smiling people on too many chronic pain web sites and in too many self help books. I told her that the field of pain management on the whole insists on putting an optimistic spin on our lives. I noted how this also happens because no differentiation is made between light and severe chronic pain and we tend to get all lumped together. We need true images, I said, of real people in real pain, documentaries, photographs, films that really show the faces and the bodies of severe pain.

Little did I know what I was in for. She contacted me the next day. Might they send a photographer to my home to take pictures throughout the day: a-day-in-the-life-of-a-chronic-pain-patient kind of thing?

My instinctive reaction was protective: "No, not me!" I am not going to show myself in great pain early in the morning when I look terrible. When the pain has drained the blood from my face. When my eyes take on a hollow look. I look 20 years older than later in the day when the pain is light, or sometimes gone, and I have dressed and fluffed up my hair. Do I want the world to see me during the worst hours?

As I thought, "Not me!" I knew simultaneously that I *had* to agree. On principle. After all, I had told her we needed images. After all, I know that people living with severe pain do not cheerfully jump and tumble through fields of wild flowers. They do not see themselves reflected in funny cartoons.

They are not dressed nicely ready to go off to community college or to their job. They do not have a job. I had to have the courage to show myself in pain.[45] And courage it took. I also decided I was not going to change a thing about my appearance, my night wear, the appearance of my house.

I was shocked when I saw the pictures of myself taken early in the morning, sitting up in bed, still dazed from pain, trying to concentrate. The hollow look in my eyes. It took a few days to feel at peace with letting the world see the private side of living with pain.

"But that is what you look like, mom, when you are in a lot of pain," my daughter said. Nothing but the truth will do.

Many people living with pain contacted me and thanked me for having the courage to show the intimate face of pain. A very good friend, who visits regularly (though always in the afternoon or evening when the pain has settled because I do not allow anyone to visit in the morning when being social can be too difficult), told me that looking at the pictures she realized that it was so much worse than she had thought. A picture tells a thousands words. We believe only what we can see. We make generalizations from what we see. Thus – cheerful representations of us are terrible barriers to the truth of the lived experience of chronic pain. And nothing but the truth will do to accomplish the hard work that remains to be done.

SITES OF FAILURE

3 Our health care: problems and wish-lists

Dr. Scott Fishman, in his reaction to my memoir, says,

> I have heard innumerable stories that highlight the central dilemma of this book: that, for many patients…the health-care system itself is a major source of pain and suffering.[1]

It doesn't take long when one sits with a group of pain patients to hear stories about having experienced disbelief, neglect, misdiagnosis, no diagnosis, endless trials of drugs, being sent from one doctor to another, seeing so many of them that in the end no one really sees you – and still, the pain continues. While in recent years chronic pain is taken more seriously, many problems remain. How the world of medicine describes and treats a disease sends strong messages to society about the nature and seriousness of the disease.

The invisibility of the disease, an invisibility that silences us in a culture where believing demands seeing, both within medicine and in society at large, is surely at the heart of the many problems we encounter. As physician David Biro says, until we have a "pain machine" that can definitely measure pain (as some neuroscientists believe we may some day), "we must continuously acknowledge the most important criteria in assessing pain: the word of the sufferer."[2] And that truth has been extraordinarily pernicious for those living with persistent pain.

The 2011 "Relieving Pain in America" report, a major review by the U.S. Institute of Medicine –the medical branch of the National Academy of Science– notes the problem of chronic pain to be even worse than previously acknowledged in terms of numbers of people living with pain, the cost, suffering, and the high rate of suicide.[3] Says Tara Parker-Pope, "For patients, the acknowledgment of the problem from the prestigious Institute is a seminal event."[4]

Yes, and that is tragic. Perhaps I should be happy our problems are finally acknowledged by a prestigious institute, but I thought instead, "This is unbelievable. It is 2011!" Taking it personally, I felt an impulse to be sarcastic. I had lived with intense constant pain every day for about six years, and with considerable pain for another 10 years. Millions of others can say the same. Finally, the country's prestigious institute "acknowledges" our problems. Not, "a cure found." Not, "we are really making great progress in effective treatments." But "acknowledged."

This history of disbelief and neglect has allowed pain management professionals to be cheerful about our lives. A woman I befriended in a pain management program wrote me the following and gladly gave me permission to use it.[5]

> I go through spells where it just becomes too difficult and I feel very tired and drained. I saw my doctor at one of these awful times and apparently did not smile. The next visit I was back up and able to smile again. She said to me, 'Terri, this is how you should be, this is the way people like you, it is so much nicer when you smile." I knew that she in no way understood what I was going through.

Imagine a doctor saying to a patient with advanced cancer, or first stage cancer for that matter, or any other major disease, "Anne, you look much nicer when you smile. You should smile more!"

Terri dropped her doctor.

Inadequately educated practitioners

Our family doctor is typically the first we encounter in our search for help. But the help we receive is for most of us very inadequate, and can even be harmful, such as the "Let's wait and see," approach I, and millions of others, received from our family doctors. It is now understood that doing nothing is harmful as it allows chronic pain to develop.

Physicians' education in chronic pain has been inadequate or absent, as has been documented over and over. Veterinarians receive anywhere between three and six times as many hours of pain education as do physicians. Pain management is typically not an essential part of the medical curriculum. Chronic pain does not have its own status as do other major diseases such as oncology, rheumatology, cardiology, internal medicine etc. As Heather Young and Scott Fishman note (respectively associate vice chancellor for nursing and chief of pain management at the University of California, Davis), there are no consistent or nationally endorsed competencies in the U.S. for pain management for physician and nursing education programs.[6] Health care professionals, they say, learn about the diagnosis and treatment of pain randomly and incompletely through clinical practice rather than intentionally and comprehensively through their education programs. (In 2011, Young and Fishman received a grant to develop a pain management curriculum.)

Kevin Pho reports that in 2011 only five of the 133 medical schools in the U.S. have required courses on pain.[7] Pho does not mention how many –or how few– hours are involved in these courses, nor what is actually taught in them. Another 2011 study at John Hopkins University showed that, of 117 medical schools in the U.S. and Canada, a majority did address one or more core topics in pain, but many did not report any pain teaching and most others devoted less than five hours to pain education.[8] The authors conclude that though pain is by far the leading reason people seek medical care, pain education at North American medical schools is limited, variable and often fragmentary.

Given this deeply inadequate knowledge base, "pity the patient whose MRI is normal," the Chronic Pain Association of Canada tells us, "that person is clearly looking for drugs."[9] It is a disaster for us. How, given this minimal and haphazard approach to educating doctors, can one possibly expect society at large to take chronic pain seriously?

Major reports on the status of pain care have in recent years warned patients not to assume their doctors have enough knowledge to treat their pain.[10] In "Inside Chronic Pain" I list over fifty (fifty!) contradictory statements I received from twenty two different doctors and specialists over an eleven year period, sometimes pronounced soberly, sometimes in a shrugging, guessing manner.[11] This exuberance of contradictions pertained to several aspects: What is the diagnosis? Could I get better? Where should Botox injections go? Should or shouldn't I exercise? Is traction called for? Are my vertebrae displaced? For a large painful "glob" in my neck I received seven different diagnoses over a ten year period, which included a neuroma, inflamed lining of the bone, an entrapment of scar tissue and nerves, a myofascial contraction, a swollen lymph node, and brain fluid collecting in that area. Yet all these doctors were paid to "diagnose" what was wrong with me. Many others living with chronic pain have personally told me their list of contradictions they received. An in-depth, semi-structure interview by Dewar et al. found that receiving many contradictions regarding diagnosis and treatment was common in pain patients' experiences.[12] As one interviewee summarized, "The more physicians you see, the more opinions you get…So you're left totally confused as to what direction you should take or what is really going on with you."

It would be difficult to think of any other disease so poorly understood that its diagnosis would result in so many contradictions. If doctors are *that* confused by chronic pain, what can one expect from society at large?

The problem with "pain specialist"

When a rhizolysis (the denervation of nerves by using radio frequency stimulation) and a nerve block did not help, I was told, "We are running out of options." After unsuccessful Botox injections, and another unsuccessful nerve block by a different specialist, I was similarly told, "There is nothing else I can do for you." I received these comments in 1999 and 2003 respectively. Given the orientation of these specialists, both anesthesiologists, that *were* the only options their specialization had to offer. Their specialization was anesthesiology, not chronic pain. It took me years to come to understand that the "pain specialists" we are referred to are most often specialists in another field who apply their knowledge to pain. That does not equate being a *pain* specialist.

At a pain awareness event I attended in 2008, an anesthesiologist gave a brief power point overview of the intervention procedures he carries out (nerve blocks, injections with chemicals, rhizolysis). After his short talk, several people in the audience (95% of them people living with pain) asked him what kind of other things, besides the procedures he had mentioned, could they do to ease their pain? What do you think of meditation? I have been using a lot of supplements, do you think they can help? What do you know about osteopathy? What do you think of decompression therapy? (No one asked about the procedures he had been talking about which in itself is an interesting observation.)

His responses still echo in my mind because they simultaneously were surprising, yet anticipated. He repeatedly said, "I don't know." "I can't tell you." Then he said, "But I know a lot of you here and there's a lot of expertise among you and you can teach each other." (Several people in the audience had been or were his patients.) He sincerely attributed a certain kind of expertise to us. But he, the specialist, did not feel he had that particular kind of knowledge. Perhaps this specialist considered our knowledge not "real" medical knowledge. More like lay-person's knowledge. Whatever went on in his head, it was stunning to see the specialist and his audience so disconnected. And one wonders why any knowledge of what may help should lie outside of the purview of the medical profession.

The phrase "pain specialist" then is a deeply confusing construct, to us and to society at large. People think that a "pain specialist" can take the pain away. I can't count the times that someone has said, "But can't you see a pain specialist for that?"

"Yes. I have seen 15 of them."

Fifteen is the exact number as I write this in February 2014, not counting family physicians and the numerous alternative practitioners I have also seen.

The fragmentation of pain care is stunning. As a pain patient you really do not know which "piece" of you will get attention when you are referred to a specialist. Your nerves? Your vertebrae? Your posture? Your chemical balances? Your joints? Your ligaments? Your brain? You cannot be certain if there is a relationship between the pain problems you have and the knowledge of the specialist you see.

A pain specialist can be a neurologist, an orthopedic doctor, an anesthesiologist, a physiatrist, a rehabilitation specialist, an orthopedic or neurosurgeon, a specialist in electro-diagnostic medicine, or perhaps a combination of two or three of these. And this person then applies her/his knowledge to people living with pain. But rarely does a specialist have the tools to pull it altogether, says Scott Fishman.[13] He adds,

> The average neurologist may not be considering the impact of joint arthritis from disuse. The rheumatologist may miss the early nerve damage, while the physiatrist may focus on physical therapy but fail to notice that the patient's insomnia and depression are driving a downward cycle of dysfunction.[14]

And unlike those patients with other major diseases, we cannot count on our general physician to know which specialist is best for our specific pain problem.

We encounter similar problems with chiropractors, massage therapists, acupuncturists, osteopaths, biofeedback specialists, and physiotherapists, in that they too practice their specialized knowledge on us, but there is no guarantee that it is the right kind of knowledge for our particular pain. Our friends and family will add their favorite therapist of whatever kind to this smorgasbord for us to try out.

Will Rowe, former CEO of the former American Pain Foundation says this on the matter,

> If you have heart problem you go to a cardiologist and get it taken care of. If you have complex diabetes, you go to an endocrinologist and get it taken care of. If you have cancer, you go to an oncologist and get it taken care of. Where do you go if you have pain? You might think you go to a "Pain Specialists." Who might that be?[15]

In my case, had someone *early on*, presented me with *all* options, which would have included prolotherapy and myofascial release therapy, the two treatments that have helped, years of suicidal pain could have been prevented. These treatments existed back then, but I had to stumble upon them myself which took years. Finding out about prolotherapy was a lucky outcome of a general advice I received from my favorite pain specialist in Toronto, Dr. Gorden Ko, who suggested I see Dr. Nasif Yasin in Vancouver who "is good with his hands." Luckily, one of the things Dr. Yasin was good at with his hands was prolotherapy which he practiced in the way it was originally developed.[16]

Thus, the two treatments that took a decisive chunk of the pain away were not part of the many treatments I received from the mainstream world of pain medicine (numerous drugs, nerve blocks, steroids injections, rhizolysis, Botox, intramuscular stimulation, physiotherapy, osteopathic and chiropractic treatments, acupuncture) none of which helped and some making the pain worse. Doctors and specialists at the time didn't even know what prolotherapy and myofascial treatments were. Too many still don't. In July 2013, a year after I immigrated from Canada to California, my new family doctor had never heard of prolotherapy.

The narrow training in chronic pain doctors receive is maddening. What makes it even worse is that doctors get paid more for giving injections than for most other kinds of pain treatments, and that the injections are often dispensed at for-profit pain clinics owned by the physicians holding the needle.[17] "People get injections because they've walked in the door..."[18] This generally haphazard approach to chronic pain management, at times infused with financial motives, encourages society's endless misunderstandings of our problems.

Assessment: relevancy problems and biases

> The 1-10 pain scale. It is more confusing than the pain itself. How would you rate your pain on a scale of 1-10? I have been asked this question throughout these past two years about as many times as I have been asked my own name... To answer this question correctly you must first determine what 10 represents and what 1 represents. Well 1 is easy, 1 stands for no pain... It's the 10 part of the question that I find the real stumper... Let's say 10 is the worst pain you can imagine, as I have been told many times to do. OK so 10 is being burned, while being run over by a train while having your hair pulled, while watching a puppy die, while...you see where I'm going? If 10 is the epitome of all pain then any pain you may be experiencing at the time seems to be minor in comparison. You may rate your pain as a 2 or a 3, then the person who has asked the question thinks that your pain is not that bad. It is somewhat ridiculous to ask someone to compare what he or she is experiencing to the limitlessness of his or her imagination. [19]

This eloquent objection to the ubiquitously used 1-10 scale was written by a 15 year old patient of a physiotherapist who encourages his adolescent pain patients to express themselves through art and the written word.

I myself find the 1-10 scale exceptionally inadequate and misleading. It lacks interpersonal validity but also, and more importantly, especially for clinical care, it lacks intrapersonal validity. There is a substantial difference between a 1 and a 9. Or between a 2 and an 8. But as the distances between the numbers get smaller, the meanings of these distances start to blur. I still don't know what the difference is between a 6 and a 7, or even a 6 and 8. I would interpret the difference differently on different days, depending on many factors, as the number itself is not connected to anything. And when I mark a 6 on a certain day, I cannot remember what the pain was like when I marked a 6 at a previous time – something I should be able to if the scale is to have intrapersonal validity. As Newsweek (June 4, 2007) in a special issue on chronic pain phrases it, the scale is "absurdly imprecise."

But I had missed this young woman's insight, that when you tell a doctor that your pain is a 2 or a 3, or a 4 or 5 on a scale from 1-10, the doctor can easily think that your pain therefore is not that bad. After all, it is not a 9 or 10. Few patients will say their pain is a 10 when talking to their doctor even if they are sitting there thinking they are going to faint from pain (an experience I am well familiar with). For something can always be worse in life. "What *is* a 10?" this young woman asks. You really do not know how to imagine the worst pain possible. Or to remember the worst pain you ever had. You may remember the event –a nail through your hand, a very painful childbirth, a badly sprained ankle– but the pain *itself?* The objective-looking scale, she points out, can protect a doctor from really listening to the patient and to make judgments that diminish the patient's suffering.

These observations by a fifteen year old offer significant phenomenological and methodological insights for anyone attempting to improve assessment of chronic pain: *One cannot imagine a pain one has not had. One cannot even accurately remember a pain one did have. One cannot imagine the worst pain possible.*

In my own experience, once the pain has settled, I cannot even remember the intense pain I woke up with that morning. I remember *that* intense pain woke me, but the pain itself? Equally important, when I am in several hours of severe pain, I cannot remember what it is like to have no pain. I cannot think outside of intense pain when I am in it. Intense pain is an alternate state of consciousness. Language does not live there. What all this means for assessment of severe chronic pain is profound. For when I sit in that doctor's office, being asked to rate my pain, I cannot get to the correct answer which lurks somewhere outside of my memory and outside of language. Often, frankly, I just say something that sounds halfway reasonable, always aware that I cannot get to the truth.

Pain is a "wordless terrain" says David Morris, "where all communication threatens to come to a halt…"[20] It exists outside of language. It also lies outside of memory. As Alan Basbaum, of the department of anatomy at the University of California, San Francisco, a medical researcher, similarly notes, you cannot "re-experience your pain."[21] How, then, can it be assessed?

What other ways might there be for us to communicate the nature and severity of our pain to a doctor? And what other ways might there be for the doctor to understand the pain we live with? By extension, how do we do that within the larger society?

With regard to assessment of a condition about which the knowledge base is so inadequate, the contradictions of its diagnoses so multiple, even the very "thing" that is to be diagnosed so elusive, assessing the condition becomes a terribly difficult task. Hence, I almost feel badly to say anything negative about existing procedures. Nor do I have a lot to offer in terms of improvement. But knowledge of the difficulties pain patients experience with standard approaches to assessment should inform any attempt to improve them.

Those who have lived in severe pain for many years, are left wondering, when one treatment after another has not worked, why we have to fill in the same scale or questionnaire again and again, after doing so has not resulted in anything helpful. They become like boring worksheets in school. We can easily become sloppy in how we fill them out. I know I do. There is a sense of doom when I see the same scale or questionnaire again. Why do I have to do this? There is no way to get it "right" anyway. We also sense that perhaps one of the reasons we are asked to mark scales and fill out questionnaires so often is so doctors can cover themselves: There is after all a file on us containing lots of charts and scales.

Several of the standardized questions asked can be trivial. In 2008 I saw a new specialist in Vancouver. He knew I had driven in from Victoria. That means driving one hour to the ferry, being on the ferry for one and a half hour, then driving an hour into downtown Vancouver. It was a very difficult drive for me but I did it. At the beginning of the first meeting I started to relate my medical history by telling him what other specialist, had said. He interrupted.

"Forget about what they said. I don't want to hear what other doctors have said. I want to hear your story."

"Wow," I thought. "This is great. He wants to hear my story!"

So I started to tell him my story. I can't remember how much I told him when he suddenly grabbed a questionnaire in front of him, interrupted me, and started to ask me a series of questions.

"Can you dress yourself?"

I was surprised by the sudden control he took over "my" story, and by the silliness of the question. I remember thinking, "Do your really think there is a possibility that I cannot dress myself, but I can drive to the ferry, and then drive an hour into town to see you?"

I struggled for the truth, "There are mornings when the pain I wake up with is so intense, that I would have a hard time dressing myself right away…" but halfway he interrupted me again.

"Yes or No?"

"Obviously yes, given I am here," I said, "but the first few minutes in the morning…" I started to repeat what I intended to say because it seemed to me that the particular patterns of fluctuation in my pain problems would be important for him to know about. But he interrupted again.

"Yes or No?" he repeated with a stern kind of charm.

"Well, Yes."

"Can you climb stairs?"

"Look, I am here…" I said. Even to get to his office you had to climb some outside stairs.

"Yes or No?"

I shrugged… "You know the answer."

He looked disturbed but marked the paper. I am sure he marked "Yes."

We had rapidly gone from my story to his 'story' – which was the countable story of "Yes or No."

These questions were trivializing and not rational. I felt weird. I felt as if he was using the wrong questionnaire. He was insulting my intelligence.

The doctor will say, but I need baseline data. To that I say, How can you "measure" something when you use a silly and wrong starting point? If there are mysterious reasons why these questions must be asked, then at least the doctor could say, "I know of course that you can dress yourself and climb stairs, otherwise you wouldn't be here on your own, coming all the way from Victoria, but I need to ask these questions." Or, he could have simply marked the questions on his own without asking me as he knew the answers as well as I did.

I am not being picky. People living with chronic pain are already misunderstood and mis-assessed by society in so many ways that trivialize our suffering ("But you look good!" "What do you do all day now you don't work?" "Must be nice to be able to sleep in!"). We are already approached with so many misperceptions and trivializations, that these kinds of silly questions from doctors only add to these indignities.

Of course there is a rationality to these instruments qua instruments. Logically speaking, they are methodologically rational to the point where they force our responses into small fragments that can be easily counted and statistically analyzed. I am forced into something countable although nothing about my pain is countable. What is utterly rational for a statistical model can become utterly irrational for those who live in pain.

A clinical psychologist who works with many pain patients wrote me, that after reading my memoir, he had eliminated a number of questions from the various assessment tools he uses with new pain patients. With his permission, this is what he wrote me.[22] Of the usual intake questions, he says,

> Many clients find the questions too obtuse, and annoying. This is particularly so for the person who has already seen 10 to 20 health professionals, most of whom ask the same types of questions (as you know). So the idea of asking the client "How do you wish me to be of help to you?" strikes many as unhelpful if not irritating, so I have given it up... Like wise, "If you could take a photograph of your pain, what would it look like?" leaves many clients cold... Asking someone what they have lost as a result of their condition usually results in the answer of "EVERYTHING" in capital letters. It touches a raw nerve, and since the question is answered almost always that way by all clients I have eliminated it... Most people don't like questions about their childhoods in the middle of a pain questionnaire so I have taken them out... For some it feels too intrusive and they fear the information being used against them... I've never had a useful answer to questions about "What have you gained as a result of your condition." This and related questions always lead to curt, often cranky answers. Possibly the most troubling question for most people is the question, "What do you think you can do to make friends with your pain"? This question has been entirely unwelcome for all but perhaps a handful of my clients, and I suspect they were too polite to say anything. It strikes them as insensitive and, putting it bluntly, rather stupid.

Indeed, I have often shaken my head over these kinds of questions. Many are useless, misleading, or loaded questions. Many of them originate from psychological theories that have nothing to do with chronic pain. Some, indeed, are plainly stupid. We feel treated like children. Often I have wanted to ask: "Are you serious?" "Don't you want to rethink that question?" These kinds of questions show at a deeper level that there is an absence of knowledge about what living with persistent pain is like. And no real interest in listening to find out. An absence that reflects the assumed superiority of psychologized and standardized ways of knowing over the realities of our lives.

Some of these questions show in their very phrasing the built in biases against us: "what have you gained...," and "making friends with your pain."

Presumably, there has to be a positive side to living with pain, an assumption that feeds the accusation of seeking 'secondary gain,' a view already so prevalent in society. These kinds of questions stand in the way of true listening. They allow the healthcare professional to *think* that he or she now understands our lives, while these kinds of questions in fact prevent understanding.

Coralie Wales, president of Chronic Pain Australia, has this to say,

> As a counselor who specialized in chronic pain, there was a time early in my career that I used psychological tools to "assess" people in pain. I had to "justify" my work to the insurance industry…However, as I became more aware of the depth and breadth of the lived experience of pain I felt increasingly uneasy about using them. I realized I was participating in a dishonest culture where research is based on "subjects" rather than people. *The "subject" is often unaware of the real aims and objectives of the research.* I decided that using psychological tools was harmful and they in fact impeded my ability to help. Once I abandoned these tools my therapeutic value went up greatly. It liberated me to concentrate on an honest relationship where I could be real and make crucial connections with the person in pain (emphasis added).[23]

A deeply helpful therapist I used to see, a clinical psychologist with a Buddhist orientation, never subjected me to a list of questions. I told him at the first meeting that I needed someone to listen. That I needed to hear myself talk about my suicidally difficult life. An astute and honest listener, he provided just what I needed. The underlying soulful message was that my terrible experiences were worthy of his understanding. No standardized assessment, ever, has given me that message. Had he said, "Okay, but I first need to ask you some questions," and had he proceeded to read standardized questions from a list in front of him, I would not have returned. I would have instantly felt flattened into a caricature of "the pain patient." I would have seen him as a stranger. And I don't tell strangers my difficult truths. An honest relationship cannot be built on unequal power relations which are inherent in subjecting someone to a list of questions of which a number are not relevant, are biased, are trivializing. It is honest relations that we need more than anything else. As Arthur Frank stresses, the listening on the part of a professional should not be seen as a therapeutic technique, another psychological strategy…[24] Instead, says Frank, the listener must be a witness honoring the suffering, and hear exactly the story that is being told.

Standardized assessment tools largely ignore fluctuation and context. Many assessment tools ask the pain patient to mark a pain rating as it is "Today," or "Now," or even "Right now." This assumes an underlying stability across appointments that for most of us does not exist. I have often wondered if the doctor draws a conclusion about the relation between the number I mark and the way I look and behave during the appointment – a conclusion that likely will be invalid. I also find myself often editorializing my ratings with "sometimes," or "only in the mornings," or, "the pain often fluctuates." A questionnaire I was asked to fill out that stipulated I could mark only one of five choices for various aspects of the pain experience was so mind-boggling to me, because in several cases two or three possible responses equally applied, that I simply stopped and wrote at the top, "I am finding these questions impossible to answer because they do not take into account context or fluctuation." Done.

If scales and questionnaires must be used, it would be better if the assessor would simply talk to us, listening carefully, ask us to elaborate on the nuances of our pain problems, making notes of what we say, and unobtrusively filling out whatever scale or questionnaire they feel they need.

Another urgent problem impacting assessment are the well documented disparities based on the gender, race, ethnicity, class, and/or appearance of the pain patient in terms of assessment outcomes, access to pain care, access to pain medication, and in what is and is not offered as treatment.[25] While pain itself has no preference for race, gender, ethnicity, or appearance (except for certain kinds of pain that occur more often in certain groups than in others), professionals are influenced by race, gender, ethnicity, and appearance. A societal model of chronic pain pays very close attention to these biases.

Making assessment more relevant

Given the outside-of-language and outside-of-memory nature of chronic pain, assessment that is relevant to both doctor and pain patient is very difficult: the more reason to be as creative as possible. Its purpose must be to learn about the nature of the pain and pain patterns, but equally important is for the doctor to understand what the pain does to the patient's life. Means for assessment should be open to whatever ways pain patients can come closest to their truths. I believe one of the first questions a doctor or therapist should ask goes something like this: "What do you think are some of the most important things we need to know about your life in pain?" Followed by a respectful listening.

As neurological surgeon and anesthesiologist John Loeser observes, "The simple act of listening to someone's story of suffering may be a therapeutic encounter."[26] In contrast to acute pain which does not depend heavily on narrative, chronic pain, says Loeser, is encountered on a different playing field. Narrative is essential to the assessment and treatment of chronic pain.

> The patient must have a provider who will listen, not just to what the acute illness consisted of, but to what the chronic pain has done to the patient's life...*In no other disease is the role of narrative so critical* (emphasis added).

Indeed, I always yearn for a doctor to really listen...And I yearn for doctors who behave as did my favorite family doctor, who never asked me to mark any scale, never threw any kind of assessment tool at me – but who served as a sounding board, a sharp listener, a consultant of whom I could ask anything, who would go over possible questions with me in preparation for an appointment with a specialist, who gave me ten extra minutes, who went over information with me I had found on line, who said, on parting before he moved to another city, that he had been "thrilled" to see how I tried to navigate the world of medicine, and who wrote me a note after he had read my memoir on chronic pain saying that it had been "an honor to be part of your experience." Not frustrated. Not bored. But honored. Can you imagine.

I am quite sure he assessed me all the while. And I am also sure that his assessment was far more accurate than any standardized assessment 'tool' he could have used. Nor did I mind being so assessed – in depth, within context, within meaningful conversation, with honesty, with kindness. He will always be, in my mind, the best family doctor ever. While those who behaved 'scientifically' focused on their lists of questions, firing them at me, questions often inappropriate to my situation, slip out of my mind as soon as I leave their office, feeling misunderstood, not listened to, feeling standardized.

If formalized assessment tools must be used, they need to incorporate functional language. In my memoir I argue for a scale, if scales are desired, with fewer pain levels which will make our responses more accurate and reliable across appointments, and they should be accompanied by descriptions of the consequences of each level for our day to day functioning. (In my memoir I distinguish three pain levels for myself that function reliably: light, considerable, and severe, and I note the functional consequences that describe each level.[27]) Pain specialist Chester Buckenmaier takes a similar direction.[28] Buckenmaier, director of the Army Medical Command's Defense and Veterans Center for Integrative Pain Management at Walter Reed Army Medical Center, maintains the 1-10 scale but adds functional language to each rating, however minimally. But it allows a patient to rate their pain based on the language accompanying each number. For instance, a rating of 2 has the following accompanying language: "Notice pain, does not interfere with activities." A rating of 4 says, "Distracts me, can do usual activities." A rating of 7 says, "Focus of attention, unable to do anything." A rating of 10 says, "As bad as it could be, nothing else matters."

When functional language is added, I can identify. Ratings now call up experiences and contexts – all of which I can remember, whereas the pain itself I cannot. I can have greater confidence that my ratings will be more accurately understood by the doctor and by others. When doctors believe actual words we say, words that describe our life, the disease becomes real. There now is an external referent: pain's consequences for our lives. The doctor is now looking at our lives. Not just at a mark on a scale, an abstraction we have guessed at. And even though doctors will see the numbers behind the words, they do read our words and can identify with them. Our *words* are believed. That is a powerful message in a society and in a medical system that often do not believe our words or have no idea what they mean.

Fragmentation of knowledge

In 2008, a new family doctor decided I needed a thorough check up and ordered a series of tests. I liked this doctor. She was empathetic. A good listener. All results came back "fine." Even excellent.

"That is the irony," I said. "I have always been so healthy up to the accident." "But you are still healthy!" she said, with enthusiasm.

Her words took me by surprise. I was sitting there, exhausted, with a lingering headache, having been woken by intense neck and head pain around 4 a.m. that day, as was the case virtually every day.

"No, I am not…" was all I could say, shaking my head, not knowing how to defend myself against her diagnosis of being "healthy." If my life was a healthy life, then I would not know what being ill meant. Daily serious pain, month after month, year after year, pain waking me up early, sleep deprivation, flare ups of intense neck and head pain during the day, not able to work, to hike, to travel alone – and I am healthy?

I thought a lot about this exchange. Any other condition that would take away someone's working life, many physical and social activities, not allow for a normal night's sleep, any condition that would cause severe exhaustion

– surely, any doctor would see that as being ill. If all tests would come out fine the doctor would say, "These tests came out ok, but you are obviously not healthy. So we need to look further."

But chronic pain turns out to be a different matter. I was by definition seen as healthy – because all the visible, measurable pieces were healthy. Pain, this "thing," existed as something mysterious, something outside of the normal range of markers of health. This particular doctor believed me. That was not the problem. Nor did she ever attribute my problems to psychological causes. Yet, even in the mind of this fine doctor, the notion of "health" co-existed with a life pretty much ruined by pain.

This is the socially split personality we have to live with: ill to ourselves, healthy to the world. Healthy, also to doctors who are trained to see health as absence of measurable disease.

Reluctant doctoring

Surgeon and Harvard scholar Atul Gawande admits, pain patients are distinctly not a doctor's favorite patients.[29] Dr. Micheal Stein tells how he used to find his patients' pain to be unknowable.[30] It felt far away, he says. A patient's pain used to bore him. And as Will Rowe says, we are our doctors' " least favorite patients to treat."[31] We are too difficult to deal with. We do not fall in the "diagnose and cure" category. Doctors cannot *see* or *measure* anything and that makes them feel incompetent, for "competence" for many doctors, lies in seeing and measuring. Most doctors are not (yet) trained to show empathy for our suffering as a "skill" they need to have. The medical system, in Meghan O'Rourke's words, is "emotionally deficient."[32]

Physician Matthew Bair and his colleagues surveyed twenty general practitioners about their experiences in caring for chronic pain patients.[33] They found that caring for us takes a "real toll" not just on us but also on our doctors. These physicians felt they were providing ineffective and unsuccessful care. They felt frustrated, ungratified, and guilty. They dreaded seeing our names on their clinic schedule – knowing it would be another unsuccessful interaction at best and difficult or hostile at worst. What, then, does it mean for doctors *to care* for us?

Inevitably, we come to sense our doctors' dislike and feeling of incompetence toward us. We sense that we frustrate them. Many of us give up on the medical system. Of the five chronic pain patients I know in Victoria, three of them have given up altogether on the idea the world of medicine has anything to offer them. We try to find our own pain relieving strategies, often in desperate ways: In Canada, one in six chronic pain patients have given up on doctors and resort to alcohol and illegal drugs to dull their pain. The National Institute on Alcohol Abuse and Alcoholism cites a figure of 28% of people living with chronic pain turning to alcohol, and notes the many risks associated with it.[34]

Perhaps worst of all, and I can attest to this, the bad doctors "haunt you for the rest of you life," as a pain patient told me. Indeed, I will never forget the worst of my doctors as I have told about them in "Inside Chronic Pain." It is sad and ironic, that I spent much time in my therapy sessions – at $120 an hour– talking through the negative experiences with doctors. (I never had negative encounters with doctors before the chronic pain became the reason for medical appointments.) It is crucial however to also mention that I will never forget the few fine doctors –my tales about them also in my memoir– for their skill and their humanity. As is, physicians will invariably underestimate, just as does society at large, the intensity and amount of pain we live with. As medical researcher Allan Basbaum says,

> We never know the magnitude and quality of someone else's pain… If as a physician you *think* someone is a crock, send him to someone else. Because you are doing him a disservice. It happens all the time. People inevitably underestimate pain.[35]

I want to say to all physicians, and to all researchers, please stop thinking "exaggeration," "malingering," "emotional," "hostile," "catastrophizing," or "amplifying" when we try to talk about our pain. While you think we are stumbling and being unclear because we are trying to manipulate you, or are simply whiners, we are desperately seeking for the right words to describe our pain and its consequences while knowing full well that there are no right words. Take the risk that by believing us you may miss those very few who, in fact, do malinger, rather than disbelieve and not care for the many who you think are trying to fool you but whose pain is slowly destroying them.

As Jerome Groopman says of his own labeling of patients who were very difficult to work with as "recalcitrant," and "noncompliant," he and other doctors did so to rationalize the difficulties these patients presented them with. By using these labels, says Groopman, the problems became the patient's problems and not theirs. Programs to educate doctors to acquire better "bedside manners" do exist of course.[36] But as long as such programs do not explicitly address chronic pain, even the most well-intentioned doctors may still distance themselves from their "difficult" chronic pain patients. When I came upon an article on chronic pain titled, "What and who is the "difficult" patient?," I immediately and instinctively crossed out the word "patient" and wrote in "doctor."[37] That is how deep the negative experiences are buried.

"There is nothing else I can do for you" hides, what physician/writer Abraham Verghese calls, "*the conceit of cure.*"[38] That is, the view that curing is the only true medical task. As medical technology took off in the 1970 and 1980s, says Verghese, the world of medicine thought there was nothing that couldn't be cured. At some level, he says, doctors became "plumbers." The "conceit of cure" concept explains a lot about poor pain care. Chronic pain, by definition, cannot be cured. The conceit-of-cure is operative in these words by a pain specialist,

> They have a chronic illness, chronic pain, and I see them when something new or unmanageable is going on. There's no point. There is nothing more I can offer them.[39]

Or, when in the same study, another specialist says,

> We are used to clinical markers of disease in our work, usually. And here the markers are distress and suffering, and we are not trained to treat distress and suffering.

When I am told by a doctor, "We don't know what to do about chronic pain. What refill do you need?" the conceit-of-cure that inform those words paralyzes me. I did not come in for a cure. I have learned not to expect one. I need to explore possibilities for pain relief with someone who understands more of the body than I do. I need advice. I need a listening ear. I need to talk about some changing patterns in my pain to see if that means anything.

In fact, the last few years, when I see a new healthcare professional, I say something like, "I don't expect you to cure me." I am trying to put the person at ease, so that he or she does not panic thinking I expect a cure they cannot deliver.

No amount of money or research will correct the conceit-of-cure attitude, though education and awareness raising might. Without a profound attitudinal change many of us are doomed to superficial refill-appointments. Doctors must see suffering as worthy of their attention. As a well known surgeon told physician Pauline Chen, "We have two jobs as doctors: to heal and to ease suffering. And if we can't do the former my God we better be doing the latter."[40]

Increasing doctors' knowledge, honesty and empathy

> We decided to honestly inform our patients of the current state of
> uncertainty that exists in Pain Medicine, both in regard to diagnostic
> and therapeutic practices. [41]

This stance is taken by Stephanie Davies, Christopher Hayes, and John
Quintner, who restructured the pain clinics in Australia where they work to
become patient-oriented and patient driven. They use a group based education program to teach people who live with pain what exist in pain management, after which patients are then free to select particular treatment options
on the basis of risk/benefit information.

I wished I had been given extensive and honest information about all
available treatments and their possible adverse effects, honest information
about success rates, and what "success" actually means (as it does not necessarily mean becoming free of pain). I wished I had been told up front that
the medical profession has no way to tell us, with any kind of certainty, what
might and might not help. It took me roughly six or seven years to finally
understand this. No one was upfront about it. This set me up, each time, for
high expectations, followed by failure of the treatment, even at times resulting in increased pain, the possibility of which I had not been told either. It
was devastating. Being honestly and fully informed up front would at least
have prevented the crashing of hopes.

A key question is, of course, how fully informed are the professionals
who guide a program such as outlined by Davies et al.? Would their knowledge include the entire range of alternatives? Would it have included the
non-mainstream treatments that helped me? Would it include knowledge
of professionals in the community who practice alternative approaches to
pain relief? None of that is made clear. There has to be excellent professional
education first before being honest in informing pain patients can actually
take place.

In medical education, Verghese uses illness literature to foster empathy. Others use "narrative medicine" which involves the careful listening to
the structure of what a patient says and the writing of stories by physicians
themselves. Because pain is "plotless" (that is, there is uncertainty of cause),
says professor of clinical medicine Rita Charon "certain issues are irrevocably
central: trust and trustworthiness (and) steadiness of commitment and invest-
ment in the patient's future…"[42] Pain medicine, she says "makes the doctor

honest – not able to overlook the use of the self in the service of the patient, not able to sidestep the inevitable mutuality of suffering." "As a doctor," says a physician who studied under Charon, "you are really a co-author of patients' experiences and you need to hear their story."[43]

Arthur Frank's view of the place of narrative in medicine is similar to my own.[44] Frank would like to see an emphasis on non-fiction writing about medicine, such as anthropology, ethnography and patient's narratives. "What would it be like for ill people to tell their stories and for doctors to read them?" he asks.

In my book I tell tales of my interactions with the 22 physicians and specialists I had seen since the accident. I could tell wonderful tales about four of them (two specialists and two family doctors), doctors who attended to my suffering as well as to my damaged neck. They behaved as Verghese and Charon would have wanted them to behave. I referred to them as the "fine ones" and will give some additional examples below of fine doctoring that I have encountered since, such as a young family doctor in Victoria who took me on after my favorite doctor left town. She shook my hand at the first meeting. She smiled. She listened carefully. At times nodding her head in empathy. At the end of the meeting she said,

"Anything else you want to ask?"

I couldn't believe my ears. No doctor, ever, had asked me that. Quite the opposite. Often, there are signals that they want to end the appointment. Some even stand up and walk to the door when I am still talking. She shook my hand again on parting and said: "A pleasure to meet you." One of my fine specialists, who I ran into as I approached the outside door of his clinic, said, "Hi, Lous. I was just thinking of you…" I couldn't believe it. This busy, busy specialist thinking of me when he is crossing the parking lot. Even remembering my name. And my miracle doctor, Dr. Nasif Yasin, whose skillful prolotherapy treatments took half of my pain away, said at one point, "Every time I put a needle into you, I pray I will do it right." A blessing with every needle.

When I called for a long appointment with my favorite family physician, as the pain had been terrible and I wanted his advise on a particular treatment, the secretary said, "He doesn't make long appointments. But I will schedule an extra ten minutes anyway because he has such empathy for people who live with pain. I am sure that will be all right." Writing of these encounters with my fine doctors, now years later, I still feel moved. Grateful.

I tear up. Their empathy and kindness swirl around in my pained brain and soften the difficulties of my life.

A friend of mine asked what made these doctors so good in my eyes. I was surprised hearing myself listing these basic civil behaviors: They are kind. They look you in the eye. They believe you. They empathize. The don't abruptly cut you off. You feel that no question you have is unimportant. They will listen to information you bring them, and help you to think it through. That's about it. Pretty simple.

Physician Heidi Pomm summarizes research that shows that pain patients consider "listening" and "being believed" as the most important qualities in their physicians, regardless of whether or not the doctor can help with the pain.[45] She suggests physicians ask "Is there anything else?" And, "Let me see if I understood you correctly." And, "It is very difficult to live with pain, and I know it affects all areas of your life." How hard is that.

Atul Gawande observes that display cases in pain clinics contain letters from patients to thank the doctor, not for a cure, but for taking their pain seriously, for believing them.[46] Teresa Flynn describes a fruitful relationship between Kate, a pain patient, and her primary care physician, who has: "a personable demeanor, an invested interest in her pain, and an engaged and consistent dialogue."[47]

I feel a bit stunned when I read all this, because these attitudes and behaviors reflect straightforward, civil, human intercourse. The kind of interactions you would expect to be the *basics* of pain care, the more so because pain is so complex and invisible. Yet we find such doctors hard to find. Attending several pain management programs, when sitting around the table and the topic floats to our doctors, someone invariably will say, "He has no clue," or, "He doesn't care."

But doesn't he? Or she? I have slowly come to the insight, that at least some of the not-so-fine doctors may well feel empathy but do not know how to express it. What do doctors fear might happen if they expressed their empathy? If they said something comforting, and showed some interest in our pained lives? Why do they decide, consciously or unconsciously, to stay aloof and on guard? Pain medicine needs to learn a great deal more about this if pain care is going to noticeably serve us better.

Gina Kolate makes the observation that patients usually do not confront doctors.[48] Instead, they rant to friends and family or simply change doctors. Exactly what I have done. Hence, most doctors do not even know they behave badly. "The reality is that a lot of these doctors don't have a source of objective comments", a director for quality management at the Tufts Health Plan in Massachusetts tells Kolata. Kolata's following observation caused a sting of recognition in me,

> ...doctors who are generally pleasant and communicative act differently toward certain patients, affected more than they realize by their personal prejudices against particular patients, like fat people, hypochondriacs *or people who complain about pain* (emphasis added).

A gastroenterologist who treated abdominal pain and then developed it herself said, "I had no idea that when patients said pain, this is what they were talking about. It was so much beyond words."[49] She couldn't describe it. Patients, she added, have to learn to really convey as powerfully as they can when talking about their pain.

The lovely family doctor who asked me "Is there anything else you want to ask?" read my book. The next time I came in, she didn't even say "Hi," but launched into a kind of confession, telling me that she had been convinced that she knew what her patients suffering from chronic pain went through. But to read it all in one place, she said, she realized she didn't know. She had been stunned how bad it really was. "I now hear your voice when a patient tells me about their pain," she said.

A doctor who came down with severe chronic pain himself has this to say,

> I'd survived the traumas of a major motor car accident, the ignominy of a prostatectomy, and the despair and exasperation of three separate cancers and their harsh therapies, but nothing had prepared me for the greatest challenge of my life, dealing with chronic pain... no matter how diligent or knowledgeable (a doctor is) one does not even begin to fathom the circumstance that is chronic pain until experienced first-hand... It challenged my psyche, mocked my considered strengths, and upended my confidence. The realization that each morning pain will be the first experience on awakening and the last experience at the end of the day dominated my thoughts, imposed all plans and restricted all activities. [50]

How do we bring this kind of knowledge to the public at large? How do we bring it to doctors and therapists and psychologists who want work with us but often have minimal insight into our lives and whose theories and attitudes stand in the way of gaining such insight? How can we expect any better from society at large?

At least one important response to these questions is to invite other ways of knowing. What is seen as objective knowledge, offering "hard data," which are by definition abstractions of the lived experience, have not made doctors or society noticeably more understanding of and empathetic towards pain patients. It is imperative that different ways of claiming knowledge about chronic pain become mainstream if our lives are to be more accurately assessed and understood. These include documentaries, journalistic accounts, poetry, letters, prose of various kinds, paintings, drawings, video, photography – any mode of expression that can break through the shell of others' aloofness, ignorance, and dismissal. Other ways of knowing forge a moral imperative to attend to us more fully, to genuinely listen, to care in embodied ways that mainstream quantitative knowledge does not. (Some examples of other ways of knowing in pain management research will be noted in chapter 11).

I'll end with two poems by people who suffer from severe chronic pain. The first one by a pain patient I befriended who had never written poetry before:

That ever present ruler of my life
That goddamn soul stealer
That day taker, it wastes away my time
If I'd never met pain, my life would be mine[51]

And this from someone, skilled in writing poetry, who lived with severe pain for thirty years and who recently passed away:

The silent woman sits and breathes -
Do her unspoken words fall into the leaves
To be as lost as spilled wine?
Her unexpressed emotions
Do they fly into the commotion of the wind
As it flows around her
Do they blow away from her busy mind?
Is she lost in thought?
Or just lost
In pain's unending bind.
If she tries to recover her spilled wine
Surely it has turned into vinegar with time.

The mystery of the silent woman
Is as mysterious as pain itself.
Subject only to those who live in it's steel trap-
To feel and interpret it's rap rap rap!

This poem was published in the research journal, "Pain Research & Management," the journal of the Canadian Pain Society.[52] I was both stunned and delighted to see it there. The person who submitted it, physician Peter Watson, asks, "Can we become more sensitive to nonverbal expressions in the arts of drawing, painting and poetry, or are some sufferings beyond our understanding?"

The fact that some sufferings are beyond our understanding, including the suffering that comes from relentless pain, does not mean that we can not find ways by which we can *increase* understanding. It is not all or nothing. *Any* increase in understanding, in empathy, in a doctor's invested interest in our pain, in the willingness to listen and talk things over with us, is progress. For that to happen in pain management, we need all the possible ways of knowing we can think of.

4   Over-psychologizing chronic pain: stripping context, forgetting the body

Pain, my brother, is an unseen and powerful hand that breaks the skin of the stone in order to extract the pulp.

Kahlil Gibran, *Self Portrait*

The pills he is given every sixth hour wash away the worst of the pain, which is good, and sometimes send him to sleep, which is better, but they also confuse his mind and bring such panic and terror to his dreams that he baulks at taking them. *Pain is nothing*, he tells himself, *just a warning signal from the body to the brain. Pain is no more the real thing than an X-ray photograph is the real thing.* But of course he is wrong. Pain is the real thing, it does not have to press hard to persuade him of that, it does not have to press at all, merely to send a flash or two; after which he quickly settles for the confusion, the bad dreams.

J.M. Coetzee, *Slow Man*

Reading through much of the research on chronic pain, I get a bit perplexed. My life over the last 20 years has been dominated for six of those years by intense daily pain and the rest of the years by considerable pain. Further, there have been the many adversarial aspects of society that intensify that bodily pain. These include an unprepared medical system, insurers' mean-spiritedness, the trial-and-error nature of the effects of drugs and their debilitating side effects. For many others in pain there are employers who don't believe them, impoverishment that sets in when jobs are lost and insurance and disability claims are denied. Chronic pain involves a hyper sensitized nervous system, and is directly made worse by stress. As pain specialist Scott Fishman states: "Pain patients respond to stress with increased pain."[1] The many pain-related social and societal stresses become, by definition, disease factors. Any person living with severe pain –and their families– will tell you that.

Yet, many articles in chronic pain research are solely preoccupied with our psyche. Once it became clear that the biomedical model can only do so much for us, the focus of theorizing and researching did not shift to include the social and societal conditions that stand in the way of pain relief and can make the pain worse. Instead, maintaining the mind/body dualism inherent in the biomedical model, psychological theories took over, shifting the focus from the body to the psyche. I often think I am reading articles in psychological journals rather than in pain management.

Had the "social" in the "psychosocial" model been understood as the *actual* social and societal forces that impact chronic pain, we would have seen a turn, not just to psychology, but to narrative inquiry, to sociology, ethnography, and anthropology, and I would now be reading carefully documented accounts about what we have to cope with from day to day; what happens in doctors' offices as doctors listen, or don't listen, to their pain patients; what kind of knowledge transpires there and what kind of knowledge is absent; what actually happens in hearings with insurance companies and what outdated theories of pain are used to deny claims; what is involved in companies adapting employment practices or failing to do so. I would be reading articles chronicling what the perceptions are about chronic pain held by family members, colleagues, friends, and society in general, and articles about the social politics and the politics of representation that invariably run through all of this.

But rarely do I read any of this in the professional literature about chronic pain. Instead psychological research using standardized methods is now common, putting our psyche front and center. This research focuses on a long, long list of psychological correlates that practically always involve negative personality and cognitive traits already predetermined to characterize people living with chronic pain, before researchers even approach us. We become psychological "cases."

The dominance of the psychological model, I believe, has become detrimental. It over-psychologizes us, heaping the burden of chronic pain onto assumed cognitive, emotional or behavioral deficiencies of one kind or another. Never mind that researchers writing these articles may have no direct and intimate knowledge of the actual day-to-day lives of people who live with pain. Such knowledge is not a prerequisite for their work. Knowledge of psychological traits and measurement instruments are. And before we know it, our problems are defined as psychological in nature. Relieving pain now shifts to working on our assumed psychological weaknesses and pathologies. The problem of pain, over-psychologized, is now entirely ours.

"You are *the only one* who can control your pain," we are told.[2] Reading the psychological research on chronic pain and the Self help books that are typically based on it, I am essentially told that I am responsible for just about everything: for the quality of my communication with doctors and with others (we have 'communication difficulties' and need to learn various communication skills), for the quality of our relationships (we are too withdrawn and need to be more outgoing; or we are too angry and need to learn how to manage our anger; or we inhibit our anger, and need to learn how to express it), for raising our 'self-esteem' (which is automatically is assumed to be low and therefore we need to engage in positive self talk and self-affirming statements), for dealing with the ignorance of society (we need to try to kindly explain our pain), for dealing with our isolation, and so on. Essentially, I have to work on everything myself, as if these presumed personal weaknesses are, in fact, true.

I want to say: "Are you kidding?" I am in serious pain every day. I can no longer work. Doctors have no answers. Society mostly does not believe us. Insurers play horrible games with us. All of that directly impacting my pain. But I am the one who is in control? And I am responsible, with the help of activities and worksheets you provide, for correcting all these presumed personal weaknesses you are superimposing on me?

Of course we can do several things ourselves. I devote a entire section of "Inside Chronic Pain" to just that. Here I am pointing to what happens when chronic pain gets over-psychologized. How realities are distorted. How our pained bodies are pushed aside. How all responsibility is unfairly and unrealistically put on our psychological shoulders. And all that because we have answered questions on a questionnaire or responded in an experiment in a certain way. This dominant psychological measurement approach absolves the concrete real life forces that negatively impact our pain.

It is telling that the literature that psychologizes chronic pain, rarely, if ever, shows an understanding of what lives lived in severe pain are actually like. There is virtually never even as much as a reference to actual accounts of our lives. The researchers seem blissfully unfamiliar with them. The starting point instead lies with existing psychological constructs and measurement procedures that were typically developed to study problems *other than* chronic pain, and which are then applied to a disembodied construct of "chronic pain." Studies often use laboratory experiments that inflict a quick minor pain stimulus. The findings are then unproblematically generalized to "chronic pain." But as Patrick Wall also observes, employing a short pain stimulus (from which research subjects can withdraw any time) has no relation to lives *lived* in persistent pain.[3]

A seemingly unending range of mainly negative psychological constructs are employed. For instance, in an overview of psychological approaches to researching chronic pain by Keefe et al., constructs said to be related to our pain experience include: catastrophizing, fear, anxiety, poor adjustment, problems with coping skills, readiness for change (which we lack), pain behavior, helplessness, self efficacy (which we lack), confidence (which we lack), pain reduction efforts, distraction, redefinition, venting emotions, seeking emotional support, maladaptive responses, extreme pain reports, graded activation, pacing, precontemplation not intending to change, precontemplation intending to change, interpersonally distress, and having a dysfunctional profile.[4] Other researchers add to this list cognitive disengagement, the experience of defeat, intolerance of success, interpersonal relationship problems, aggressive emotions, disturbed early family relationships, early psychosocial adversities, panic disorder, and mental disorders.[5] We are further measured for having an "immature defense style."[6] Still others think we may also have problems with problem solving, dysfunctional beliefs, and anger management. We show inhibited anger, make cognitive errors, and have distorted interpretations of our pain such as believing that pain is harmful. Furthermore, we use a disproportionate amount of downtime (apparently the researcher knows what the appropriate amount of downtime is), and on top of all that we are difficult and hostile. I am sure that if I kept on searching the pain literature I would find still additional pathologies assigned to our personalities.

The length of this list is plainly bizarre in that it is clearly unending. It is constrained only by a researcher's imagination. I often feel that just about any psychological construct, no matter for what problem or for whom it was originally developed, is fair game to throw at our invisible, unmeasurable and therefore easily distorted disease to see if it sticks. How, possibly, do we keep our dignity in the light of such assaults?

People with cancer, heart conditions, or other measurable diseases, are not bombarded with measurement instruments to see if any of the endless personality weaknesses noted above can be correlated with their illness. I believe this is so because of the tyranny of measurement and method: Researchers must measure, even if there is nothing to measure. With other illnesses there is something concrete to measure indicating reasons for the illness. With invisible and unexplainable pain, the empty space left by not being able to measure *has* to be filled with some measurement procedure to satisfy the scientific impulse. Enter psychological and psychiatric researchers, with plenty of measurement instruments already available to subject us to. We are blank slates upon which to project just about anything one can think of. Further, if those with other kinds of illnesses are perceived as "negative," or "hostile," or "emotional," it will be typically attributed to the suffering their illnesses bring on rather than to newly discovered personality pathologies.

In the meantime, we struggle with relentless pain which goes where ever we go. With exhaustion. With loss of jobs and income. With losing our social life. With doctors, friends, employers, and insurers who do not understand what we live with. The problems we encounter are huge and multiple. I actually think that psychologically, most of us are doing quite well given all that.

With acute pain none of this is relevant. People in acute pain are not given psychological tests as there is no assumption that the pain is caused, maintained, or associated with psychological problems. For the most part, acute pain has an immediate cause. It is or soon will be explainable. It is when the pain does not behave as it should (that is, go away), that the unexplainability needs to be filled with something else that is supposedly measurable. For measured it must be.

Chronic pain forces us to live in pain *while* we live in society. We encounter a range of social and societal problems which make our pain worse and which cannot be explained away by psychological theories. Others with chronic illnesses, of course, also have to live in society. But given pain's invisibility, the world throws some very unique and specific societal problems at us as noted throughout this book that directly impact our pain. The long list of assumed psychological problems attributed to us constitutes, however unintentionally, acts of denial, disavowal, distortion, and betrayal.

I am convinced we have barely started to understand how chronic pain's invisibility permeates and complicates every layer, every aspect, and every minute of our lives, wherever we are, with whomever we are. How it impacts societal ignorance, wrong judgments, harsh assessments, misunderstandings, misdiagnoses and disbeliefs. Our psyche cannot be asked to own the effects of all that. Yet, that is exactly what the over-psychologizing of chronic pain asks of us.

The slippery slope toward causation

None of this is to deny that aspects of our psychological lives are not involved in chronic pain. Of course some are. It couldn't be otherwise. It is to point to the obsession in pain research to try to correlate just about any possible psychological problem a human being can have with our pain states. Then, before we realize it, things are turned around and it is suggested that psychological problems bring about and maintain chronic pain. The slippery slope of confusing correlations with causation at times forces itself into print. For instance, Gundel and Tolle agree that "Many psychiatrists or psychologists ask their patients if they can imagine that *some initial psychological pain may have turned into physical pain* (emphasis in text).[7] Jingai Cui, Eisuke Matsushima, Katsuko Aso, Akio Masuda, and Koshi Makita refer to a line of research that points to "inhibited anger as the cause of pain in chronic pain."[8] Richard Chapman and Ernest Volinn describe the cognitive-behavioral model which believes that "the patient failed to return to normal experience and function (that is, to the pre-pain experience) … because the patient holds maladaptive beliefs and attitudes and/or engages in maladaptive or counter-productive behaviors."[9] Robert Teasell and Harold Merskey also take a strong stance against the attribution of causality to psychological factors in chronic pain patients, as does Patrick Wall.[10]

Severe chronic pain as a form of living-in-the-world

When sharp pain wakes me at 4 a.m., what I first am aware of is the hard brutal fact of sharp physical pain – not the thought, not an emotion, as I am essentially still asleep and certainly not yet thinking or feeling. Then, as I groggily struggle to sit up, I am instantly and acutely aware that my world at that moment is entirely different from the world when I am not in pain. It's a different planet that I am on. The awareness is one of an intense aloneness, of being an alien in this world, which is a social experience as much as it is a psychological one. For me, it is a social, existential experience before it is a psychological one. It is the living in the world that persistent pain changes dramatically. As David Morris says,

> Chronic pain may push us toward an area of human life we know
> almost nothing about… It places people in utterly different worlds of

feeling. It surrounds them with silence. In many ways the person in chronic pain might as well be standing on the moon.[11]

No battery of psychological tests can reach us there.

Cynthia Toussant, founder of "For Grace," an organization devoted to the ethical and equal treatment of women in pain, told me that the "isolation" that came with her pain was the worst. Toussant suffered from Complex Regional Pain Syndrome after she injured herself in dancing practice.[12] It took 13 years to be diagnosed. Doctors had dismissed her pain as attention seeking, as a psychological problem. She spent a decade in bed, her legs and then her body on fire. Being so isolated is not in the first instance a psychological problem, although it of course has a major psychological impact. But the nature of the problem is in essence first a social one: a problem of living isolated in pain in a world that can not see pain.

The unimportance of our lives

As noted, the invisibility of chronic pain is not acceptable to mainstream research approaches which demand quantification and measurement in order to make knowledge claims. This makes it necessary for researchers to operationalize (i.e., to make quantifiable) chronic pain, and turn it, somehow, from something immeasurable into something measurable. Within this methodological framework, the shift to the psychological and the psychiatric realms, where measurement protocols already exist, was almost predestined to occur. Knowledge is claimed from our responses to predetermined questions, not from carefully listening to us or observing our actual lives. There is of course no way we can make the complexity of our lives clear on a questionnaire where questions, informed by psychology or psychiatry, predetermine the parameters of our responses.

Those willing to truly listen will find that most of us are dealing admiringly well with our extremely challenging circumstances. Researchers who over-psychologize us will simply never find out. As noted earlier, rarely do I find references in the psychological literature to narratives of our lived experience as documented by qualitative studies or by the work of journalists.[13] Rarely, if ever, do I see references to historical and cultural descriptions of lives in pain[14], to novelists writing about their own lives in pain,[15] to professionals who talk about their own pain,[16] and to the many, many voices of regular folks who speak of living with pain on various web sites of pain organizations. All that is essentially absent from the psychological research on chronic pain. Our actual lives and our voices and perspectives are not considered.

This absence is stunning. One would think that publications that address in-depth what it is like to live with chronic pain would be central to any attempt to study chronic pain from a psychological perspective. That this is not the case reveals the insular and reductionist world of the dominant research paradigm. Courses are now offered in narrative medicine at some medical schools, but I doubt there are any requirements in the education of psychologists or psychiatrists to read texts that inform what it is like to live with persistent pain, or a requirement to get to know our lives first hand.

Over-psychologizing using standard measurement protocols, is so pervasive a habit that even when a more comprehensive view is promised, it does not happen. For instance, the editor of a special issue of "The Pain Practitioner" on pain and depression, promises in his introduction a "complementary" and "inclusive" approach that will unite many opposites, such as "the internal and external milieu, body and brain, brain and mind, physiological and phenomenological, and "ultimately the self and other(s)."[17] I felt pleasantly surprised when I read these words, particularly about the "self and other" part, as that would bring us squarely into the actual social and societal realms. Or so I thought. But it doesn't happen, except for a fleeting reference (no discussion) to the work by David Morris and Elaine Scarry. The researchers in this issue focus instead squarely on the individual in pain and what are seen as their psychological problems. "Social factors" and "environmental factors" are referred to only as abstractions, to be related to existing psychological constructs steeped in assumptions of pathology, when stating for instance, that "social factors" may be contributing to the development of "negative schemas" or "learned helplessness."[18]

The "social factors" *themselves* are not to be found in this issue until the very last article, written, tellingly, not by a researcher, but by Dan O'Neal, a person living with pain. O'Neal tells us, how, when still working as a contractor, his employer told him that if he filed a "Workman's Comp" because of injuries he incurred on the job, he would be most likely let go.[19] This, as he notes, was of course illegal. He indeed loses his job when his employer is not willing to let him come back to work on light duty, which O'Neil thought he could handle. His story then tells of his struggles with Workman's Compensation, having no income, and living on credit cards. "One step close to homeless," he says.

All of this was building up and I was ready to blow at any given moment. I was ready to blow my brains out or swallow a whole bottle of pills… So now I am out of insurance and I don't know what to do. I'm scared… I would find a private place in my home where I could go to cry. And let me tell you, I did my share of crying… I was depressed to the point that I really wanted to check out of life.[20]

That reality is something quite different from scoring high on a "learned helplessness" scale used in psychological research which completely ignores the concrete specifics of real life context. To diagnose O'Neil with "learned helplessness" does him no good. He doesn't suffer from "learned helplessness." He is experiencing intense frustration as he is unjustly treated in ways that are detrimental to his life. What he needs is help with his insurance claim. And with his threatening employer.

The mean spiritedness and the immense societal barriers O'Neil experienced are precisely the kind of "social" and "environmental factors" which directly impact and increase pain states. Yet psychological research turns them into abstractions. A researcher doesn't even have to observe these actual "social factors." The strategies that are offered (positive self talk, cognitive rephrasing, minimizing 'catastrophizing') are equally contextless. They do not address these "social factors."

In contrast, O'Neil makes clear in describing his struggles how "social factors" actually do their work. He shows how the "self and other" function interdependently in his real life. He shows how the specifics of these forces contribute, not to psychological constructs such as "negative schemas" and "learned helplessness," but to his existential despair, which is an entirely different matter. Moreover, O'Neil shows us his courage, endurance and persistence (attributes which never show up in the literature that psychologizes chronic pain) in spite of these negative barriers. He even gets involved in a pain advocacy organization and becomes a "sort of social worker" for others in pain.

Of course, I too experience bouts of anxiety, hopelessness, and depression – as existential distresses. They are correlates of living with persistent pain, with the 'nightmare of losses' that accompany it, and with the unbelievable efforts we are forced to engage in to get access to help. These existential distresses are not psycho-pathological problems, but are the co-emergent outcomes of the physical, social, societal and political difficulties that we encounter. Outcomes which demand an embodied and far more complex research approach than presently offered by psychology.

Again, my critique here is not to say that the psychological is not involved. I am objecting to the *dissolving* of the chronic pain experience into psychological pathologizing. This literature is no longer about the life of the person in pain. It is about the life, and the language, of a particular approach to psychology.

Pain behavior

"Pain behavior" is a central construct in behavioral theorizing. Behaviorism holds that all behaviors are conditioned, and that there is a predictable pattern between stimulus and response. If you can control the stimulus, then you will also be able to control how humans behave. Operant conditioning specifically holds that learning occurs by the use of rewards for desired behaviors and punishments for undesired behaviors.[21] In pain management research, the purpose of operant conditioning is to reward "non-pain behaviors" and to extinguish "pain behaviors" (e.g. grimaces, verbal complaints, and postural pain movements), and to minimize our supposed identification with the sick role.

Thus I read, "... specific rewards are provided when exercise quotas or activity goals are met, and pain behaviors are not rewarded by attention from the therapist."[22] These words make me think of the popularity of behavior modification in the 70s and 80s in institutions for the mentally challenged and the mentally ill, but behaviorism's popularity has diminished even in those fields. Hence, I was very surprised to see it still used in pain medicine. Within pain research, others too have commented on the outdated nature of behaviorism.[23]

It can get a bit bizarre, when researchers conclude that "provision of desirable and/or reinforcing responses such as expressions of sympathy may be more important to patients than reductions in pain or disability."[24] Hence, spouses in these studies were taught to ignore their spouse's pain behaviors, thus presumably "extinguishing" them. Thus, when people in pain elicit help or emotional support from their spouses by telling them they are in pain, they want sympathy rather than help with managing the pain.

It could ruin a marriage.

Hasn't it occurred to the researchers that the person in pain may just have a fine relationship with their spouse and that they do not need to hide their pain as we routinely have to? Hence we can relax and tell truth, which in turn can lower pain levels. Have they ever considered that spousal support may have to do, let's say, with love, with affection, with caring? When I am in a good relationship, I simply express what is going on at the moment, because our relationship welcomes that. I show moments of pain as well as moments of humor, of affection, of intellectual exchanges, and so forth. But a behavioral researcher, focusing narrowly on "pain behaviors" would not see any of that. Moreover, as pain physician Pam Squire points out, there is a complex nociceptive system, but there is also an equally complex "anti-nociceptive" system.[25] Anti-nociceptive signals include placebos, exercise, and "comforting." Asking for empathy and comfort can be pain reducing acts. When my daughter makes me a cup of tea when I collapse on the couch in pain and need to rest my neck, I am, according to behaviorism, using my 'pain behavior' (resting on the couch, telling her my neck hurts) to obtain her sympathy, not to reduce my pain. In fact, her making me tea, glad she can do something for me, helps me to relax which lowers pain intensity.

For those who truly exaggerate their pain in order to get attention: Who cares. There are always people in life who exaggerate to get attention. Many a reader may perhaps even blushingly admit that they themselves at times exaggerate to be the center of attention or otherwise get what they want. It is utterly bizarre to me, to say the least, to focus on an extremely vulnerable group of people whose lives are already terribly difficult, to see if we are "sympathy getters" by showing "pain behaviors."

Accepting, committing, and distorting

It is surprising to me, that the machine model of human behavior shows up in one of the latest approaches to pain management. Acceptance and Commitment Therapy (ACT). To be sure, as Keefe et al. also note, acceptance theory within pain research is not clearly defined.[26] Some warn that the emphasis on "acceptance" can create an additional barrier between chronic pain patient and healthcare professional.[27] Still others, such as Dahl and Lundgren, use "acceptance" to weave a mechanistic story that turns physical pain into an apparently insignificant 'thing' we can chose not to pay attention to.[28] According to these authors, pain is no more than what our thoughts or make of it. If only we turn our attention to what we really want in life, we can live the life we want. Such a complete cognitive-behavioral redefinition of chronic pain reflects and reinforces a general attitude in society that says to a person in pain: "Just think of something else."

Thus, when sharp pain wakes me around 4 a.m. every morning, that is not a problem. But the moment I think: "Oh, god, I cannot do this for the 7003rd time...," now, then we have a problem! For even the thought "I am in pain," Dahl and Lundgren argue, is the actual problem that messes us up. Do away with negative thoughts and the pain is no longer reinforced.

When physical pain is said to be caused by our thoughts we are silenced all over again. Dahl and Lundgren are an extreme example of utter cognitive reductionism and of the continued use of the outdated mind-as-machine metaphor in pain management, but softer versions of the "just say no to pain" movement are rather wide spread. Employers and insurers and society at large will welcome it: By attributing pain to the thoughts of the sufferer, everyone else is off the hook.

ACT was developed for psychological problems by psychologist Steven Hayes who himself suffered from panic attacks and was helped by using the psychological principles of ACT (none of which relate to the body in pain).[29] We can all benefit from observing the way we think about our problems and becoming more flexible in our thinking and in the words we use, but to *dissolve* physical pain into cognitive principles is an entirely different matter.

Here are some of the real world word-pictures of pain and its relation to thought and language by those suffering from it (including a well known novelist, a well know physician, a well known journalist): "The pain changes everything. It makes it hard to speak and difficult to concentrate, and nearly impossible to stay human. It crowds every other thought out of your brain."[30] Or, "Pain changes you, washes over you in waves and erodes away at the very core of your being. It eats away at your spirit ... our lives shut down to prepare for what we have to endure. Conversations with others are impossible."[31] Or, "My pain is so definite and overbearing that I am losing my ability to think clearly."[32] Or, "Intense pain is all-consuming. It takes over your life, and it's impossible to focus on much else."[33] Or, "Pain blots out the horizon, fills everything...Pain stops me from thinking."[34] Or, "Because of relentless pain, I couldn't work, I couldn't move, I could hardly think."[35] When in great pain," says Elaine Scarry, "the contents of consciousness dies."[36] "Pain," says physician Biro, "is an all-consuming internal experience that threatens to destroy everything except itself..."[37]

Just think of something else. For the millions who suffer from severe ongoing pain, the "just think of something else" approaches to pain management are an affront. They bypass reality. They trivialize. And one must wonder, for whose benefit they were developed.

Suicidality

Given the unacceptable high numbers of suicides among us, I decided to highlight suicidality to note, how even with regard to this final act, our lives in pain are misrepresented when over-psychologizing chronic pain. For instance, a review by psychologist Nicole Tang and psychiatrist Catherine Crane of 12 research studies as well as of additional "empirical" and "theoretical" work on "risk factors" for suicide, identifies the following factors: type, intensity and duration of the pain, insomnia, helplessness and hopelessness, the desire to escape from pain, pain catastrophizing and avoidance, and deficits in problem solving abilities, all seen as "psychological processes."[38] The authors conclude that there is an urgent need to examine how these psychological factors "mediate or exacerbate suicidality, and to develop enhanced interventions for pain patients at risk." Tang and Crane specifically propose "enhanced intervention" in the two areas they conclude are highly correlated with suicidality: "pain catastrophizing" by having us tone down our supposedly exaggerated negative self talk, and "deficits in problem solving abilities" (it is left unexplained what the actual intervention to address our supposed deficits in problem solving would look like).[39]

People living with serious chronic pain, who didn't already have a major mental illness before chronic pain entered their lives, have a different view: What comes to mind when we read "risk factors for suicide" is, foremost, Pain. We experience the actual pain as a brutal fact that itself is unbearable and can directly lead to suicide. The foremost reason I was seriously suicidal during a stretch of roughly six years, was Pain. For as George Clooney said, whose excruciating pain after a fall was fortunately taken away with surgeries (though even his complaints were initially also dismissed), "You'll have to kill yourself at some point, you can't live like this."[40]

Tang and Crane however insist on psychological factors that "fuel" the desire to escape pain, such as "defeat" and "entrapment."[41] These factors then can be used according to these authors as intervention "targets" – and *that* is precisely where the problem comes in.

Of course constructs such as defeat, helplessness, and hopelessness are involved in ending our lives, but they do not pop up out of nowhere. They come from somewhere. And that is completely ignored in the over-psychologizing of chronic pain. They are not independent "variables" that serve directly as "targets" for interventions. Proposing that psychological processes need to be intervened directly, can in fact present barriers to come to an accurate understanding of why we end our lives. Nor do we end our lives because, according to other research cited by Tang and Crane, we have "greater difficulties in making specific plans of how to achieve desired goals in the future."[42] I am stunned when I read these kinds of research results. I write in the margin, furiously: "You forget that we have *Pain*. Debilitating pain." Planning for desired goals in the future implies a degree of control, resources, health, energy, ability. All of which those living with severe pain have lost. When intense physical pain prevents you from even knowing what you can do this day, your efforts are focused on getting through the day, often hour by hour. We are assigned psychological deficiencies that are completely out of tune with what living with persistent severe pain does to a life.

Tang and Crane's conclusion after their lengthy review of the literature, that "pain catastrophizing forms a logical target for intervention" to try to prevent suicide, as well as teaching us some "problem-solving skills" is mind-boggling.[43] If during my intensely suicidal years a psychologist would have told me to stop "catastrophizing" and say positive things to myself instead, and work on problem solving as the two means to suicide prevention, I would have left. I would have gone home and listened to beautiful music, meditated, and cuddled up with my cats instead to keep the desire to end my life at a distance.

If such disciplines as sociology, ethnography, and anthropology were considered as important in pain research as psychology, we would have a very different picture of what the risks are for our far too frequent suicides (see also chapter 13).

It is all so obvious to us. When I read that a researcher concludes that "relatively little is known about potential risk factors," I shake my head in disbelief.[44] "Have you ever asked us?" I want to say. But I already know the answer: "No." Because what people in pain say themselves is not "scientific." It is "only" anecdotal. Hence it cannot be seen as trustworthy knowledge. I want to say, "Just invite a dozen of us for an evening, create a trusting atmosphere, and we will tell you about what gets us to want to end our lives. Do not bring questionnaires. Just be prepared to listen attentively, respectfully, and carefully." To date, I have not come across such a study.

"Have you ever lived with us for a week or so to learn why we are suicidal?" I want to ask. But again, I already know the answer: "No." For the field's privileged research methods are not designed to look at our real lives. If researchers would genuinely listen to us, or live with us for a while, they would find many possible reasons for our suicidal ideations and attempts.

As one of the limits of their overview study, Tang and Crane do note that several studies have not controlled for social and demographic factors that may confer increased suicide risk, such as "older age, financial hardship, unemployment."[45] However, such aspects of our lives that indeed contribute to despair and suicidal ideations should not be statistically "controlled" so that psychological problems can be better isolated. They should be carefully observed in their own right and policies developed as to what can be done about these actual risk factors.

In the end, what has been most striking to me in the literature that over-psychologizes chronic pain, are *the intensely negative attributes ascribed to us*. The list of psychological features researchers associate with chronic pain, bizarre in its unending nature, are virtually all negative ones. Reading this literature feels like being hit over the head, over and over. We become even more voiceless than we already are by pain's invisibility: Being accused of so much pathology, how can anything we say still be seen as rational?

Nowhere in the psychological literature do I read how chronic pain can bring out courage and persistence. Nowhere do I read how chronic pain can increase compassion for others who suffer. I do not read about the immense endurance and patience many of us develop. Or how we develop our resourcefulness in spite of all that works against us. How so many of us still manage a semblance of family life, even work life which, given persistent pain, demands extraordinary determination, sacrifice, and resourcefulness. And that perhaps, is the most damaging outcome of the over-psychologizing of chronic pain. An outcome that takes our dignity away, and misinforms the healthcare profession and the public alike.

5   *Please don't do this to us... the psychiatrizing of chronic pain*

...confusing similarity in form with identity in nature....
Victor Frankl, *The Doctor and the Soul*

The problem is that the diagnostic manual we are using in psychiatry is like a field guide, and it just keeps expanding and expanding... Pretty soon, we'll have a syndrome for short, fat Irish guys with a Boston accent, and I'll be mentally ill.

Paul McHugh, in *Unhinged.*
The Trouble with Psychiatry

The reason for addressing psychiatric research in a book that focuses on the broader societal forces that impact the chronic pain experience, is two-fold. First, choosing to apply psychiatric constructs to chronic pain sufferers distorts the reality of our lives and who we are as people. And second, in doing so, negative societal stereotypes held by society at large, and born of ignorance, are reinforced. Below I will outline why there are profound problems with psychiatric assessments for people who had no psychiatric problems before they encountered chronic pain.

In my own case, I was sent to a psychiatrist two years after the accident that caused persistent and intense pain. The referring pain specialist told me the reason for the referral was that the psychiatrist could order an MRI quicker than the pain clinic could. But it took only a few "yes" responses on my part to a list of questions the psychiatrist fired at me read from a sheet of paper, to be informed that I needed to see him again. When I asked why, he told me that he saw "his patients" once a month. I had become "his patient," a psychiatrist's patient, in no time, because I had said "yes" to a few questions – questions not even related to my life in pain. This is not to suggest that there aren't still excellent psychiatrists around who listen attentively and offer helpful advice or that prescribing psychiatric medications might not be the right thing for some of us.

Never having been to a psychiatrist before, I had automatically expected we would have a real talk about my actual life in pain. But, no. He listened to no more than the basics of what happened, then asked me if my parents had been happy, and if I had a "boyfriend" (I was fifty five at the time). Then he turned to his list of questions. Done with the questions, he immediately pre-scribed Prozac (which I refused) without asking me if I wanted it. I was not told what my diagnosis was. I am assuming 'depression,' or 'anxiety.' Or some other disorder listed in the Diagnostic Statistical Manual (DSM).

The DSM is the diagnostic handbook used by psychiatrists, by both cli-nicians and researchers, to draw "a line between what is 'normal' and what is not."[1] It is psychiatry's "peculiar bible" as Daniel Carlat, author of "Unhinged. The Trouble with Psychiatry" refers to it.[2] Says Thomas Insel, Director of the National Institutes of Health (NIH), "(I)t is, at best, a dictionary, creating a set of labels and defining each… (ensuring) that clinicians use the same terms in the same ways."[3] The diagnostic labels, and the symptoms that accompany each label, create a common language for describing pathology, thus creating a measure of reliability. But, says Insel, "The weakness is its lack of validity."

The history of the development of the DSM should worry any person living with chronic pain who is sent to a psychiatrist: The DSM now contains so many possible disorders (297 in the 1994 edition) that one could be di-agnosed with some of them just by getting a few questions "right" almost by chance. For given the immense complexities and difficulties of lives lived in pain, and given that severe chronic pain works itself into every niche of life, the person in pain will experience 'symptoms' that, according to the DSM, belong to certain psychiatric disorders, and will respond with a "yes" when asked about these symptoms. The required number of "yes" responses for a particular diagnosis to be made is essentially subjective. As I have learned since, the cut off number to receive a particular diagnosis is the result of a committee vote.

Carlat, in an interview with Robert Spitzer, the main figure in the de-velopment of the DSM, asked Spitzer, "How did you decide, for example, on *five* criteria as being your minimum threshold for depression?"[4]

"It was just a consensus," Spitzer answered. "We would ask clinicians and researchers, 'How many symptoms do you think patients ought to have before you would give the diagnosis of depression?' And we came up with the arbitrary number of five."

"But why did you choose five and not four? Or why didn't you choose six?" Carlat persisted.

"Because four just seemed like not enough. And six seemed like too much."

I had to take a deep breath, reading this exchange.

My fate, my status of being 'normal' or 'not normal,' is in the hands of psychiatrists who essentially bypass the major ongoing crisis in my life, ask me a number of questions from a sheet of paper, and then see if I have given the "consensus" number of responses to qualify for a particular diagnosis.

Psychiatrists, says Carlat, no longer learn psychotherapy.[5] "Psycho-pharmacology," he says, "was infinitely easier to master than therapy." "I *don't* do psychotherapy because I *can't* do psychotherapy," he says.[6] He was never taught how to do anything else but prescribe drugs. Instead of talking and listening, psychiatrists learn to ask the "right questions" to get to a diagnosis.[7] Psychiatrist Donald Levins tells how years ago he often saw patients ten or more times before arriving at a diagnosis.[8] Now he makes that decision in the first 45 minutes. "You have to have a diagnosis to get paid...I play the game," he explained. Says psychiatrist Nancy Anderson, "DSM has had a dehumanizing impact on the practice of psychiatry. History taking –the central evaluation tool in psychiatry– has frequently been reduced to the use of the DSM checklist."[9] Precisely my experience.

Consider also, given chronic pain's fluctuating nature, it is quite possible that had I had a pain free day when I saw the psychiatrist and said "yes" to fewer questions, I might not have given the required number of "yes" responses. Had I had a terrible day and answered "yes" to more of his questions, heaven knows what other diagnoses I might have received. Severe pain overwhelms, and the level of pain on any given day shapes one's outlook on life. Thus, my assumed psychiatric disorder could be "diagnosed" one day and not another day based on my pain level at the time of the appointment.

The DSM is updated approximately every decade. And 'updated' has meant, without exception, that new mental disorders have been added with each update.[10] Psychiatry, Carlat states, has nothing anymore to do with its original mission – to discover the causes of mental illness and to treat those causes. "Our diagnostic process is shallow," states Carlat. Carlat's book is an honest story of how he himself got caught in this shallowness.

Psychiatric diagnosis has gotten out of hand, says Allen Francis, chair of the DSM-IV Task force. Having functioned in that role, Francis takes partial responsibility for this "diagnostic inflation."[11] The latest 2013 DSM-V edition, he says, reduces the thresholds for diagnoses even further and "recklessly" introduces new ones. As I came across more and more articles in pain research written by psychiatrists and psychologists assigning us a wide range of pathological conditions, I realized that not only shyness and stage fright and grief and other normal problems in living have been hijacked by psychiatry, but also chronic pain. I often feel I am asked to forget about the pain I live with and think of myself instead as someone afflicted with all kinds of psychological and psychiatric problems. And when I happened to read the two articles I critique below, by Iorio et al. and by Datz, on the same day, I felt pushed over the edge. [12] I pretty much blew up.

Iorio et al. report on their study titled, "Examining the Prevalence of Psychiatric Features within a Chronic Pain Population." Two hundred and one chronic pain patients were given an extended version of the Mini International Neuropsychiatric Interview (M.I.N.I.), a diagnostic inventory which explores 17 disorders based on the 1987 version of the DSM. The M.I.N.I. is a "short, semi-structured diagnostic inventory." All we are told of the "population" is that there are 84 men and 115 women (plus 2 sex unspecified) with a mean age of 47, accessed through pain clinics. We have no idea what kind of lives these pain patients are living. How bad their pain is. What losses have occurred because of their pain. Have they lost their jobs? Their income? Have they had to move to a basement apartment? Do they have a good doctor? Or do they feel, as so many of us do, that our doctors would rather not see us? Does their pain specialist listen to them? Has their spouse or their friends withdrawn? Are they in a terrible fight with their insurance company or compensation board? Can they no longer travel, hike, or ride their bike? Are they homebound? How do they take care of children when in constant pain? We know nothing about these critical aspects of lives in pain, and for all we know, nor do the researchers.

After filling out this one "short, semi-structured" inventory (which given my own experience with inventories, might take roughly half an hour complete, maybe even less) there are apparently enough data to decide if these pain patients suffered from one or more of the following: "major depressive episode with or without melancholic features, dysthymia, bipolar I or II, panic disorder, agoraphobia, social phobia, specific phobia, obsessive compulsive disorder, generalized anxiety disorder, substance disorders (alcohol dependency, alcohol abuse, substance dependence and abuse), anorexia, bulimia, somatization disorder, hypochondriasis, body dysmorphic disorder, pain disorder, and/or suicidality."

Anxiety disorders were found to be the most prevalent (in 72.86% of this group of pain patients), with mood disorders following closely behind (70.85%). In the end, between 20 and 80 out of 201 pain patients, that is between 10% and 40%, came down with at least more than one psychiatric condition, some with more. Iorio et. al. conclude that the prevalence of psychiatric disorders for chronic pain patients is "substantial." Pain patients have "comorbid psychiatric disorders" which, they say, should be treated. "Treated" is not further defined, but given the pharmaceutical orientation of today's psychiatry it most certainly translates into prescribing psychiatric medications.

Given, the authors say, that psychiatric disorders often go "undetected" by primary care physicians, pain management needs "enhanced detection" of these disorders so that treatment "may be increased." "Enhanced detection." Just keep probing me with enough questions of an abstract nature (that is, not directly related to, nor showing any interest in, my actual pain experience), and I will be rendered a psychiatric case.

Reading the Iorio et al. study I flipped. I wrote furiously in the margins: "Please, don't do this to us!" "Don't flippantly assign us mental illnesses on top of what we already have to deal with." "This is unconscionable!" – because assigning mental illness to someone can be extremely consequential, particularly if the person does not have the background to know how it is done and believes he or she is now also a 'psychiatric case'. To be assigned a mental illness carries an enduring stigma.

Once I calmed down, I thought a lot about how it is, that people suffering from ongoing pain end up being seen as having mental illnesses. That doesn't happen to people living with cancer, heart problems, or diabetes. Their irritability, their anger, their despair, their moodiness are seen as directly tied to the difficulties their diseases create and their justified worries about their future – rather than as signs of personal pathology. Again, given researchers see themselves as measurers, they have a hard time with the vagueness of chronic pain. But they can, they think, measure psychological and psychiatric conditions, so at least *something* can be measured and related to chronic pain.

And, as the Iorio et al. study shows, there are plenty of mental disorders to be 'found.' Clinical psychologist Geralyn Datz, Director of the Pain

Management Program at Forrest General Hospital in Massachusetts, further suggests testing pain patients for "histrionic or borderline tendencies," "hypochondriasis," "hysteria," "neurotic, psychotic, and impulse control disorders," "antisocial traits", and is also on the look out for "narcissistic" pain patients.[13] While Datz' assessment is to detect who is at risk for opioid abuse, it is not acknowledged that those who abuse opioids are often people not suffering from chronic pain who managed to get hold of pain medications, or pain patients who have not been properly prescribed, and many of us have not been. All opioid abuse is implied to be a result of assumed psychiatric problems.

What is so deeply disturbing about the Datz article is that it tells the reader, over and over, that assessing pain patients for all these pathologies is an easy task. Unbelievably, there are eleven references to how quickly and easily these instruments can be administered and scored, and how important it is to have tools that are easy and quick to administer. Datz refers to eleven questionnaires, designed to detect the mental and personality disorders listed above, and comments on them as follows:

> "It is an easy-to-use questionnaire that can be completed in less than 10 minutes;" "A shorter, 14-item version of this measure also exists;" "...is a 5-item, yes/no self-report questionnaire...;" "... in some settings, brief measures are a good choice...; an array of "practical problems" (mentioned are shortage of staff, lack of access to an experienced psychologist) "may influence the use of brief psychological testing;" "For some practices, hand-scored, quick measurements are the only option for assessing psychopathology." "...are useful for quick screening purposes..., "...takes about 10 minutes to administer and score. It has been widely used to document the depressive symptoms and outcomes in samples of chronic pain patients." "... takes little time...;" "...a 44-item measure designed to quickly assess psychopathology." "...is shorter, easier..."[14]

The message here should anger those living with pain: assessing people living with pain for serious psychopathology is a piece of cake. Apparently, our personal pathologies are so pronounced that 'finding' them is easy. Would these short, quick instruments be used for patients who suffer other illnesses –cancer, heart disease, diabetes– to see if they "have" psychiatric illnesses that cause their ailments? Would they be so flippantly and quickly diagnosed to be hysterical, histrionic attention seekers, anti-social, narcissistic, and all the rest of it? This is psychiatry run amok.

There is a reference in Datz' article to the "clinical" interview that "must be comprehensive and take into consideration 'the whole person.'"[15] It is difficult to see, however, when everything has to be done quickly, as there are "15 patients still to see and you have a consult at the hospital" (thus Datz introduces her article), how comprehensive the "comprehensive" interview can be. When there is "lack of access to an experienced psychologist, time constraints, cost limitations, and staff availability to administer, score, and interpret results," says Datz, "hand-scored quick measurements are the only option for assessing psychopathology."[16] Gone is the comprehensive interview. Gone is "the whole person," a phrase which appears twice and is written both times between quotation marks, as if there is an underlying awareness that "the whole person" cannot be assessed using quick and easy to use instruments.

Marcia Angell, in a discussion of recent books that critique the psychiatric profession (she includes the books by Daniel Carlat and Robert Whitaker) notes how the number of people diagnosed with mental illnesses has risen at a "mind-boggling rate."[17] She notes two reasons: the expanded nature of the criteria for mental illness so that nearly everyone has one, and the fact that the psychiatric profession has allied itself with, and is manipulated by, the pharmaceutical industry. I would add a third reason: the ease and speed by which a doctor or researcher supposedly can diagnose a mental illness.

The questions psychiatrists ask are mere tools to come up with a diagnosis. The psychiatrist I was sent to definitely had no interest in my life lived in pain. "I realized I barely knew most of them," admits Daniel Carlat about his patients.[18] Checking the articles I critique above, I can find no references that would have informed the researchers what it is like to actually *live with pain*. How is it possible that researchers' and clinicians' stories of pathology trump ours about our real lives at every turn? Why are theirs so privileged? And our stories so de-privileged? Erased, in fact?

> There is such a thing as absolute power over narrative. Those who secure this privilege for themselves can arrange stories about others pretty much where, and as, they like.[19]

Novelist Chinua Achebe, a keen observer of the privileging of certain stories over others, speaks of the need for "re-storying." In pain research, the privileged stories are those of medicine, psychology, and psychiatry. Not of the humanities, phenomenology, ethnography, anthropology, autobiography, art, sociology – fields of study that address the specific and the real life conditions of our lives, which we very rarely see represented in the professional pain literature.

During the worst years of my life in pain I would often break down in the office of my wonderful therapist.[20] He listened. He never pathologized. Never judged. Therefore, I was at ease. It is miraculously freeing to be with a professional who really wants to understand what you are trying to say – my devastating experience was worthy of being understood. One day, in the midst of a stretch of days filled with relentless pain, I asked him, "Am I crazy? Am I exaggerating? Is my life not as difficult as I say it is?"

What *if* he had said – "Well, let's see. You surely would meet the criteria for a serious anxiety disorder. And given you are now feeling you are going crazy, that points to a major case of mental instability. I also know you feel you are no longer the person you were before the accident, so that points to a distortion of your perception of self – I'd say, we are also looking at a personality disorder. You further told me you often don't see your life as worthwhile anymore, so that points to a major depression. You have told me your pain keeps you from socializing and you feel detached from others. I fear that points to a avoidance personality disorder as well as a societal anxiety disorder. Your intense fear for your future would make you a catastrophizer. And your sudden mood swings could point to a bit of a borderline case – I'm not quite saying bi-polar, but something in that direction…"

I hope I would have stood up, left without paying and without saying good bye. Never to return. Thankfully, my therapist is a sane man. He said, firmly and with compassion,

> No, you are not crazy. You are perfectly sane. You have gone and are going through immense difficulties, and anyone would suffer as you do. You are not exaggerating. Your pain is exhausting as it would be for anyone. It would be unbearable for anyone.

My therapist understands pain. He understands that all my "symptoms" – from withdrawing from social contact to feeling I am at times going crazy to experiencing sudden mood swings, are a direct consequence, not of having a psychiatric disorder, but of living with relentless pain from which one cannot walk away. Not even for a minute.

That is maddening. But that does not make me mad. Just as people trapped in a war zone where grenades explode around them feel they are going crazy, are neither crazy nor depressed. Just imagine, a researcher knocking on their door, diagnostic inventory in hand, seemingly oblivious to the fact they are in the midst of a war. He starts firing off questions: Are you unhappy? Do you think of death? Do you worry about the future? "Yes?" Well, then you are seriously depressed. You suffer from... etc. Had anyone not shown any stress symptoms, but acted relaxed and content – *that* would have been cause for concern.

An outlandish comparison? Not really. People who live with constant severe pain are not of this world. They live in a world akin to war. Pain specialist Scott Fishman's book is called: "The War on Pain." You don't fight a war if the situation is not war-like. Many writings on chronic pain use war metaphors such as "conquering," "targeting," "winning the war on pain." Chronic pain evokes war metaphors because it, itself, is war-like. It is harmful, unpredictable in its attacks, and can lead to death when suicide presents itself as the only solution left for pain control.[21]

Assigning psychiatric disorders to people living with relentless pain who have no prior history of psychiatric disturbances, because we have 'symptoms' of disorders noted in the DSM, illustrates the category confusion Victor Frankl points to:

> Suffering may well be a human achievement, especially if the suffering grows out of existential frustration... Existential frustration is in itself neither pathological nor pathogenic. A man's concern, even his despair over the worthwhileness of life is an *existential distress* but by no means a *mental disease*."[22]

To judge the responses that people living with pain give to questions on a psychiatric inventory, and then to attribute the mental disorder to the chronic pain patient, is a case of mistaken identity. What is happening, says Victor Frankl, recounting an analogous situation, is a case of "confusing similarity in form with identity in nature."[23]

Scott Fishman too implies the habit of "confusing similarity in form with identity in nature" where he states,

> Patients who are trapped in [the medical maze] are easily labeled. We say the patient is "amplifying" because they're angry or frustrated. Or maybe we say they have a "personality disorder." In fact anyone who is stressed enough will look like they have a personality disorder. Then we blame the patient.[24]

Patrick Wall, co-author with Melzack of the gate-control theory, similarly comments with a measure of irony, on the notion that depression, anxiety, and fatalism, so commonly seen in people suffering from relentless pain, morph into the primary cause of pain rather than being understood as a consequence of the pain.[25] This stance, he says, is particularly popular among doctors committed to a therapy that has failed their patient and now blame the patient. He then gives an example from urology about patients who suffered from terrible pain and developed deep depression and anxiety and became heavy users of opioids. Once successfully treated, the pain disappeared and what had been considered psychiatric disorders disappeared.

Once you lose your job, your relationships, your marriage, your social life, your income, the ability to engage physical activities you used to do, *on top of* having relentless pain – it would be strange, to say the least, not to develop depression, anxiety, irritability, despair, panic, all resulting from these *existential crises* rather than from psychopathology. Polly Young-Eisendrath tells of a man named Dan, who became a quadriplegic in a major car accident:

> Still in the hospital in an intensive care unit, and in great pain he was trying to communicate his agony to the staff, but they showed little understanding or empathy. Instead, they sent a psychiatrist to treat him for depression. When the doctor began asking Dan about his relationships in early childhood, Dan demanded that the psychiatrist leave the room.[26]

I admire this man for sending the psychiatrist away.

What happens to assumed psychiatric disorders when the pain disappears?

Another way of looking at the problem of "confusing similarity in form with identity in nature", is to ask the question, what happens when the pain disappears?

In 2008 one of my daughters, then living in Hawaii, delivered my first grandchild. I so much wanted to go and we planned a two week visit. Travelling alone is extremely tricky for me, having landed me twice in an ER room when an intense pain attack in the plane immobilized me. Because of this, my pain specialist timed cortisone injections to correspond with the time of my visit. They stopped the pain. Miraculously. I was so happy. It felt as if the accident and its aftermath of endless pain had never happened. I jumped on the plane, happy and free from worry. Ideally, the cortisone effects could last up to three months and then the injections could be repeated. I secretly counted on it. Eleven days into the visit, just before I had to return, the pain came roaring back. The trip back home was disastrous.

What happened to whatever mental disorders I might have been assigned? After the injections, finally able to sleep, I slept for almost thirty hours straight, woke up, and felt fantastic. My head and heart and mind and brain were clear again. I recognized myself the way I was before the accident. Energy came back. A sunny disposition came back. Anxiety, depression, irritability – *poof!* Gone. Had I had a psychiatric disorder, cortisone shots would not have taken it away. My daughter was correct: "You are not a depressed person. You have very depressing times." She saw me becoming myself again when the true cause of a despondent pain state decided to stay away for a while.

Merskey and Teasell too note that psychological complaints "remit dramatically" after successful treatment of pain and conclude that psychological behaviors from pain should not be treated as psychological illness but simply as "markers of distress."[27]

In psychiatrizing the chronic pain experience, there are two research directions that particularly irritate us: the research on "catastrophizing" and the research on "secondary gain." Both reflect, and thus reinforce, societal misperceptions and stereotypes.

Catastrophizing: whose hyperbole is it?

Since the 1990s, the notion of 'catastrophizing' has taken hold in pain research. Catastrophizing is defined in various overlapping ways – but all echo stereotypes society in general believes about us. For instance, "Pain catastrophizing refers to a negative view of the pain experience. It is exaggerated or blown out of proportion."[28] Catastrophizing is "the tendency to focus on and exaggerate the threat value of painful stimuli and negatively evaluate one's own ability to deal with pain."[29] Catastrophizing is a "cognitive error."[30] It is a "negative distorted belief about oneself or one's situation."[31] It is a "thinking error... the tendency to predict the future negatively without considering less extreme, more likely outcomes."[32] Catastrophizing is "characterizing pain as awful, horrible, and unbearable."[33] It is "a form of extremely negative thinking represented by a person taking the view that pain or a situation related to pain will lead to or is associated with a physical or mental catastrophe."[34] "Pain catastrophizing [is] a pervasive set of dysfunctional beliefs or appraisals of one's ability to manage or tolerate pain."[35] Catastrophizing is a perception of the pain that "makes it worse than it is."[36] "Catastrophizing involves an exaggerated negative orientation toward noxious stimuli."[37] Catastrophizing is "the tendency to misinterpret or over-interpret nociception."[38] "Catastrophic thinking is associated with difficulty in cognitively disengaging from pain."[39] In catastrophizing…we find ourselves caught in an ever-tightening web of our own creation."[40] It is all in our head after all.

If I were to fill out the catastrophizing questionnaire, I would say "yes" to questions asking if I am fearful that my pain may get worse? Who wouldn't be? If I am envious of those who can hike, bike, drive across the country, and do lots of other things I can no longer do. Who wouldn't be? I would say "yes" if asked if I worry I will never be able to engage those activities again. During the scoring of my responses, my sadness about these losses and my justifiable fear about the future, will morph into personal pathologies: I will undoubtedly come out as an exaggerating, magnifying, catastrophizing pain patient.

My pain specialist told me that as people living with pain get older, for one third of them, the pain diminishes – it "burns itself out," he said – but for two thirds it does not. Several years ago I was told by another pain specialist that for problems like mine, the pain "tends to get worse." Other doctors and specialists have told me over the years that there was nothing they could do for me – as millions of other people living with relentless pain have been told. One excellent specialist told me: "You have a plumbing problem and there is no good plumber in the house." My fear is exaggerated? A dysfunctional belief? A thinking error?

When I am 90 years old, I may well still be waking up every early morning from freakin' pain, as it has been the case for the last 7000-some days. There is no believable reason why it might not continue after 20 years of it. The only thing that helps in the middle of night when pain wakes me is to get out of bed, stretch my neck, move around, take pain medication, use ice packs. But at 90, suffering quite likely from other frailties or illnesses, I may not be able to get out of bed by myself anymore in the middle of the night. Then what?

Am I "catastrophizing"? Or are my fears and worries reality based, and totally reasonable? My case is not at all unusual. Most people living with serious pain have heard plenty of messages from their doctors indicating that their prognosis is poor. "There is nothing I can do for you." "We are running out of options." We have all heard it. Fear of the "unknown" and of "further incapacitation," says Thomas of her research participants, was "pervasive…There is no assurance that the agony of this moment will end; the future is unfathomable."[41] In another qualitative study, a participant says, "You keep wondering if it's going to last the rest of…your life. And would it get worse?"[42] Says another participant, "I'm scared to ask if it's going to get worse. 'Cause probably they're going to say yes. And I don't want to know that either."

One of my many frustrations with the research on 'catastrophizing' is that it is based on our responses to statements on paper about 'pain.' Just 'pain.' As if pain occurs in a vacuum. Statements such as, "I become afraid that the pain may get worse." "I worry all the time about whether the pain may end." "There is nothing I can do to reduce the intensity of the pain." "I can't seem to keep it out of my mind." "I keep thinking about how badly I want the pain to stop."[43] Note, how, during the scoring process, the words "worry" and "afraid," both based on specific individual/social realities, morph very mysteriously into the construct of "catastrophizing," a construct that assigns various forms of pathology to our personhood. Those filling out the questionnaire do not know this is going to happen.

The statements on the catastrophizing scale then, sever chronic pain from the contexts within which it arises. Pain becomes a 'thing.' There are no contextual statements on the questionnaire such as: "I worry about how am I going to get dinner ready tonight given my pounding, relentless headache." "I don't know how I am going to keep up with the rent and feed my kids while living on government benefits of $800 a month." "I have lost my job and I do not know how I will have enough money to live on when I get old." "This relentless pain makes me unresponsive to my spouse and I worry what will happen to my marriage." Those are the things we worry about when we say "yes" to the contextless questions on the scale. I could add dozens of such embodied, reality-based worries people living with pain have, worries that have no easy or even possible solutions because there is rarely an adequate treatment for severe chronic pain. Our responses on the catastrophizing scale then are not "maladaptive coping strategies" as researchers would have it, not "catastrophizing tendencies."[44] Leaving out the actual contexts and reasons for our worries is what makes possible the process by which our reality based worries get translated into pathology. Their absence is necessary for the assumption of pathology to enter. Pain *must* be 'thingified' for this line of research to even exist.

The statements on the catastrophizing scale are similar to trick statements: The nature and parameters of possible responses are determined a-priori both by the particular phrasing of the statements on the questionnaire and by the demands of the measurement units and research procedures. What will be listened to, and what cannot be listened to is already fully predetermined. In this case, the statements are phrased so that scoring responses according to the construct of "catastrophizing" can be carried out. Since that is not explained to the person responding to the questionnaire, I see them as trick statements. Of course we are afraid our pain will get worse. For Pete's sake, who wouldn't be, when the world of medicine shows itself helpless. Who would say: "Oh, well, I have had severe pain now for five years and my doctors have no clue what to do and cannot tell me it will get better – but, No, I am not at all afraid it will get worse." And of course, we can't keep pain out of our minds when it overwhelms our minds – as severe pain does by definition. And of course, I want the pain to stop.

In reality, many of us are dealing courageously and as effectively as possible with our lives. Dealing as well as possible with our lives and simultaneously fearing the future or wanting the pain to go away are not mutually exclusive. But unfortunately, mainstream research approaches conceive reality in either/or frameworks. The leading statements on the catastrophizing scale are not designed to absorb the complexities of our embodied lives.

Concerning research methodology, the first time I read an article about catastrophizing my instinctual reaction was something like this:

> *Wait a minute.* How can they say we have "irrational" and "exaggerated" thoughts about our pain which they cannot even see? That we are engaged in a "cognitive error" about something they cannot see or measure? That we have "distorted beliefs" about something that cannot be seen? That we think our pain is worse than 'it' is when the 'it' is not accessible to them in any way or form? There is no way they can know what our pain is like or show evidence that we are making our pain worse than 'it' is. It is logical to conclude that the researchers are the ones who are irrationally engaged.

The most treacherous aspect of all this is that, given pain's invisibility and immeasurability, it is not possible for people in pain to construct a counter argument: to *prove* that we are *not* catastrophizing, that we are *not* out for secondary gain, that we are *not* exaggerating, *not* malingering, *not* engaged in fake "pain behaviors", and all the rest of it. We are totally defenseless according to the methodological habits of mainstream psychological and psychiatric research on chronic pain. The power imbalances are extraordinary. People in pain will forever lose this game as long as researchers use methodologies that do not relate to real life, yet claim their methodologies are the scientifically privileged ones. As a result researchers can heap upon us, or so they think, an entire range of negatives by the mere use of instruments specifically designed to "find" these negatives. It is a predetermined "finding." It is really a fake finding. Researchers then claim to know what they cannot know. For, as Mark Sullivan also argues, the nature of standards used in the analyses of "exaggerated pain behavior" (which is closely related to research on malingering and catastrophizing) are moral and social.[45] They cannot be scientific. If the pain experience is private, as of course it is, it is not available to scientific investigation.

Further, when I have a medical assessment done, I know beforehand what the purpose of the assessment is. I will learn about my cholesterol level. I will learn what my blood count is. I have been told what is being measured and for what reason. Regarding the catastrophizing scale, are subjects informed what it is that the researchers are looking for? That they will be assessed for possibly "exaggerating"? For "catastrophizing?" For having "distorted" beliefs? For having "difficulty in cognitively disengaging from pain?" For making "cognitive errors?" Do they know that "worry" and "fear" will morph mysteriously during the scoring processes to "blowing things out of proportion?" I am rather convinced that they are not being informed. What are the ethical implications in a society in which full disclosure in research is the norm? It is hard to believe any person living in pain would participate if they knew how their responses are actually being processed. This psychiatric/linguistic secretive slippage from reality-based "worry" and "fear" into psychological pathology is one of the deeply disturbing aspects of this line of research. It is a profoundly ethical and moral problem which needs to be raised as such in the literature.

And finally, this line of research ignores and has no interest in how many of us engage in the opposite of catastrophizing: We *hide* our pain. We mostly keep our fears to ourselves. In the darkness of the night we fight our demons alone. When with others we say, "I'm OK," while in pain, we pull ourselves together to try to behave 'normal' so we can stay in their company. Qualitative studies, autobiographical and journalistic work amply show how we hide our pain. "Like the wounded animal that separates itself from the herd," says Melanie Thernstrom, who talked with hundreds of chronic pain patients, many patients keep their pain to themselves and often end up alone.[46] "I don't even tell my wife about it…" says a pain patient in a study by Sandra Thomas.[47] Another patient in the same study tells how she makes jokes and forced herself to laugh in order to maintain a normal façade. How I, and millions of others, relate to that. The need to hide pain, says Thomas, was a prominent element of the narratives of her research participants and, she says, is also noted by other researchers.[48] Our culture, notes Thomas, does not offer a 'natural home' for people living with pain. "You know, I would find a private place in my home where I could go to cry," says a former business man and contractor who fell off a scaffolding and has been in pain ever since.[49] Says a woman living with considerable daily pain, "I usually feel that I have to be secretive about it. I might tell (my husband) but not always. I know that I'm afraid that if I tell people how I really feel, they'll be uncomfortable.[50]

In "Inside Chronic Pain" I record the many times I would break down as soon as I was away from people. Clinical psychologist Gary Lea, who has worked for years with chronic pain patients, told me of the "countless" number of his pain patients who did not want to be seen in pain. "Yet," he told me, "everywhere I look in the pain literature I read about 'pain magnification'."[51] It is maddening. It is insulting. It reinforces societal stereotypes by exaggerating how we exaggerate and by hiding how we hide.

Of course there is a certain percentage of the human race who truly have catastrophizing personalities. Someone who is always worried that he will not have enough money to retire even though he has two million dollars in the bank can be said, even by common sense judgment, to be a catastrophizer. Whatever that certain percentage is, it will be roughly the same among chronic pain patients. That is not the point.

The point is this: When we respond to statements on the catastrophizing scale, we bring our actual lives to how we respond. That is what we think the questions are about. We don't realize that they are not. That they are merely based on someone else's abstractions. When we agree that we are afraid the pain will not go away, we are telling the researcher that, inherent in the prospect of more pain, we are rightfully justified in fearing we will lose our job, our marriage, our social life (the researcher is not asking for this contextual information and thus does not obtain it – nor wants it). When the researcher thinks he or she is going only after 'pain' – believing that is even possible – we, without even thinking about it, bring our lives to our answers. For us, pain and our lives are not separable.

Chronic pain orients you to a very worrisome future. Says a pain patient, "The furthest that I will look ahead is about a month. I won't plan ahead any more than that because it is too scary. If I try and think of 1 year, 2 years, 3 years down the line, then I panic."[52] These could have been the words of most of us. The tragedy, of course, is that we *do* and *must* think of two, three, ten years down the road, for all sorts of reasons, we just *try* not to. A woman I befriended because of our shared pain problems, and to whom I had written in an e-mail how I worried about the future given my neck and head pain was not getting better, wrote me,

> We who have pain can't look backwards (too much trauma and losses) nor can we look to the future for worry that the pain will get worse and take away more from us. Struggling to stay positive for today only… I would say don't worry about the future but I would be a hypocrite as I worry about how I will live and pay my bills in the future. I don't blame you for your worry. It shows that you have good sense.[53]

Of course high scores on the catastrophizing scale often are associated with depression and disability, with higher rates of healthcare usage, with increased medication usage – but for most of us that is not because we catastrophize, but because we actually *are* in a lot of pain and because we *do* have plenty to justifiably worry about. Our reality, as physician David Biro observes about people living with relentless pain, "is downright uncompelling and ugly" and a "living hell."[54] The construct of catastrophizing is no match for our actual lives.

The language used by professionals can reinforce or, alternatively, correct the negative stereotypes society holds about us. The present pathologizing language widens even further the abyss that separates those who live with pain from those who do not.

Researchers often split conceptual hairs to a bizarre degree trying to further their research agenda. One reads that catastrophizing may relate to "cognitive-affective constructs," it "may reflect the cognitive component of depression," it may "also overlap with affective traits such as negative affectivity."[55] Catastrophizing "may be just a symptom of depression," or it may "mediate the relationship between depression and the evaluative and affective aspects of pain, but not the sensory aspect."[56] Catastrophizing is seen as a form of "communal coping" or a "transactional stress and coping model"; or it cannot be a "communal coping model" because catastrophizing has "an explicitly cognitive connotation" and "catastrophizing cognitions cannot serve a social communicative function."[57] Catastrophizing may have "interpersonal correlates." It may be "independently associated with patient adjustment."

There is "magnification," "rumination," and "helplessness" involved which show similarities to "primary" and "secondary appraisal processes" – the variations are endless.

In the meantime, given the *actual* catastrophe we live with, *we* are wondering how we are going to make it through the next day, week, or month – as parents, as partners, as workers, as people, financially. We worry –as contrasted to "catastrophize"– how we are going to make it through the upcoming hearing with our insurance company. How we are going to get our doctor to really listen to us. How are we going to make it financially on reduced income. The many problems overtake us. It is these problems we need down to earth help with. Hairsplitting of research variables is not going to help us in the least.

The catastrophizing literature becomes directly personal: We are not just catastrophizing, but for some researchers we are 'catastrophiz*ers*' – even "high" or "low" catastrophizers.[58] These words assign a negative personality trait. They place us dangerously in the ontological realm of fundamental characteristics of being. Yet, researchers make these judgments about us (judgments, not facts, since researchers cannot measure the pain we are said to be catastrophizing about) not by using research processes that honor our actual lives, but by methodologies that use constructs researchers are interested in.Catastrophizing researchers may well say, "We don't mean to accuse you of anything negative. We are just talking about ways people cope with their difficulties. Don't take it personal." "Exaggerating?" "Making it worse than it is?" "Cognitive error?" "Blowing things out of proportion?" "A thinking error?" "Extremely negative thinking?" "An exaggerated negative orientation?" "Dysfunctional?" Those judgments are not just neutral ways of talking about how we cope with our difficulties. They are descriptions of assigned negative, pathological personality and cognitive traits.

Combine the psychological research as discussed in the previous chapter with the catastrophizing studies I note here, and the exuberance in diagnosing pathology can't get any worse. As a person living with pain, I feel harassed by the range of pathologies I can so easily and quickly be diagnosed with. It is bizarre. I feel that if I were to visit another psychiatrist or would agree to respond to a questionnaire in psychiatry or psychology that focuses on chronic pain, I would walk into a mine field. Everything I'd say could and would be held against me.

Those who score as "high catastrophizers" may in real life also be high endurers and courageous individuals. We can both be extremely worried about our future for very good reasons and deal well and courageously with our lives in pain. They are not in contradiction. Researchers get what they ask for by the very ways they develop their questions. So they must be very conscious and careful of what it is that they ask for, how they ask for it, and what they do not ask for – as not to violate the integrity of our lives.

Sometimes I wonder if pathologizing us is not at some level, even unconsciously, done with a degree of purposefulness. For as Bonnie O'Connor, professor at Brown University Medical School notes, those who do not suffer from pain, professionals and lay persons alike, defend themselves from those who do.[59]

> We construct their ceaseless pursuit of relief as a symptom of attributed character disorders: they are 'attention-seeking' or worse, 'drug-seeking;' they are 'complainers'… they are hypochondriacally 'doctor-shopping.' In making these judgments we distance ourselves from those in pain…if they are not like us, the we are not like them; and if we are not like them, then we are not susceptible to their terrible affliction.

O'Connor told me –as did another reader of my book– that she had become afraid while reading my memoir. Afraid that what happened to me could easily happen to her – an accident, a second of inattention. It is therefore easy to turn away, to stop interacting with us, as to not to have to deal with the thought of such possibility for the self. That also holds for healthcare professionals and researchers who choose to deal with us superficially, shielded by methodology and research protocol. But as James Baldwin states it so well,

> The questions which one asks oneself begin, at least, to illuminate the world, and become one's key to the experience of others. One can only face in others what one can face in oneself. On this confrontation depends the measure of our wisdom and compassion.[60]

Another explanation for the ease of labeling us in pathological ways may be reflected in these words, also by James Baldwin: "If I am not what I've been told I am, then it means that you're not what you thought you were either."[61] If I and millions of other people living with pain are not the pathological characters researchers and clinicians make us out to be, then those who measure us into pathology are not what they thought they were either. If I am not the pathological person they measure me to be then they are not the authority they see themselves to be.

Daniel Carlat's book "Unhinged" in many ways illustrates this. His revelations that what he does is mainly listen for 'symptoms' listed in the DSM, match them to diagnostic labels, prescribe drugs, and hardly knows his patients, is a humbling story of his realization that he is not the authority he once thought he was. Carlat speaks admirably of a colleague who takes a large cut in income so she can take time to talk with her patients and develop deep connections with them. She tells him, "Most of the people I see have misery and unhappiness, rather than major depression. They are miserable because of problems in relationship or difficulties coping with their life's circumstances."[62] Exactly so for people living with relentless pain. Most of the time, no psychiatric story of pathology is called for.

Elaine Scarry's words, from her influential book, "The Body in Pain" go right to the heart of the matter:

> For the person whose pain it is, it is "effortlessly" grasped (that is, even with the most heroic effort it cannot *not* be grasped); while for the person outside the sufferer's body, what is "effortless" is *not* grasping it (it is easy to remain wholly unaware of its existence; even with effort, one may remain in doubt about its existence or may retain the astonishing freedom of denying its existence; and, finally, if with the best of effort of sustained attention one successfully apprehends it, the aversiveness of the "it" one apprehends will only be a shadowy fraction of the actual "it").[63]

Those who measure our pain into pathology do not grasp "it"; instead they retain the "astonishing freedom" to misconstrue our distresses into something else entirely.

David Buchanan, senior lecturer at the school of Nursing and Midwifery at the University of Tasmania, himself a person living with pain, also notes that the notion of "catastrophizing" is in fact a hyperbole that is not with the suffering of the pain patient but with the construction of the professional interpretation of our pain.[64] "In short, it makes them feel better about not understanding my pain," he says. And when we are referred to as "catastroph-izers," he adds, the person in pain acquires a constructed identity. What was intended to be a clinical interpretation, becomes a hyperbolic declaration that stigmatizes and stereotypes the sufferer. The term is harmful, says Buchanan, not merely muddled, and directly involves the age old problem of interpreting pain when an observer or researcher cannot comprehend what is happening.

The insult can be sharp, such as in this flippant comment reportedly said by a formal presenter, and reported by a healthcare professional attending the 2010 IASP conference on pain,

> Ask catastrophizers to *not* think about pain, and guaranteed they think about it more. Ignoring the catastrophizer doesn't work: they just turn up the volume.[65]

It could of course be that this quote was not accurately recorded. But that does not matter for the person in pain: These words about us appeared in a formal publication. They lived in someone's mind. Turning up the volume.

Secondary gain, secondary losses, professional secondary gain

Teasell and Merskey broadly define "secondary gain" as that

> vague, all-encompassing term that also includes the effects of compensation (and that) suggests the individual is somehow rewarded economically, physically, or emotionally as a consequence of having an illness.[66]

The suggestion that ill people are out for "secondary gain" shouldn't even be considered unless benefits from an illness outweigh the burden of the illness, say Merskey and Teasell. In relation to chronic pain, they say, it is not plausible that individuals living with pain who often have worked consistently and well for years would 'fake' themselves into a situation where they receive sharply reduced benefits, their family situation becoming increasingly tense, and debts piling up.[67] There is absolutely nothing to be gained from living with ongoing pain.

When living in Victoria, B.C. for several years, I came to know five people who live with severe daily pain. Four live in basement apartments, having lost their job and having to watch every penny. Only one, a married woman, can continue her normal life as her supportive husband takes care of her needs. I myself, fortunate as I am, have had very good extended healthcare and disability benefits through my work, although I lost close to half of my income and of course, the working life I greatly enjoyed – the life I enjoyed. All of us lose, and then lose some more. It is a sign how little others who suspect we are out for "secondary gain" know about our lives, and that includes researchers who engage such line of research.

There are of course always the classic tales such as the one I read somewhere about a person in pain on disability leave who was seen in Europe playing in a rock band. Here too, a certain percentage of us will be out for secondary gain simply because a certain percentage of human beings habitually are. Reliable data on how many of us actually abuse the system is simply not available.[68]

What is well documented however is how routinely many of us are damaged by the system. Says Gary Lea, a clinical psychologist who has worked for many years with people who live with pain, "No discussion of secondary gain should occur without a discussion of 'secondary wounding.'"[69] Secondary wounding entails disbelief by doctors, employers, insurers, and society at large; lack of empathy; encountering immense ignorance; having no access to pain care; hearing one's pain problems being translated into psychiatric problems, and so forth. For those who are involved in personal injury suits, Lea notes delays in medical assessments, repetitious evaluations, delays in reaching settlements, symptom minimization or denial, difficulties in securing documents relevant to their injury, and outright accusations of seeking secondary gain in the form of financial gain, attention, unwarranted sympathy, or work avoidance.[70] Lea is convinced that 20 years from now, the pain related complaints by people who are now seen as seeking "secondary gain" will be found to be valid as more powerful assessment technologies will become available.[71] Tales of secondary wounding abound on web sites of pain organizations where people living with pain get to tell about their lives. "I had never been accused of being dishonest before, but...I had no way to prove I was telling the truth," said a woman with the horrible pain condition of complex regional pain syndrome, whose doctors initially did not believe her and said so in the medical records they kept on her. It would take eight years before she found a doctor who understood her problems.[72]

In formal research studies on chronic pain, the construct of 'secondary gain' can be used casually or even obsessively. Vranceany et al., for instance, note that the "psychosocial" model refers to cognitive, affective, behavioral, social, and cultural factors.[73] A number of examples are noted for each of these factors to describe what they mean. To describe what the "social" factor means however, only one example is given but is repeated several times – that of "secondary gain." I felt we were being portrayed as petty criminals. As Teasell and Merskey observe, "The suggestion of secondary gain as causing or perpetuating chronic pain is infuriating for patients who cannot work because of pain and who are well aware that they would be better off financially continuing with their employment."[74] As Fishbain dryly observes, "the chronic pain patient incurs a large number of secondary losses as a result of allegedly seeking secondary gain."[75] The "secondary gain" accusation is mind-boggling.

Scott Fishman, Chief of Pain Medicine at the University of California, at Davis, points to the hypocrisy (my term) that surrounds attributing the secondary gain motive to people living with pain. Secondary gain, he says means that the person has an unstated reason for doing what they're doing that isn't being directly dealt with in the examination room.[76] While of course that sometimes happens, that decision, he says, is very hard to make, because we all want all sorts of things for complicated reasons. Moreover, Fishman notes, the reality is, "that everyone has some secondary gain agenda." Doctors, he says, are not exempt from this. Doctors are supposed to focus only on the best care of the patient. But doctors are certainly guilty, he says, of being focused on reimbursement.

How often have I walked out of an doctor's office, having had an eight minute or even shorter meeting, resulting in no more than a refill, thinking: "He gets paid for *that*?" Says a pain patient, "He didn't even want to listen to what I said. He just wrote out a prescription."[77] And another cited in the same study, "You wonder are they really trying to help or are they just trying to take the money?" There are many such observations on web sites of advocacy organizations where people in pain get the chance to speak. While some changes are occurring in the healthcare system, for the most part doctors still get paid just to see you, whether they help you with your pain or not. They get paid for ordering a test, not for ordering the right test. Psychiatrists get paid for matching our answers to their list of symptoms, and for prescribing drugs – not for listening to us and helping us to navigate our difficult lives. Pain researchers would be well advised to drop the entire line of "secondary gain" research that gets it all wrong by blaming the victim and hiding their own interests.

I heard myself say to a pain researcher: "Instead of all these labels of pathology, people living in pain should be receiving praise and awards for courage and endurance!" Endurance of constant pain, of great losses, endurance of the ignorance we encounter everywhere, of a medical world that is ill prepared for us – awards for all we have to put up with. In the future we may well look back at how easily lives lived in pain are now pathologized and wonder if the psychiatric profession itself had gone mad.

6   Health economics: who pays?
what is paid?
what is not? why?

In 2002, to escape the harsh winters of Toronto where I lived, winters that made living with pain even more isolating, I moved to the milder climate of Victoria, B.C. I moved into a rented house, where, due to intense pain, I was confined for the first few days. Finally, the gods, in their mercy, lessened the pain to where I could go out. Still groggy and tired, I showered, dressed and drove downtown. I had to have a soft, soothing Starbucks latte. Resting at Starbucks. A place for recovery of sorts.

Then I went shopping. Entering clothing stores, I am transported back to health and youthfulness. I pick out a soft light grey sweater. I buy impulsively. I am vaguely aware this is not my style. I am more practical than that. But not today. I am on automatic. Handing the clerk my credit card brings another return to normalcy. The feel of the card, when I put it back into my wallet, erases for a moment this life of restrictions and shrinkage.

As I walk out of the store I have already forgotten what I just bought. I put the bag into the car and go blank. What did I buy? I drive home with a sweater I don't need.

In a flashback, I remembered a young woman I'll call Anne. I was volunteering in 1991 in a Toronto halfway house for young mothers with criminal records. My task was to accompany them on outings and make sure they stuck to a set of rules. Most had been victims of abuse - "it comes with the territory," the director of the halfway house told me. One day I took a few of them shopping, their favorite activity. Anne just had received her monthly check. We were in a drug store and Anne grabbed a shopping basket. What followed stunned me. She filled her basket so quickly it left me speechless.

"Do you need all that?"

"No," she said, without missing a beat, "but would you rather have me buy drugs on the street?" The bill came to over $200.

When I now feel the urge to grab a sweater that I do not need, I think of Anne. I was not raped. I am not a victim of incest. I am not living in a half-way house with my children taken from me. I "just" have pain. But the same drug will help.

This is health economics at its most intense personal level.

Most economists would probably not see health economics reflected in me buying sweaters I don't need. But according to Wikipedia's explanation of health economics, "the demand for health care is a derived demand from the demand for health." For many women living in pain, grasping for the image of an attractive appearance is a desire for health – attractiveness being closely related to the impression of health. And we want our health back. More than anything else in the world. Efforts to do so take many, many forms when it comes to lives lived in pain. And it cost us a lot of money.

"There is nothing like pain to put people into poverty"

Physician Carmen Green, Professor of Anesthesiology at the University of Michigan, points out that particularly those of low economic status descend rapidly into poverty when they encounter chronic pain.[1] She further comments that doctors rarely are tuned into the personal cost of trying out treatments for chronic pain. They do not ask their pain patients if they can afford what they prescribe. (None of my many doctors ever did.) Doctors must consider, Green says, how having less resources impact their patients.

I often feel guilty. And grateful. Teaching at a university, I have had excellent extended healthcare and disability benefits while many people living with pain who can no longer work live on marginal government disability payments. They end up in rented rooms or basements, cannot afford massages, or acupuncture, or osteopathic treatments or expensive traction treatments – highly likely none bringing a cure but all having the potential to temporarily relieve at least some of the pain. They are not be able to buy a new mattress that may be better for their back or neck, or travel out of town for treatments elsewhere, or afford to go out for a nice dinner on a good evening. At a self help meeting I attended, I talked to a woman who, being in constant pain and living in a basement, had to give up her beloved German shepherd she could no longer pay for. Her eyes flooded with tears when she said, "But I do have visitation rights…" A man went from an income of $60,000 to less than $10,000, also now living in a basement apartment, trying to save money to buy some Christmas gifts for his grandchildren. The stories go on. Everywhere.[2]

Imagining myself in these situations, I freeze. I will note below the various treatments I have been able to try out, two of them which helped considerably –prolotherapy and myofascial release– but which were not paid for by insurers, and they were expensive ($25,500 including travel cost). Where would I be if I could not have had them? People living with severe chronic pain, as compared to those living with other major illnesses (assuming they are covered by insurance), may well be among the worst off when it comes to becoming financially ruined. There are a number of reasons for this.

First, there is no sure path to pain relief. Finding pain relief means trying out a wide range of treatments, both traditional and alternative, that just might bring some relief, but then they also might not. No one knows for sure what might and might not help. Also, when a treatment helps it often stops working after awhile. Then, the search is on again. Out of despair we'll try anything and everything, depleting our savings.

Second, pain knows many pathways to the brain. When only one is targeted, it can well lead to compensatory effects in the others. Which is why pain relief often needs to be approached from many angles at the same time. Hence, many of us regularly visit different healthcare professionals for different treatments.

Third, insurers do not readily pay for an invisible condition. It is easy for insurers to deny the reality of invisible pain – they do it routinely. And we end up paying the bills ourselves.

And fourth, severe chronic pain, in oneself or in a loved one, is so devastating, that it becomes unbearable to live with or to witness. One will do anything to get rid of it. As Barbara Kivowitz says,

> When you are in pain, you will use up savings and retirement accounts, cut back on frills and basics, take out a second mortgage, and maybe even dip into your children's college funds, if you think there is a chance that you can get relief…It bears repeating that when you are in constant pain you will try ANYTHING.[3]

One hears this over and over in autobiographical writings. We'll spend anything we have and don't have, if there is even a sliver of hope. As pain specialist Scott Fishman says of his patients, they will try anything, even risking total paralysis or death.[4] Spending all your assets goes right along with that. Nothing else matters but getting rid of the pain. Living with severe pain invariably means losing one's job. With less than $1,000 a month for those lucky enough to be granted disability income and high expenses to try and find relief, poverty arrives rapidly.

In her first year of living with pain, Kivowitz spent roughly $30,000 out-of-pocket. These were her personal expenses: special pillows, $250; a TENS unit, $186; a loose fitting wardrobe to reduce pinching tender spots, $750; heating pads, $175; elimination diet, $250 per month; co-payments to see the many doctors and specialists we end up seeing, $1,200; an expert appraisal out of town, $1750; acupuncture, first visit $350, $100 for each treatment totaling $3,350; physical therapy, $3,525; chiropractic, $3,250; supplements, consultations included, $2,250; psychotherapy, $5,000; homeopathy, $375; massage, $900; Eye movement desensitization and reprocessing therapy, $1,200; Reiki treatments, $720. This does not take into account a year of lost wages, Kivowitz concludes.

This list may sound a bit much to the reader, but it is completely familiar to me but for the special diet and wardrobe, and the co-payments to see doctors and specialists which in Canada you do not pay. Co-payments can add up because we end up seeing so many different doctors and specialists.

And so the cost keep adding up, for us and for the healthcare system. One of the pain patients Melanie Thernstrom interviewed, spent "six figures of her own money" on treatment after treatment for eight years before she found something that worked.[5] "If you have chronic pain chances are you have discovered that getting the care you need at a price you can afford can be, well, excruciating," says Michelle Andrews.[6]

Jeanne Lazo notes how throughout her chronic pain years her family spent more than $6,000 annually in out-of-pocket expenses for pain relief which depleted their savings.[7] Many physicians, she says, did not realize the financial impact of the tests and treatments they suggested. And as Susan Okie's observes, physicians do not learn and do not know much about the cost of medical treatments, the financing of healthcare, and the impact of high medical bills on their patients.[8]

Writing this in 2011, almost fifteen years since the accident, my own list of out-of-pocket cost for finding pain relief, estimated for 15 years, has been as follows: Pillows (two Tempur-pedic ones, an Obus pillow, a Japanese pillow, a water-flow pillow, feathered ones, soft ones, pre-shaped ones) approximately $590; a special mattress, $900; a magnet mattress cover, $700; four sessions with a wellness physician, $1,000; non-covered massage, $5,250; non-covered chiropractic treatment, $700; supplements prescribed by a naturopath, $200; small medical devices (over the door traction systems, self massage device) $90; twelve prolotherapy sessions, $5,500 including travel cost; computerized decompression treatments for two months, $2000; private residential pain clinic for ten days including travel cost, $5000; five treatments of a different approach to prolotherapy including travel cost $3,700; and three weeks of intensive daily myofascial release treatments at a private clinic in Arizona, including travel cost, $20,000. And a few hundred dollars for a never ending amount of cold and heat packs, lotions that promise miracles, and endless over the counter pain medications. This amounts to a total of roughly $44,000 for the fifteen years, or about $3,000 per year.

Most people living with pain do not have the generous extended healthcare coverage I have had. In addition to my out of pocket expenses, an estimate for treatments paid for by extended healthcare over fifteen years for medications, physiotherapy, psychotherapy, massage, chiropractic and osteopathic treatments, and naturopathic consultations adds up to $90,000.

Further, living in Canada, I have not had to pay any co-payments or deductibles. To date, I have had approximately 160 pain related appointments with family doctors and approximately 70 appointments with specialists of one kind or another (not counting the ones noted above I had to pay for myself). No co-payments for two nerve blocks, a rhizolysis (nerve burning procedure) and related assessment processes which involved five consultations and assessment injections. Nor for two sets of Botox injections, cortisone injections, trigger point injections, three MRIs, six X-rays, a SPECT scan, three nerve tests, two bone scans, two cardiovascular tests, and two ultra sound scans. I don't even know how to calculate all these cost in co-payments and deductibles had I lived in the U.S.

Watching Larry King one night, I realized something. He was speaking about his foundation that provides financial help to people who suffer from heart disease but cannot afford treatment. There are foundations for all kinds of diseases where those who cannot afford treatment can apply for financial help. I am not aware of any such foundation for people with chronic pain who have become impoverished and can no longer pay for pain relief.

The problem with "mainstream"

"Fewer than half of all back surgeries are successful in relieving chronic back pain," says neurologist Bartleson of the Mayo Clinic.[9] In the residential pain clinic I attended, I met one woman who had had twenty-three back operations and was still in great pain. Another person had had six operations and was still in pain. I overheard one of my pain specialists tell a colleague he had just seen a new patient who had thirteen operations on her neck and was still in pain. As David Morris notes, between ten and twenty operations for the same problem is not uncommon.[10] Rates of back surgery failure are astounding: I have read figures of between 30% and 74%. Not infrequently, patients end up with increased pain. Fishman refers to this phenomenon of back surgeries making the pain worse as the "failed back syndrome."[11] The phrase "failed operation syndrome" would be more accurate.

These not so successful operations continue on a large scale and are paid for by insurers of one kind or another: They are mainstream. All my own traditional medical interventions were paid for: nerve burning procedure (which made the pain worse and generated nerve pain as well), Botox injections (did not work), and nerve blocks and other kinds of injections with chemicals (did not work). Then I was offered an open neck surgery to remove the entire nerve ganglion at the C1 level. No guarantees offered. A major and delicate operation requiring a five day stay in the hospital. All would have been paid for. (I refused. According to a second and third opinion it would be too risky an operation.)

In 2003, I finally came upon a treatment that made perfect sense given the nature of my injuries: prolotherapy. I received twelve monthly sets of injections with dextrose in my neck into the ligaments which the accident had overstretched and made useless. The injections deliberately cause inflammation. As the body heals the inflammation over a period of about four weeks, new collagen is deposited and the ligaments develop new fibers, tighten, and become a bit stronger. Voila – after the fourth set of injections I could feel my ligaments starting to work again! I could hold up my head for longer times. There was less pain. After twelve months, prolotherapy, as practiced by the physician at the time (I found out years later that different specialists do it differently) took approximately half of the pain away and made me much more functional. I could move my head again without my neck "going out" and causing a pain attack. I could look over my shoulder again. I could look again at the person next to me during a conversation. Before, I always had to hold my head straight or else sharp pain would instantly develop.

The Canadian healthcare system, nor my car insurance, nor my extended health insurance through the university, paid for the prolotherapy. When the fourth set of injections started to work, I called my extended health insurance company in the hope they would pay for the rest. Absolutely not. It was not a "mainstream" treatment, I was told.

"But it worked!" I exclaimed.

"It is not mainstream."

I argued that the many mainstream treatments they, in fact, had paid a lot for had not worked. But prolotherapy did. And at $350 per treatment it was not cheap but not that expensive either. I argued that prolotherapy had been around for decades. I argued that there were a number of clinical studies, as well as experimental studies, that show great success. I got nowhere.

How is it determined that something is "mainstream"? *Who* determines that? Using what criteria? In a field so unorganized and fragmented as pain management, with seemingly no one in charge who understands *all* options, *who* can fairly judge what should be paid for and what shouldn't? What kind of traditions and politics shape these decisions? How is it that when a surgeon decides that a major risky operation is called for, it is automatically paid for, even if it may not be the best treatment, and it could even make things worse? The surgeon I saw clearly had the deciding voice. Had I agreed, the assessment procedure for the operation would have been scheduled right then and there.

Do those who decide whether a treatment is "mainstream" use accurate data on the "success" of procedures they pay for? How is "success" defined? What does it take to bring a procedure such as prolotherapy into the "mainstream" category? Or myofascial release treatments which also helped but which no one paid for? How long do pain patients have to beg for a defendable way of determining what gets covered?

Healthcare professionals have privately told me that prolotherapy is not covered because of vested interest: It does not enrich traditional medicine which uses interventional "cut and burning" procedures and injections with chemicals. It does not enrich the pharmaceutical industry as dextrose (the substance used in prolotherapy) is merely sugar water. Whether that is so or not, it is peculiar that an often successful intervention that essentially triggers the body into healing itself was not covered.[12]

Fishman notes, that an insurance company would much rather pay him $1,000 to give a patient an injection in the spine than spend an hour with a pain patient to figure out which treatments would be best for them.[13] The insurer, says Fishman, will balk at that. They will make me fill out papers, make me make telephone calls to toll-free numbers (and make me wait) and defend myself. On the other hand, they will immediately, with no questions asked, accept my charges if I do the standard procedure. Although it would cost far less to spend the hour with a patient and their family, the reductionist model of medicine ironically assures that potentially less effective –but also more costly– treatments may be offered.

This is so, says Fishman, because the insurer thinks they can patrol traditional objective treatments. The insurer says, I know he used a needle, he used a drug, he has images to show what he did, and I know exactly how the procedure is performed. It is all objective, therefore we will pay you for it. But they don't know what to make of the hour I spend with a patient…How do they know what happened during that hour?

"We have become plumbers," says physician/writer Abraham Verghese.[14] Do something *to* the patient (cut, poke, sew, burn, insert, inject, stent, re-move) and you get very well paid. Do something *for* the patient, Verghese says (listening, consulting)… not so much.

It is all irrational, Fishman concludes. To me, it is an excellent illustra-tion of how 'objectivism' has its utterly irrational dark side. What objectivists consider as "merely" subjective (talking things through, procedures that treat tissues that cannot be readily seen on a scan such as ligaments and myo-fascia tissue) is not valued or taken seriously because it can not be patrolled. The notion of 'control' as an *idea* undergirds this process: Only that which can be kept under control can count as data. When the "objectivity" is worshipped to the point of ideology, when we have reached the *habit* of "objectivism," those with an invisible disease such as chronic pain fall between the cracks. And they pay for it dearly.

7   Drugs: my hate/need affair

In February 2010, a few months after my book about living with pain came out, I received the following e-mail from the pharmaceutical company PriCara,

> Dear Dr. Heshusius,
> Your book, *Inside Chronic Pain: An Intimate and Critical Account*, offers important insight into understanding chronic pain to ultimately improve treatment outcomes. On behalf of PriCara, Division of Ortho-McNeil-Janssen Pharmaceuticals, Inc., I was hoping to set up a call with you next week to discuss potential partnership opportunities with PriCara for an unbranded campaign to address critical issues in pain management.

"Oh, no," I thought. "Are you kidding? I don't work with those I do not care for."

I do not care for pharmaceutical industries because I was swallowing lots of Vioxx during the years when Merck, the company that made it, already knew of the serious cardiac problems Vioxx caused resulting in a number of deaths, but didn't tell anyone about them. An estimated 80,000 additional heart attacks occurred before the company was forced to take the drug off the market in 2005.[1] I was on Risperdal, developed by Janssen Pharmaceutica Products for schizophrenia and bi-polar disorders, a fact I was not told about. Risperdal was prescribed to me off-label. The drug agitated me beyond description. It earned the company two billion annually. The company has admitted to minimizing the risks involved in taking Risperdal and to making "false or misleading" claims in promotional materials.[2] I was on Neurontin, a drug developed by Pfizer for epilepsy, also an off-label prescription, which I was told. But back then I didn't even know what "off-label" meant. Nor was that explained to me. I had not yet learned anything about pharmaceuticals and I was in too much agony to pay attention. Back then, I would have swallowed anything a doctor would have prescribed. (Now I decide myself).

I learned later that Pfizer faces more than 1,000 lawsuits for illegally promoting Neurontin for unapproved uses and because of the drug's link to suicide.[3] I immediately could put a name to that awful side effect I felt myself when taking Neurotin: a sharp increase in that chaotic, suicidal stir, already so prevalent in those living with severe pain. Pfizer also pleaded guilty in a high-profile fraud case for illegally marketing its painkiller Bextra, paying a 2.3 billion dollar fine, the largest fraud and False Claim Act case in US history.[4] I was on Inderal, a beta blocker made by Wyeth for hypertension. By 2008, over 5000 lawsuits were filed against Wyeth because its hormonal replacement drugs Prempo and Premarin caused increased risk of breast cancer, heart attacks, and strokes – I used Premarin too. I still take Oxycodone and used Percocet made by Purdue Pharma who pleaded guilty to criminal charges for misleading doctors and patients by claiming that Oxycontin (the slow release version of Oxycodone) was less prone to abuse than other opioids.[5] Purdue further claimed that one dose provides relief for 12 hours, more than twice as long as generic medications.[6] Purdue knew that for many pain patients this was not true, but Oxycontin's high price hinges on the promise of 12 hours relief. The fact that pain relief is shorter for many patients can cause them to have acute narcotic withdrawal symptoms which fosters addiction. I was on Imitrex, developed by GlaxoSmithKline, who knowingly sold contaminated baby ointment and 20 other tainted drugs made at their plant in Puerto Rico that had been rife with contamination for many years.[7] The company also settled law suits linking it's drug Paxil to suicidal behavior and birth defects.[8] Its best selling diabetes drug Avanda, earning the company 13.8 billion in 2009 alone, caused over 100,000 heart attacks – a dangerous "side" effect GlaxoSmithKline was aware of before the evidence became public. I took Celexa, made by Forest Pharmaceuticals who pleaded guilty to off-label marketing of the drug. Celexa has been linked to birth defects and suicidal behavior.[9] I was prescribed Prozac (which I refused) made by Eli Lilly, and referred to as the "ugly" story by investigative journalist Robert Whitaker.[10] This story shows how from the beginning there was only marginal efficacy over placebo, and there were problems with suicidal ideations. Subjects were getting manic and psychotic responses. But these data were covered up by re-coding serious adverse effects such as "suicidal ideation" simply as "symptoms of depression." Thirty-nine thousand adverse effects, including suicides, hallucinations, and convulsions were reported to the FDA MedWatch which is estimated to be only 1%-10% of the actual number since reporting is voluntary. Yet, the drug was manipulated into the medical journals and clinical practice as a wonder drug. Eli Lilly managed to quietly settle over thirty lawsuits. And lastly, I was prescribed Mirapex, developed for Parkinson's disease by Boehringer Ingelheim Pharmaceuticals and marketed in the U.S. by Pfizer. There are two hundred lawsuits filed against the company for hiding the fact that the drug can cause compulsive behaviors (e.g. gambling, binging, sex, buying).[11] By then I had been on so many drugs, many of them making me very sick, that I decided not to fill the prescription. I was done with being a guinea pig.

That's nine powerful drugs I was prescribed specifically for my pain, made by nine major companies, all losing lawsuits for product liability and eight of them found guilty of criminal actions. Four of the nine drugs were developed for major illnesses I do not have – I am not schizophrenic, I don't have Parkinson's, I don't have epilepsy, and I do not have hypertension.

And then there is Tylenol, thought of as a harmless drug by most people, and that used to include me. But the *American Journal of Respiratory and Critical Care Medicine* linked long term daily use or frequent use of as little as 1000 mg of acetaminophen (just two extra strength tablets) to respiratory illnesses such as asthma, chronic obstructive pulmonary disease, and decreased lung function, and other studies note high blood pressure and kidney damage.[12] I've had to use 1000 mg. of Tylenol daily and many days much more, since that fatal day of the 1996 accident. What lies in store for me?

As every pain patient finds out, prescribing pharmaceuticals for pain relief is a trial-and-error process. We are routinely exposed to this array of potentially very harmful drugs, as both doctors and patients can get desperate to find *something* that may help. Hence, we are prescribed one drug after another.

To this day, I do not 'get' off-label prescription. Drugs are tested and therefore proclaimed safe. Then they are given to doctors who are told: You can also prescribe this drug for conditions for which it has not been tested or approved by the FDA. You can do your own small, uncontrolled studies. And although we may pay you for doing these studies we will not supervise them. Doctors can also prescribe off-label just because another doctor tells them it works. Or they read somewhere that it works. Off-label prescribing is not regulated. It is legal for doctors to do so, while off-label marketing by the maker of the same drug is not legal. I feel like a fool: I had always thought that the formal testing process resulting in FDA approval would protect me from precisely such unregulated experimentation!

As Laurie Magid, U.S. Attorney for the Eastern District of Pennsylvania, said when commenting on the Eli Lilly lawsuit for illegal marketing activities, the off-labeling marketing "circumvents the very process put in place to protect the public."[13]

Worse, a doctor might not even know that in the past, a pharmaceutical company may have applied for the approval of a certain drug for a condition for which the drug is now prescribed off-label, and was turned down.[14] Now, *that* is scary. I am protected better against flaws in my toaster than I am against quite possibly deadly flaws in my medications.[15]

Then there are the major financial ties between drug companies and the medical world where researchers hold equity interest in companies that sponsor their research, the quid pro quo expectations resulting from pharmaceutical representatives visiting doctors, the hiding of negative data, the hijacking of a huge part of medical research, education and clinical practice such as funding research institutes, educational programs, endowed chairs, funding awards, giving money to advocacy groups, sponsoring seminars and medical conferences, and ghostwriting scientific articles, even ghostwriting an entire book, which, in the words of a former FDA commissioner, "is a new level of chutzpah."[16] I could present many additional sources for every one of these charges, but my mind refuses to go through the pile of articles on my floor that are these sources, thrown over the years into a box. It nauseates and scares me. As Steven Hall comments in his review of books that critique the pharmaceutical industries, the details are "stomach turning."[17] All this is deeply personal given that my accident threw me right into the middle of this unethical and too often deadly mess of betrayals.

Back to the invitation I received from PriCare to discuss a possible partnership because of the "insights" in my book. More than 2,600 lawsuits have been filed against Ortho-McNeil-Janssen of which PriCara is a division, for not providing adequate warning about tendon ruptures from their antibiotic drug Levaquin while they were aware of the problems.[18] The parent company of Ortho-McNeil-Janssen and PriCara, Johnson & Johnson was found guilty of paying bribes and kickbacks to win business in Poland, Greece, and Iraq, and is also under investigation for paying kickbacks to induce "Omnicare", the nations' largest nursing home pharmacy, to recommend Risperdal to the elderly.[19]

So, no, PriCara, I'd rather not partner with you.

Then a pharmacist friend of mine encouraged me to check it out as, he convinced me, pharmaceutical companies do a lot of good things particularly in their research departments. Just perhaps I could do some good by holding on strongly to my own experiences. And I was curious as to how they handle "partnerships" (I had not yet read Daniel Carlat's and Robert Whitaker's books which provide detailed pictures of how these processes work).[20] And I was curious why they contacted me in the first place, given that in my book I critique the pharmaceutical industries for their various unethical practices and I say many negative things about the adverse effects of the many drugs I have been on.

I agreed to an initial phone conversation.

The representative was certainly pleasant and sympathetic enough. So we first talked a bit about the difficulties of living with pain. Then we moved to the potential partnership. I asked her what she saw me doing. She proposed the possibility of being part of a web-cam where people could interact with others about my experiences. That, in itself, seemed a good idea. For a split second I got interested. Then came the question:

Could I talk "at a high level" about safely prescribing opioids and the use of medical devices? I was so stunned by these questions that I was distracted for a second. How could anyone, having read my book, ask me if I know about safely prescribing opioids? Or talk about medical devices about which my book doesn't say a single word?

"Have you actually read my book?" I asked. I heard the incredulous tone of my own voice as I spoke.

No…she had not…but she had ordered it…and it should come in a few days… and she couldn't wait to read it…

I told her that if I had any expertise at all, it was about what living with chronic pain is like. Nothing else.

"Perhaps we should wait till you have read my book and then see if there is anything that might work for both of us," I said.

She agreed. As I expected, I never heard from her again.

I felt I had been the recipient of pushy behavior, and a straightforward lie, having been told by PriCara how important my book was. A white lie perhaps, but still a lie to try to buy me for their purposes. This seemingly little incident, that amuses those I have told about it in that 'what do you expect' kind of way, is a microcosm of what pharmaceutical industries do in the wider world.

Pharma, Oil, and Tobacco, are the three least trusted industries in America according to a 2010 Harris Poll.[21] It is easy to see why Oil and Tobacco are mistrusted. But Pharma? The industry that cares for our health? Their cheating is a betrayal of the worst kind.

The aggressive PriCara e-mail reminded me of what happened during pain support meetings I attended two years in a row in Victoria B.C. We were organizing events for Pain Awareness Week. Both years a pharmaceutical company had provided a few hundred dollars to buy food for the events. Both years there was suddenly a new person attending the meeting. They were not introduced. They were just sitting there, listening. (I still regret that, both years, I didn't have the presence of mind to ask who they were right then and there.) When I inquired afterwards I learned these folks were representatives of Pfizer, the company that had given us money for refreshments. The group leader didn't really know why they were there. Just sitting in. The web site of the pain support group (designed to provide only local self help pain management information) suddenly carried the Pfizer logo. All this a small reflection of what Alan Cassels refers to as the "infiltration" by Pfizer of the Canadian medical landscape.[22]

I have no doubt that these representatives were there to listen to how we talked about our lives in pain so it could be used to improve their marketing. Fair enough, isn't it. They give us a bit of money for sandwiches and carrot sticks and we give them access to a marketing research site. What I object to is that, while all other decisions were group decisions, this one was not. The quid-for-pro thing was automatic. No one questioned their presence. Pharmaceutical companies count on silence about their practices by giving money. And money buys them the "right" to "infiltrate" just about any organization they want to. And it seems that almost no one who receives their dollars is objecting and holding them accountable.

As it is, patients cannot make an educated decision about the side effects of the drugs we are prescribed. I can't even trust my doctor when it comes to pharmaceuticals, and that is not because I don't trust my doctor.

The pot calling the kettle…

In a Self help program for pain management we were cautioned about alternatives and natural remedies. Just because "it is natural doesn't mean it is safe" the work book said. "These remedies are not standardized." The group leaders reiterated this. The words "tested" and "standardized" seem sacred to them.

Lazarou, Pomeranz, and Corey calculated the number of "serious and fatal adverse drug reactions" in U.S. hospital patients, while in the hospital or causing admission to a hospital.[23] They *excluded* "errors in drug administration, noncompliance, overdose, drug abuse, therapeutic failures, and possible adverse reactions." "Serious" was defined as those adverse drug reactions that required hospitalization, were permanently disabling, or resulted in death. For the year 1994, an estimated 2,216,000 such serious reactions occurred, which was 6.7% of all hospitalized patients. An estimated 106,000 patients died. All this from properly prescribed and properly taken drugs. More directly relevant to pain, twelve to fifteen thousand people die every year from NSAIDs.[24] Many thousands more end up in emergency rooms. In Canada, Health Canada reports over 8000 adverse reactions a year to properly prescribed pharmaceuticals which is estimated to be only 1%-10% of the actual number, as reporting is voluntary. Are these figures comparable to problems with herbal medicine and supplements?

I mentioned some of these figures in the Self help meeting. While unregulated supplements can undoubtedly also cause harm, I am always baffled when I hear warnings by those who are invested in making, selling or prescribing pharmaceuticals about the dangers of supplements – as if their own products are truly safe. Their self righteousness is quite stunning.

In a different pain management program, a pharmacist who gave us an overview of pain medications similarly warned us that we needed to be cautious when taking herbal products, because, she said, "these companies may not have your best interest in mind." She too added that herbal products are not tested and standardized.

"We test," she added authoritatively.

Yet, with all that testing, there are many thousands of dead and ill people from taking properly prescribed drugs every year.

And while regulations are now in place for negative studies to be published, these regulations are not necessarily reinforced. Drugs given to children (typically off-label, such as prescribing Neurontin to children for attention deficit disorder) are often not tested on children. The duration of the testing is typically short: a few weeks, a few months. Often not long enough to learn about long term adverse effects or even to learn if they work long term.[25] Typically, companies do their own studies which introduces bias at all levels. Further, there is the mind-boggling amount of deceit in the reporting of results which themselves are often ghostwritten. Then, there is the mind-boggling deceit in marketing strategies. "We test." I challenged her, noting some of the above items. She was not prepared for that and mumbled something in defense. I think this person had never thought about the deceit she was engaging in.

"Trustworthy evidence usually doesn't exist," the FamilyDoctor.org, an organization supported by the American Academy of Family Physicians, declares with regard to herbal products.[26] "(They) don't have to be tested to prove they work well and are safe..." Using the Mayo Clinic as their source for information, the Chronic Pain Association of Canada, while appropriately telling us to do our homework before buying dietary supplements, refers to manufacturers of herbal remedies as "opportunists" who use "big promises" to sell us their dangerous products.[27]

Because pharmaceutical experiments render "data" in a society in which the very construct of "data" and of "scientific research" are near sacrosanct, it is almost reflexively acceptable that there are so many detrimental and even deadly side effects: The method has become more important than the outcomes. "We test"... that phrase may be the best and shortest description of what the "tyranny of method" means.

In my own case, I have used many herbal products and have never experienced any side effects. Whereas the side effects from pharmaceuticals have been horrible – dizziness, nausea, vomiting, stomach pains, rebound headaches, restlessness, suicidal impulses, cognitive confusion, constipation, and heaven knows what I will come down with in terms of liver or kidney damage down the road. Someone should first conduct an unbiased study comparing adverse effects from herbal/natural products, which certainly can occur, to adverse reactions from pharmaceuticals, before condemning herbal products and favoring pharmaceuticals as a matter of course. I have not been able to find such a study.

Adverse and even dangerous effects of pharmaceuticals have been with us for so long that they have become part of the air we breath. They hardly register when the television drug commercials come on, although an alien seeing them for the first time would be flabbergasted: You think of taking those drugs? Something that can cause agitation, weight increase, weight loss, headaches, extreme fatigue, severe depression, suicidal thoughts, increased risk of death, increased risk of suicide, memory loss, fainting, heart attacks and strokes that can lead to death, new or worsening heart failure, tremors, seizures, fatal bleeding, decreased or loss of hearing or vision, uncontrollable muscle movements that can become permanent, nausea, vomiting, abdominal pain, stomach pain, blood clots in the legs, swelling of the tongue which may be fatal, dangerous decrease in white blood cells, trouble breathing, blurred vision, persistent fever, brain bleed, severe liver problems, mouth sores, severe diarrhea, varicose veins, lymphoma and other cancers, allergic reactions, mini-strokes, shaking, increase in blood pressure, high blood sugar, kidney failure, liver failure, and in the most serious cases coma or death? (This list was put together by watching a couple of weeks of television commercials.)

Many people have become inured to these warnings, having seen so many of them on a daily basis. And without knowledge of how often these side effects actually occur, and to how many people they happen, the list is pretty much a meaningless abstraction, to be overlooked. As Steven Woloshin and Lisa Schwartz note, what is needed is additional precise quantitative information about both how well the drug worked in trials compared to a placebo or to another drug (to say that the drug was "superior" doesn't do it), and the percentage of subjects who developed specific side effects.[28] That would at least have concrete meaning. Only then can we make an educated decision about whether the benefits outweigh the possible risks. After 33 years of deliberation, Woloshin and Schwartz note, the FDA has provided such rules for the manufacturing of sunscreen. It is high time to do so for prescription drugs. Importantly, there are many negative side effects that doctors do not report. The FDA relies on physicians to monitor product safety, but doctors say they are too busy to do the paperwork. "The standard in the medical community," a cardiologist tells Barry Meier, "is not to report.[29]

Needing them

I need them. I would have ended my life without them. Although pain-"killers" rarely kill pain, many do not work, others work only for a while, and many make you feel ill, many of us do finally find something that at least takes the edge off the pain. While pharmaceuticals toxify my body, they are what I reach for every time when intense pain wakes me in the early morning hours, still to this day, though there is always a sense of hesitancy as I put them in my mouth.

Angela Mailis-Gagnon and David Israelson view the involvement of the pharmaceutical industry in chronic pain as a double-edged sword, given the industry's emphasis is exclusively geared toward the biomedical aspects of pain.[30] While the industry might discover better pain medicine, the exclusive focus on the biomedical model, the authors say, may undermine the need for more comprehensive pain management. As Marcia Angell notes, the pharmaceutical industry is not especially innovative.[31] The majority of drugs for pain, she says, are merely variations of older drugs already on the market. The handful of truly new drugs were mostly based on taxpayer-funded research at academic institutions or small biotechnology companies, or the National Institutes of Health. Hence, most of the money people pay for their drugs goes right back into advertising.

It wasn't always so. Patrick Wall notes how by the turn of the century, when pharmaceutical companies started to spin off from chemical companies, the best brains in the universities were involved in innovative research.[32] Those heady days, says Wall, are over. Hard headed accountants have taken control. The industry now spends two and a half times more on marketing and advertising than it does on research.[33] Yet, the industry tells the public that their drugs have to be high priced to fund their research. Science has become enmeshed with marketing.

As my pharmacist friend notes, the "miraculous" power of the industry lies in acute interventions. Pharmaceuticals perform poorly when applied to chronic conditions, including chronic pain, he says, for the very chemical that performs wonders in acute situations starts assaulting the body when used for –the far more lucrative– long term conditions. The question, he said, is how can the pharmaceutical industry retain its research magic when our entire societal fabric relies on economic growth at all cost? Is there another kind of growth? My "bashing" in this chapter is fair, he told me. My argument just needs to be put in the context of what can be a great science, but which is unfortunately put into a societal economic model, a model that because of its greed puts a damper on a great science that could be. We do indeed need a societal model for understanding chronic pain.

Then there is the opioid conundrum: There are intricate but obvious configurations of mutual influence between the pharmaceutical industries, medical education, insurance companies, stigmatization of people living with chronic pain, and law enforcement's priorities and biases. These issues include the stigma associated with taking opioids for pain relief; the many deaths occurring from abusing them, very often, by those not in pain but who manage to get hold of them; and the increase in suicide resulting from withholding opoids. The "Canadian Medical Association Journal" states its concern that drug controls and fears about opioids are contributing to un-controlled pain and suffering.[34] The concern about abuse is all too real, but it must not be an excuse for failure to control pain, the journal's editorial states. It also stresses that the vast majority of people in pain are not the addicts we have to be concerned about. No one seems to have a good solution to this co-nundrum. But someone got to figure out how to deal with it without driving us to suicide as a means of pain relief. I will note additional issues involved in the opioid dilemma from the perspective of the lived experience of chronic pain in Chapter 9.

How do I reconcile this hate/need relationship I have with the pharma-ceutical industries? I have not found a way. What would help, is if I came across publications by healthcare professionals or researchers in pain care, who, though accepting funds from the pharmaceutical industries, would dare to hold them accountable. I was impressed by Daniel Carlat for the cour-age to reveal his entanglements with the pharmaceutical industry when he accepted healthy checks for giving lunch talks for physicians, talks scripted by the company. It's chilling to read of his slowly dawning realization that he was being used as a sales person, and had bit by bit accepted the compa-ny's story about products he knew were not as safe as the company told him to say they were. When he couldn't live with himself anymore, and told the audience the true facts, he was immediately reprimanded by the company's representative, who was always listening in. I fear that if I had entered a "partnership" with PriCara, I would have had 'big brother' watching me. I could not have told the truth as I have experienced it.

We need more revelations by insiders who know first hand how the games are being played by the pharmaceutical companies. And we need more of the companies' beneficiaries who dare to say: No more. I'll be your partner but only if you yourself are an honest one.

As a person living with pain, this whole dishonorable tale hangs over me as an extra burden. The pharmaceutical industry is the "eight-hundred-pound gorilla" in Marcia Angell's words.[35] It does pretty much whatever it wants to do. The industry is taking us for an expensive and shameful ride. With so many twists and turns that it makes you nauseous. There will be no reform, says Angell, without an aroused and determined public to make it happen. My "bashing" in this essay from the perspective of a chronic pain sufferer, is my contribution to this needed revolt.

8 *Don't believe the nice man knocking on your door*

> Disparagement of pain and disability in the medico-legal field also leads to the rejection of pain in other contexts.
>
> Harold Merskey & Robert Teasell,
> *The disparagement of pain: Social influences on medical thinking.*

Merskey and Teasell poignantly state the interdependent nature of various societal contexts that impact the experience of chronic pain. Of the many societal forces that impact chronic pain negatively, the world of insurers must rank among the worst. Merskey and Teasell summarize the problem when they speak of the "institutionalization of the denial of chronic pain."[1] When the world of medicine and the world of insurers deny the significance of chronic pain, it ripples through society and reinforces ignorance and denial in other social spheres.

In 1997, only 13% of claims filed by people in pain due to car accidents in Ontario, Canada, which were sent to a designated assessment center (DAC), were accepted.[2] (Doctors at a DAC are approved by insurance companies and referrals come from insurance companies only.) Thus in 1997, 87% of pain patients referred by insurers to their own doctors were denied because they were evaluated, explicitly or implicitly, to be malingering or to suffer merely from a bit of discomfort. In 1998, 83% were denied.

How does a pain patient win that battle, a battle most of us should win?

My own anger still surges when I take my thoughts back to that horrible time I when was battling Allianz Canada, my car insurance at the time of the accident. I want to say to anyone who has an accident, "Do not believe that nice man who knocks on your door a few days after an accident and tells you how well they have taken care of others in your situation." At least not when it comes to pain. When your pain does not go away, get the best lawyer in town.

Consider the letter I received from Allianz Canada in May, 1998, one year and eight months after the accident, which stated, "The MRI does not reveal anything abnormal and therefore it would appear there is no organic basis for your continuing pain." No further claims were allowed. My family doctor was furious and offered to write a letter for free. He explained to Allianz that my kind of injuries are often not visible on X-rays or MRIs. I am quite certain the insurer already knew this.

"Are they saying I am lying?"

"That's exactly what they are saying, but they know better. They just want to get rid of you."

As he predicted, the insurance paid no attention to his letter. A year later, through injections with a local anesthetic, facet joint damage, which can cause intense pain, was established – a common consequence of the kind of accident I had. Still later, severe ligament weakness was also diagnosed which causes intense pain as well, and which is not visible on an MRI either.

Ulla Bergholm, Bengt Johansson and Hakan Johansson list the kind of injuries to the neck that can result from an accident such as mine and the many symptoms that can follow.[3] Reading their list of injuries was a frightening summary of what happened to me: ligament tearing and weakness, facet joint damage and compression, instability of the craniocervical area, muscle rupture, blood vessel rupture (the morning after the accident my face was unrecognizable in a literal sense. From my mouth upward, my face was black and blue and badly swollen). Symptoms include neck pain, headaches, thoracic back pain, lumbar back pain, myofasical pain, dizziness, inability to walk on uneven ground, memory disturbance, concentration difficulties, constant fatigue, impaired stress tolerance, hypersensitivity to sound, sleeping disturbance, tinnitus (which for me comes and goes), and general muscular fatigue and stiffness. I experienced all of these, and many of these symptoms I experience to this day to one degree or another.

But Allianz, of course, wouldn't have any of it. They sent me to one of their doctors at a DAC. The doctor had not even read my file, mumbling something about having had no time as he had just done a back operation. He flipped through my file in seconds. Then a minimal exam followed. By his own admission, he was limited in both his examination and his recommendations by strict guidelines set by the insurance. As I got dressed, while the doctor had returned to his office, his assistant, a physiotherapist who had stayed with me, said, "We believe you."

Surprised I said, "You better."

"Oh," she said, "you don't know how many people come here and lie."

The doctor recommended a pain management program, saying he actually wasn't allowed to, but he was going to do so anyway because he believed me.

A hearing with Allianz followed in which they weren't even willing to do what their own doctor had recommended. In the letter in which they had told me that there was no "organic" damage, they also said, "In the event you choose to proceed with the DAC, I must advise you that we will stay with the recommendations of the DAC with regards to further treatments." But even that they refused to do, because, they told me at the hearing –which I re-member as a deeply destructive and humiliating experience– he had not been allowed to recommend a pain management program. "But we believe you have pain," they told me, "You are not a professor one day and not the next." I thought, "Oh, my God," what if I had been working as a low level clerk somewhere, or a house cleaner. I would obviously have been malingering. In the end however, it didn't make a difference after all that I was a professor and that they "believed me": They refused to pay any further claims.

When I look at the big envelope into which I have stuffed all things Alli-anz, I feel anger and my stomach tightens. Still, after all these years.

What also influences this process, I believe, is the absence of distinctions in formal pain levels, as there is a large difference between severe and light pain. Setting aside for a moment the difficulties in drawing these distinctions, if they were available, the insurer couldn't so easily deny so many of us. Now, they see us all in the same light: We have just a bit of discomfort.

Completely worn down by this cruel, destructive, and deeply unjust treatment, on top of suffering from severe pain and exhaustion and grieving the loss of work and social life, I gave up. I could "afford" to give up because I had good extended healthcare and disability coverage at work. What if I had not had such coverage? I would by now have joined the ranks of those pain patients living in poverty.

On the advice of one of my healthcare professionals I considered a lawsuit, but being in constant pain and deeply exhausted I couldn't follow through. Things went exactly as the insurer had planned. I was forced to give up a just fight. The irony is, of course, that I would have never given up on such a just fight had I not suffered from the very thing the fight would have been about.

It is mind-boggling: We are told by pain medicine that the invisibility of our disease is not an indication that our pain is not real. The injuries may not be visible. Or, as has been known now for some time, our central nervous system has changed itself so as to generate pain. But our insurers tell us: You can't have pain because nothing shows up on your MRI or scan or X-ray. *Thus, our pain care professionals tell us that the absence of a visible reason for our pain is a central characteristic of chronic pain, while at the same time, the insurer says it is proof that we are lying!*

Further, we are told by pain researchers that early intervention is crucial so our nervous system doesn't have the chance to start its own pain generating processes. But our insurers often deny early treatment in the hope we will go away or to set the stage to cut us off. *Pain researchers and clinicians stress the crucial importance of early treatments, while at the same time, our insurers often deny early treatments.*

Where is the outrage by the medical profession about this deliberate distortion of medical knowledge by insurers?

Rehabilitation services

A clinical psychologist who works with many pain patients wrote the following to me,

> There is a whole set of frustrations, fears, and despairs faced by people in pain who are in a world of 3rd party funding and rehabilitation. The powerlessness, confusion, and sometimes rage that goes with this is endemic. People have to do a prescribed treatment for fear of losing wage loss benefits. If they can't manage it, they are in an impossible bind. People who like you have no reported organic findings are cut off funding and told they can go back and do the work they used to do, often physical work… The adversarial nature of these systems increase pain and decrease the effectiveness of treatment. People's fear of poverty, loss, destitution, becomes totally intertwined with their pain… it bedevils patient and therapist alike.

Says a Canadian worker who, due to an accident at work, lives with ongoing severe pain, "All of us in the work force pay one way or the other into the system all our lives, but when we need it it disappears."[4] This person characterized his sessions with his psychotherapist as being in a "safe place." But his insurer stopped paying for it and he lost the only safe place he had.

N. Kleinfield and Steven Greenhouse describe the following situation at the Queens office of the New York State Workers' Compensation Board, which they characterize as a "subbasement of the legal world."[5] They spent 18 months actually attending hearings, reviewing cases and interviewing participants – the kind of real life based observational research we should see a lot more of.

> At some hearings, as judges looked on, lawyers chatted on cellphones, cracked bawdy jokes or read newspapers during testimony. Expert witnesses seemed biased to the point of caricature. Claims dragged on, but hearings seldom exceeded a few blurred minutes, rarely proved conclusive and were conducted in baffling shorthand.

One may argue that this may be happening in Queens, New York, but not where the reader lives. Perhaps not to such extent. But perhaps to such extent. Numerous disabled workers, says Mary Jeffords, head of Injured Workers of New York, an advocacy group, are so ground down by the process that they begin to unravel. So did I.

While fraud of course does happen, as fraud happens everywhere where humans are involved, the experts told Kleinfield and Greenhouse that "far more money is siphoned by employers that illegally underpay premiums by under reporting the size of their work force or by doctors who fabricate bills." "Relieving Pain in America," the extensive 2011 report on chronic pain by the U.S. Institute of Medicine (IOM), further notes that while there is

> some number of patients who attempt to "game the system"…data and studies to back up these suspicions are few. The committee members are not naïve about this possibility, but believe it is far smaller than the likelihood that someone with pain will receive inadequate care.[6]

An injured worker in British Columbia told Tom Sandborn of The Tyee, an independent political and cultural news organization, of the unjust ways the province workers' compensation system had handled his crippling injuries resulting in chronic pain. He did not want his real name used because he feared retaliation from the government.[7] This worker is a middle-aged immigrant who was a building tradesman with a steady work history. In the final settlement, he received $500 a month, but only to age 65. WorkSafe BC, the workers' compensation system, did not consider the impact of his injury on his ability to earn a living.

When I asked a badly injured worker why he was still going to an occupational therapy program which in an earlier e-mail he had called a "stupid" program, he wrote the following,

> When I called the therapy "stupid" it is because this is the third time I have gone through this program since 2003. The same "therapists" doing the same thing. It is forced on me and other clients through the WBC (BC workman's compensation board). I'll leave it with that as I AM ANGRY RIGHT NOW… the absolute hole this system puts you in is terrifying.

The following words are from a pain patient of physician Ruth Dubin, "Just before it settled I was either going to hurt myself or someone else."[8] And another one,

> I told my last WSIB worker and boss that I was going to burn myself in public in front of my workplace. I was lost in the system, lost in bureaucracy. My supervisor harassed me publicly…I was so angry, I thought of violence.

So many, many similar stories.

In a report called "Insult to Injury," labor lawyers with decades of experience with WorkSafe BC document retrograde steps taken in the last decade, including denial the loss of earnings, elimination of vocational rehabilitation assistance, over-complicated appeals processes, pensions that used to be paid for life now ending at 65, a 13% reduction in benefits rates, replacement of skilled health professionals with data entry clerks, and significant restrictions in compensation for psychological injuries and chronic pain.[9] Of course the two last items, mentioned as if they belong together and are similar in nature, caught my attention. Given that our pain, being invisible, is now so easily overpsychologized and psychiatrized away, we are doubly disadvantaged as insurers will jump on any hint in professional evaluations that psychological problems are the real problem.

Researchers have also documented the trap well-intended rehabilitation workers are in. Coralie Wales shows how rehabilitation professionals watch their clients and are in turn being watched by their superiors – with contradictory messages and needs.[10] The role of the rehabilitation case manager was seen to be aligned to the insurer by having to "report back" to them. Rehabilitation professionals, Wales conclude, take for granted that the insurer has the ultimate control over the case.

Where is the outrage? Where is the political fight?

There is no way we can fight insurers and compensation boards on our own.

The real question I am coming to is this: Where is the outrage by medical professionals and researchers in chronic pain about the distortion of knowledge by insurers to deny us what we have a legal right to? Where is the action?

Two major recent reports on chronic pain by prestigious institutes that are identifying barriers to helping chronic pain patients refer only minimally to the role of insurers. "A Call to Revolutionize Chronic Pain Care in America," a report by the MayDay Fund in 2009, insurers are referred to only once, when stating that everyone, insurers included, should work to eliminate disparities in access to pain care related to race, ethnicity, gender, age and socioeconomic status. That is all. What is nowhere mentioned is the institutionalized denial of the reality of chronic pain that occurs as a matter of reflex. The MayDay report was the result of a day long meeting of 22 panel members, all formally listed in the report, all well known professionals in pain research and care.[11] While psychiatry and psychology were represented on the panel, there was no representation of the insurance industries and compensation boards or of the employment sector. Clearly, chronic pain was seen as belonging exclusively in the medical/psychological/psychiatric realm. Insurers are an entity onto themselves and can do as they please. Yet, there will be many people suffering from severe daily pain who would much, much rather have their insurance and disability claims honored –avoiding descending into poverty and receiving medical care– than see a psychiatrist or psychologist.

The 2011 major Institute of Medicine report, "Relieving Pain in America," does refer to insurers' reimbursement protocols which, it says, "discourage effective pain care." Protocols mentioned include reimbursement for expensive imaging procedures and invasive and high risk procedures and surgery while limiting or denying reimbursement for multidimensional treatments, time spent with the patient by primary care physicians, and alternative approaches to pain relief.[12] "Restrictions of insurance coverage... including those of workers' compensation plans, constrain the ability to offer potentially effective treatment."[13] It does not, however, mention the denial of the reality of chronic pain itself, nor the use of outdated theories of pain by insurers to justify such denial.

Here too, representation on the 19 member committee that prepared the report was restricted to a range of medical professionals, and professionals in nursing, psychiatry, psychology, and pharmacology.[14] It did not include anyone from the insurance industries, the compensation boards, employers organizations, labor unions, or the medico-legal profession.

Why is it that major reports on chronic pain fail to directly confront the insurance industries for their deliberate and habitual denial of the reality of chronic pain? For their distortion of medical knowledge? Books on chronic pain likewise avoid the entire matter of denial by insurers. Melanie Thernstrom, for instance, in an otherwise extensive and detailed account on a wide range of aspects of the chronic pain experience, only refers to the "quick moneymaking procedures on which insurance reimbursement systems are based."[15] That's it. I think the insurance industry just smiles when reading these reports: there is nothing in them that presents them with a challenge.

"Cost containment," a phrase sounding serious and grave, is often used to explain the need to deny claims. Everyone knows it is not cost containment. The compensation of the CEOs of the top eight North American health insurance companies in 2008 totaled an average of $11,630,000 for each of the eight CEOs.[16] This is just salary and amounts to a monthly income of $969,175. Which in turn amounts to $32,305 per day, a figure I base on a ten hour work day, including weekends and holidays, year round, assuming that CEOs work unbelievably hard to earn these high incomes. This would mean an income of $3,320 per hour, which comes to $55.30 per minute. Thus, a CEO in this hardworking scenario has to work just a touch over 9 minutes to receive the $500 our injured BC worker receives per month. For an eight hour, five days a week workload, the CEO would have to work only five minutes to receive what our injured worker receives per month.

To be sure, a number of pain researchers and clinicians do voice their objections to this outrageous and bizarre state of affairs that leads to the destruction of our lives. I have already mentioned the work by Harold Merskey and Robert Teasell. They explicitly object to insurances bodies being involved in matters related to the evaluation of medical care, which influences medical opinion and diagnosis to minimize the impact of consequences of pain, and even its existence.[17] They point to the distortions by the industry of medical information – always to facilitate the denial of pain. The writings by Merskey and Teasell approach the proper tone of outrage, rather than just of observation.

Physician Ruth Dubin, in documenting her pain patients lives, objects to the destructive effects of insurers confrontational and adversarial approaches.[18] She calls for a shift from the medico-legal models to one that incorporates an "expanded understanding of the chronic pain experience" and includes up to date education in pain medicine for lawyers and claim managers.

Gary Lea, a clinical psychologist, notes the numerous reports he has heard from his pain patients about delays in medical and psychological assessments, repetitious evaluations, symptom minimization or denial, perceived lack of empathy for their condition, disbelief, blame, and stigmatization.[19] "You weren't hurt enough to be entitled to benefits." Or, "It happened weeks (or months or years) ago. You should be over it by now." Signs of distress because of pain were often interpreted as preexisting psychological problems. This "secondary wounding" as Lea refers to it, is inadequately identified in the world of rehabilitation. Lea estimates that 50% of his rehabilitation clients have actively contemplated suicide at one time or another as an outcome of such secondary wounding.

Another major problem, which also applied to me, is that most of us have no idea what is in store for us. Jeanne Lazo, a pain patient who ended up writing a book to help patients navigate through the disability maze, notes how most of us are ignorant of disability laws and are unaware that we are in a legal situation.[20] Almost all of us stumble into it. If we were out for secondary gain, we would come a bit better prepared.

We need real-life-based research that documents what goes on during hearings with insurers – if observers were allowed in. And if they would not be allowed in, that in itself would be a sure sign of how much is decided about pain care behind closed doors.

I wrote the above paragraph on March 14, 2012, the day the New York Times' Op-Ed piece by Greg Smith was published. Smith is the former executive director and former head of Goldman Sachs' United States equity derivatives business in Europe, the Middle East and Africa.[21] In his Op-Ed he explained why he was resigning, as of that day. He could no longer take the culture of corruption, a culture in which, as he stated, the interests of the clients have no longer any place in the company's thinking. The focus, he says, is on how to get your clients to behave in ways that bring the greatest profit to the company. In meetings, says Smith, you hear about "muppets" (referring to clients), "ripping out eyeballs," and "getting paid." Clients' success or progress is no longer part of the thought process, says Smith. Replace "muppets" with "malingerers," "liars," or "exaggeraters," and Smith's comments describe how people living with chronic pain are seen by their insurers.

Chronic pain being what it is, the question of criteria is of course a crucial one and a difficult one. As Mark Sullivan notes, the highly variable relation between clinical pain and tissue damage makes pain behavior validation a serious challenge.[22] Pain behavior cannot be validated by matching public pain behavior with private pain experience. The pain experience is not available to scientific investigation. We have by necessity, says Sullivan, an ambiguity that cannot be resolved by sorting the ill into accurate and inaccurate reporters of pain.

What one can say with certainty, is that the exclusive reliance by insurers on theories of visible causes for pain is wrong and unethical. And they know it. Yet they get away with it. One can also surely say that it is not possible that over 80% of people who submit insurance claims for pain and are denied are malingering. People living with constant pain cannot fight the insurers' betrayal of them. It is not a fight that can be ours. Whose fight is it? Who will fight with us and for us?

9   *The opioid dilemma as seen through the eyes of pain*

In June 2008, when I lived in Victoria B.C., my family doctor closed his practice. There was a shortage of doctors, and I couldn't find one who was taking new patients. I was also on a wait list to be seen by one of the few pain specialists in town. No family doctor, no pain specialist.

I was out of Percocet, which contains acetaminophen and oxycodone, and although I did not use it often anymore since prolotherapy four years earlier had taken a chunk of my pain away, I needed it for those times when the pain still went out of control. So I went to a walk-in clinic, where, to my surprise, the doctor on call was the medical director of the private ten-day residential pain clinic I had attended some years earlier. He had done the intake back then, and over the ten days we had had several conversations. He immediately recognized me...but he could not prescribe Percocet. The College of Physicians, he told me, did not allow walk-in clinics to prescribe opioids because, he said, "street people" go to walk-in clinics to try to obtain them.

This doctor knew me and knew a lot about me and my chronic pain problems. Yet he couldn't prescribe a pain medicine I needed. I was caught in a system that assigned me the status of a street person. And what if a street person suffers from a lot of pain? An important question given the rather expected finding that homeless people suffer proportionally more from chronic pain, yet have less access to pain care. Nor can they afford pain relieving treatments such as massage, acupuncture, biofeedback, osteopathy, and the like. As reported by ScienceDaily, almost half of the homeless who suffer from chronic pain end up using street drugs to treat their pain.[1]

Experiences like these expose some of the complex and multidimensional problems that surround the need for opioids by those who suffer from severe pain on the one hand, and their accidental overdose or their misuse – frequently by those who do not suffer from pain – leading to many deaths on the other hand. These dilemmas are often narrowly framed reducing them to pro or con positions. People in pain fall between the cracks of these arguments, and too often into the abyss of suicide. In the rightful panic about the many lives lost to the misuse of opioids, many people who suffer from severe pain, and for whom nothing else has helped, cannot find a doctor anymore who will prescribe for them the opioids they need. Their relentless and unmitigated suffering not infrequently leads to their death when they decide that enough is enough.

The complex opioid related problems in pain management demand sophisticated administrative and policy approaches, areas of expertise I do not possess. In fact, at first I didn't really want to write about this topic, given I find it too overwhelming to even just think about its complexities. Not being an administrator or policy expert I offer just a few comments from the perspective of living with pain.

Personally, I try to stay away from opioids, and did so even when my specialists prescribed them during the years of horrible pain, simply because I cannot tolerate their side effects. Morphine dramatically distorted my cognitive processes and my emotions. I couldn't finish a sentence. I could not sustain a thought. My sense of self was gone. These effects did not go away after a few weeks, as they do for some others. I was also put on codeine and tramadol, neither helped the pain and both made me very nauseated. Dilaudid did not help either. Then we tried out Percocet and oxycodone. While these changed the nature of the pain – still there but softer and in the background – they caused an intensification of my emotions which I did not welcome. However, they worked for the worst pain when nothing else did.

However, I have known several people who tolerate opioids very well, and some who without doubt, would no longer be around if they had not had access to them. I myself would no longer be around had I not had access to them during the initial horrendous suicidal years after the accident.

Also, individuals react very differently to opioid medications, both in terms of their side effects and the dose they need to obtain pain relief. The numbers of accidental deaths from overdose range between 15,000 and 27,000 a year.[2] In 2012, Sanjay Gupta reported an estimate of 20,000 people a year who die from an accidental "prescription drug overdose" of pain medicine and of sleeping pills.[3] People die often from mixing opioids with other central nervous system depressants such as alcohol or benzodiazepines not realizing how dangerous that is. Victims are often young people who find prescription pain killers in the medicine cabinet of family members. (According to one source, one in five people are prescribed opioids every year.[4]

Hence, pain killers can be found in many households.) Middle aged adults, particularly males, constitutes another group with high overdose rates. Many people think that prescription drugs are not dangerous because a doctor has prescribed them. People often increase the number of pills they take when their prescription is no longer as effective as it initially was, without knowing they are turning a dangerous corner. The high number of deaths from overdose is horrendous.

I have not seen studies that show how many who suffer from severe ongoing pain, having no longer access to opioids, commit suicide for ultimate pain control. Their stories float on the internet and are whispered when people in pain meet. And because these suicides have not received formal, systematic attention in pain research, they are as invisible as is our pain. We are ignored to the very end.

Juxtaposing deaths by overdose or the mixing of drugs on the one hand, and deaths by suicide when refused the needed opioids on the other hand, is not meant to be a risk/benefit analysis. *No one* should have to die of an accidental overdose out of ignorance or poor monitoring. But also, *no one* should have to end their life because of untreated pain. I am juxtaposing these two very different kinds of deaths only to highlight which group has received formal research attention, and which group has not. Which group is in the media spot light and which one is not, although both kinds of deaths are unwanted deaths, for when people living with pain end their lives, it is typically because they need their pain to end, not because they want to die. But by then there is no other way to end the pain than to die.

Tom Frieden, Director of the Centers for Disease Control and Prevention (CDC) says of opioids, "We know of no other medication routinely used for a nonfatal condition that kills patients so frequently."[5] I need to point out that while this professional view is correct at first glance, when viewed through the eyes of pain, it ignores the fact that for those whose pain is severe and non-stop, for years on end, it can be a fatal condition as for many there comes a point where ending one's life is the only option left to make life bearable. To simply stop it all.

There is great irony in what is ignored in the discussions on the danger of using opioids: the thousands a year who die from nonsteroidal anti-inflammatory drugs (NSAIDs), routinely prescribed or legally bought over the counter for pain (including Advil, Aleve, aspirin, Celebrex, Toradol, Voltaren, Vioxx and many others). Over 100,000 people a year are hospitalized for gastrointestinal complications caused by NSAIDs in the U.S. alone and an estimated 10,000 to 20,000 die from ulcers and internal bleeding every year.[6] Neither the media nor the medical literature seems to make a big deal about this. Whereas the thousands of deaths from overdose of prescribed opioids are rightfully discussed as an tragic epidemic, the thousands of deaths from NSAIDs seem to be merely a "silent epidemic" with many physicians and most patients unaware of the magnitude of the problem.[7] Questions arise: Why aren't NSAIDs scrutinized and made as difficult to obtain as opioids? Shouldn't doctors also be criminally prosecuted for prescribing too many NSAIDs when a patient dies from them? One major difference, of course, is that one does not get a heroin-like high from NSAIDs."[8] You simply bleed to death.

All this is a mind-boggling mess, involving among other aspects, politics, entrenched medical views, culture, the media, and the question who has the power to keep certain events silent and not others.

For people in pain, not receiving attention has for most of us been the case all along. That is our life. But not being paid formal attention to when we end our lives because pain medication is denied and we cannot bear the increase in pain any longer, that takes the neglect to a new level.

And as one person wrote,

> Don't take your anger out on [people in pain] causing *them* to die. That isn't fair…God help us all… please don't allow people who suffer (from pain) to be forced to end their lives because they can't get medical help.[9]

Someone else says,

> When you hurt so bad that you would rather die than take another breath you would take anything to make the pain stop, dependence/addiction or even death are not even remotely important to you.[10]

Says pain specialist Scott Fishman, chronic pain is so "ruthless," so "relentless," and so psychologically devastating that sufferers will try anything, even risking total paralysis or death.[11] There are many pain patients who have tried every possible treatment available to them and have found no relief anywhere, but for the pain dulling effects of opioids. This was the case for me as well during the first six years of my life in pain.

"Even if opiates were proven unsafe for long term use, I would still use them," says a pain patient.[12] "I would rather pass away ten of fifteen maybe even twenty years (sooner) instead of living to eighty or ninety in severe pain." "Amen," many pain sufferers will say to that, including me. It is the *relentlessness* at the heart of chronic pain why we would choose methods of pain relief that may shorten our lives over living out our years but in relentless pain. Pain once in a while? Even intense pain once in a while? Ok, we get through that. But all the time?

"Why can't a pain patient like me make my own choices? I should be able to choose how I want to treat my pain," says a person living with ongoing pain.[13] Withholding opioids from her, she says, is interfering with her "constitutional rights to pursue happiness." Says columnist Mark Maginn, who has lived with pain for forty-five years, and who is still alive because of the relief opioids have provided (he, too, has had a wide array of other treatments as well), "My heart goes out to people who have lost a loved one due to opioids. But untold thousands die yearly from pain (by suicide). Whose heart goes out to them?"[14]

I have had the exact same thought a person living with pain expressed upon hearing that someone she knew who suffered from severe ongoing pain had ended her life: "I never regret their passing knowing they have finally escaped the beast."[15] At the same time I feel a deep sadness for a life lost that likely could have been helped and saved with timely attention, with the right and timely treatments, a sadness mingled with anger at a society that routinely minimizes our pain. It is a sadness in me that contains a deep experiential understanding and identification.

I feel the same deep sadness for the thousands of often unintentional deaths from opioid overdose. In 2012, someone died from an overdose of pain medicine, often combined with other substances, every 19 minutes.[16] It is too much to think about. This sadness, too, is mingled with anger at society for having these medicines stored in accessible medicine cabinets; at the pharmaceutical industry for having pushed the notion that opioids are safe (as recounted earlier, I was even solicited to help them do so); anger for there not being a effective national system in place to keep track of prescriptions; anger about the inadequate education of doctors, many of whom do not know much about alternative pain management, or how to responsibly prescribe opioids, and who don't explain the dangers of opioid misuse to us.

Many who take opioids do not know that mixing these drugs with a couple of diazepam pills and washing it all down with a couple of beers is a dangerous mix that depresses the central nervous system to the point where you no longer can breathe. These things should be taught in our families and schools, *and definitely in the doctor's office*. When prescribed opioids (five different kinds over the years), I was never told a single word about these dangers. There ought to be a handout, spelling them all out. Not just to be given to the pain patient but *to be discussed.* Says Kathleen Meyers, senior researcher for the Treatment Research Institute,

> When someone is given prednisone, a steroid commonly used to treat inflammatory diseases, they are given very specific instruction… they are very direct about what will happen if the patient misuses it. You don't see that with pain medication. Maybe if we did a better job with how we communicate the effects of prescription medication when you don't take them the way they are prescribed or if you mix other substances with them, maybe we wouldn't have the number of people who are in crisis.[17]

These words were said in November, 2012. How are pain patients to feel when reading this? People with other diseases are warned about the consequences of particular treatments. But most of us are not. Perhaps the physician thinks that to explain the possibility of fatality by taking too many pills or combining them with alcohol may give us ideas. Or the physician simply doesn't have the courage to talk with us about these possibilities. Or the physician, influenced by pain research in psychology, thinks we are "catastrophizing" and "exaggerating." Let me say this: If we want to end our lives we will find a way. Careful explanations by our physicians will more likely help us not to end our lives: someone cares. Our lives are valued.

In 2016, the Food and Drug Administration finally issued warning labels for opioids, including boxed warnings about the risks of abuse and death.[18] While these warnings may help, they should not replace a solid discussion between the pain patient and her/his physician.

Sanjay Gupta ends his expose on the many accidental deaths from the misuse of pain killers by saying: "No one is suggesting we stop prescribing narcotics for pain."[19] But that is disingenuous, for that is exactly what is happening. There are many tales on blogs and pain advocacy web sites by people suffering from severe chronic pain of being refused needed opioid medication, or who have their dosage lowered to where it no longer helps, including by doctors who are convinced their patients really need them but who no longer dare to prescribe as needed.[20] Often we can't find a new doctor to prescribe opioids after our doctor has moved or closed her/his practice. Pharmacists can refuse to prescribe controlled substances. After a pain patient moved to another city, she tried five pain doctors in her new area,

> and not ONE would prescribe anything for me! They all want to shoot steroids and drugs and stuff into my back (instead). I've tried that and a million other things and my opioid treatment plan is the ONLY thing that has ever worked."[21]

In the pain support groups I attended, the topic of ending one's life when no strong pain medicine is provided was always avoided or was side tracked when it was brought up by a participant. The media too, is complicit,

> The mass media ticks me off to no end…because they NEVER talk about this issue (suicide because of unbearable pain). They ONLY talk about the problems with drug addictions and prescription drug abuse addicts and do not bring up the issue of very real human beings in very genuine pain who need pain killers. It is not balanced reporting on the issue. I feel for drug addicts but they are ruining it for people in genuine need. [22]

It is a mess all around. A mess that is not really surprising when pain is often ignored or under treated; when treatment is inaccessible for many; when thousands upon thousands have no access to a doctor who understands chronic pain; when many doctors have had little or no education in pain management; when too many doctors do not even like to see us; and when the pain's seriousness is routinely and badly underestimated by healthcare professionals and by society at large alike.

If we had a healthcare system that understands chronic pain, knows the many treatments available, where physicians are well educated in pain management, a system that deals with pain immediately, a system where people in pain are *listened to*, their intelligence respected, and a society in which people in pain are believed and supported, such a system and society would be a most important response to the opioid dilemma. For many of us a good deal of our pain might be stopped from becoming chronic in the first place. And if that cannot be prevented, and other treatments don't work, opioids would then be prescribed responsibly to those who need them. But we are far from that.

Another major problem is that the views by those who actually live with pain regarding what we are willing to risk in exchange for pain relief are not honored, or even invited. We are never asked what kind of long term side effects we are ready to accept in exchange for being prescribed opioids for relief of pain *now* when relief has not been otherwise obtained.

Yet, we can write a living will, an advance health directive, in which we tell the medical world what we do and don't want in case we encounter a medical emergency. These documents are legally binding statements that tell doctors not to resuscitate us, not to force feed us, not to keep us artificially alive, only to provide comfort, and to let us die – although our wishes on paper may go against the instincts of most doctors who see keeping us alive as their main task. And this is for a hypothetical future situation about which we have no idea if it will actually happen.

But when it comes to prescribing the strong medicine we need for severe chronic pain that is actually happening now –an ongoing medical emergency– we have no say in the matter. We always feel we are begging, trying not to be that stereotype of an aggressive pain patient, not to come across as that drug seeker. But we are not asked to voice how we weigh relief of severe and ongoing pain now against possible negative long terms effects. Many of us would choose long term negative effects, less years to live, the development of tolerance, even of addiction, for less pain now, driven as we are, now, to craziness and suicide by relentless 24/7 pain. It is the "24/7" that others, including doctors, do not understand.

For pain patients to be able to decide for themselves that relief from pain *now* outweighs the possible negative long term side effects from opioids, would be similar to the writing of a health directive but for reversing the arrow of time: one focuses on the future, the other one on the here and now. But in both cases, the patient's wishes are decisive with regard to a crucial medical situation; in both cases the patient takes responsibility for the outcomes; in both cases the patient is seen as an intelligent adult with rights and responsibilities; in both cases the central issue is the quality of life.

Of course, in my scenario, the pain patient would also need to sign statements, similar to a health directive, that transfer responsibility for possible later consequences from doctor to patient, always with the fullest possible knowledge, clearly communicated to the person in pain, of what long term use might do to our bodies and minds. Strict prescription protocols should be in place. But we should have our say. Just as it is now possible for us to decide how we want to die in an unknown future: with drastic interventions or with no interventions at all. Yet, in the known present, there are thousands of people living horrible lives in constant pain who could be helped, but who, for reasons that have to do with culture, politics, policy matters, and bureaucracy, are now not allowed to have medications that can soften the suicidal pain and make it bearable and manageable.

Ann Martino cites a lengthy list of reasons why physicians under-prescribe for pain which include: avoiding the risk of being disciplined by federal or state legislatures; fear that drugs for pain will lead to addiction; desire to avoid pain patients because pain management is difficult; fear of being duped by a "drug-seeking" patient; lack of knowledge about pain medicine; inability to differentiate between physical dependence and addiction; long held and incorrect belief that patients are poor judges of the scope and severity of their pain; failure to conduct thorough and frequent reevaluations of pain patients' status; hospitals that operate on a disease model that does not reward pain management; reimbursement policies of health insurers centering on "medical necessity" that have resulted in inadequate or uneven coverage for long term pain care; multiple copies of prescription forms that are cumbersome to complete and are frequently not available in an office or clinical practice setting; inadequate medical school and post-graduate training in pathophysiology of acute and chronic pain; the perpetuation of an outdated mechanistic model that characterizes pain only as a physiological impulse or a response to disease; the cultural fear of pain and death resulting in an unwillingness to engage in political dialogue about appropriate policy; and the general fear of drugs including legitimate use of opioids that is an unintended consequence of the U.S. War on Drugs.[23] *None* of these reasons, says Martino, releases a doctor's responsibility to relieve pain.

High quality pain care, accessible to all who need it, as soon as they need it, offering a wide range of mainstream as well as alternative approaches to treatment, must be central to reducing the number of opioid prescriptions, reducing deadly abuse, and easing the high suicide rate among pain patients.

In the meantime, people living with ongoing severe pain must be approached as people who are living terribly difficult lives, *now*, and who have the human, medical, and legal rights to get the help they need so they do not get to the point where ending life becomes the only painkiller left.

10 Social stigma

People living in pain are stigmatized for living in pain. Here, the first phrase "living in pain," refers to the person's reality. The second phrase "living in pain" refers to how others understand that reality. It is in the space between the two that stigmatization takes place.

With diseases that have a visible cause, the reality of the person living with the disease may not be fully understood by society, but it is not trivialized and stigmatized, or not nearly to the degree chronic pain is. After all, the test results are there. There clearly is a disease. There is a treatment. A likely prognosis.

With chronic pain, it is nothing like that. There may be scans and X-rays, but these provide guesses rather than causes. If two people were to have the exact same scan, one may be in pain and the other might not. A good part of my memoir "Inside Chronic Pain" is devoted to the multiple diagnostic contradictions I and others have received and to the trial and error approaches to treatments. As far as a prognosis is concerned, forget it.

With that much uncertainty for a condition that is invisible and hard to put into words, it is not surprising that stigma slips in effortlessly. As neurosurgeon Kenneth Follett, contributor to the 2011 Institute of Medicine Report "Relieving Pain in America" states succinctly: "Many Americans believe people in pain are whiners who are trying to avoid work, get attention or obtain drugs."[1]

Although I have not used the word "stigma" so far in this book, stigmatization can be seen as a thread that runs through nearly every chapter. The original meaning of the word "stigma" is a "sign" or a "branding mark," a physical mark indicating disgrace, infamy, or dishonor.[2] And although some people living with pain bear physical marks from their injuries, I am here not referring to physical marks. I am referring to "social stigma," to the processes of distancing, excluding and discrediting which are based on perceived negative social characteristics that serve to separate the person from the rest of society. Those so stigmatized are made to feel they do not have a normal, desirable identity. The seminal work by sociologist Erving Goffman is often referenced in discussions of social stigma.[3]

While acute pain is foremost a bodily event, and typically traceable to an observable cause, chronic pain is, by its very nature, more like a blank slate: anyone can interpret it in any way and almost anyone does. When moans and groans of acute pain slowly become internalized, the pain gets *swallowed.* Unless one lives with persistent pain, I dare say that one cannot understand what "swallowing one's pain" means – how it is possible, and how it becomes necessary to do so.

Researchers who look through interpersonal social and societal lenses have started to address the social stigma people living with chronic pain are subjected to. They look at functions of theory and uses of language, how labels come into being, how power relations determine these processes, and how various institutions reinforce stereotypes that benefit the institutions but silence the person in pain. They point to discriminatory attitudes and practices that flow from exclusive adherence to traditional bio-medical and psychological models.

Cohen, Quintner, Buchanan, Nielsen, and Guy address stigmatization with regard to the relation between the clinician and the pain patient.[4] They argue that health professionals inadvertently contribute to the stigmatization of chronic pain patients because of the Cartesian body/mind dualism which is perpetuated in medical thinking. The biomedical and psychobiological models, state Cohen et al., are based on the traditional philosophical conception of the Cartesian mind/body split and hence shape approaches to diagnosis and treatment. Pain sufferers appear to many clinicians either as a disordered body or as a disturbed mind: When no cause for the pain can be found, the absence of evidence of a "disordered" body defaults to an inference of a "disturbed mind" resulting in iatrogenic stigmatization.[5] Further, to impute a mental disorder upon a person in pain is also scientifically inappropriate, Cohen et al. state, because of recent understandings of neuroplasticity which provides a plausible neurobiological explanation for various kinds of chronic pain.

Thus, while the body/mind split rarely causes a problem with acute pain since acute pain typically points to a disordered body, when pain becomes chronic the assumed body/mind split shifts the focus away from the body to the only place it can go within a Cartesian dualism: the mind. There is nowhere else to go.

The most insidious consequence of iatrogenic stigmatization, Cohen et al. note, is a loss of voice: People in pain literally become the "unheard."[6] A disturbed mind cannot rationally speak for itself: The psychiatrizing and over-psychologizing of chronic pain as discussed in chapters 4 and 5 directly reflect this scenario.

Cohen et al. conclude that models of chronic pain must redress iatrogenic stigmatization and must discard dualisms that attribute to the person in pain a "weak mind" when a bodily cause cannot be diagnosed (or, as I have discussed in chapter 5, a secondary gain-seeking mind, a catastrophizing mind, a drug-seeking mind, an attention-seeking mind, an exaggerating mind, a malingering mind). This will not happen, Cohen et al. state, as long as the stigmatizing group keeps its hold on power. Neuroplasticity asks of clinicians to give up their paradigmatic power and enter an intersubjective space of engagement in which the pain patient is an equal participant.[7] For that to happen, the authors conclude, it is not enough to say that one is against stigmatization: A much more fundamental change in explanatory frames is necessary, which, as is also the message of this book, requires the willingness to deliberately have existing frames made explicit.[8]

Amanda Nielsen, drawing on a narrative study involving twenty people living with chronic pain, concludes that stigmatization cannot be addressed at the individual cognitive level, and that this social dimension of chronic pain must be addressed at a policy and social practice level.[9] Stigma exists, Nielsen notes, when the elements of labeling and stereotyping occur in a power situation that allows for these very processes to unfold. Indeed, the world of medicine, the helping professions including psychology and psychiatry, politics, insurance companies, the world of litigation, and employers –the entire web of societal forces involved in framing chronic pain– hold the power to bend our pain experience to their biases and needs.

Pain patients, says Nielsen, have their own strong attitudes and stereotypes of doctors (e.g. lacking compassion, ignorant, arrogant). But doctors cannot be said to be a stigmatized group as a result of pain patients' views of them: Pain patient simply do not have the power to stigmatize. Nielsen quotes Link and Phelan,

> Groups both with and without power label and form stereotypes about the other groups…But what matters is whose cognitions prevail - whose cognitions carry sufficient clout in social, cultural,

economic and political spheres to lead to important consequences for the group that has been labeled as different.[10]

Similarly, family physician Ruth Dubin chronicles the lives of six of her pain patients and notes many stigmatizing experiences they endured, such as disbelieving and confrontational attitudes by health care professionals, insurers, employers, and, in litigation, by lawyers and experts who attack the pain patient's veracity and reality.[11] Numerous accounts by pain patients on many advocacy web sites and blogs similarly tell of such explicit attacks on the reality of their pain by the very institutions and professionals that are supposed to help them.

Anthropologist Jean Jackson notes how problems of stigmatization are caused by the discrepancy between "pain experienced and pain communicated."[12] Jackson, who conducted 196 in-depth interviews with people living with chronic pain, uses the construct of "liminality" to illuminate the processes that occur when people living with pain defy existing categories. In anthropology, liminality is the ambiguity that occurs when people are in the midst of rituals of transition from one stage of life to another: Their previous role or status is no longer tenable, but the transition to the next stage or the new status has not yet been completed. They are temporarily liminal creatures. When the shift cannot be completed, their liminality becomes permanent. They belong neither here nor there. They can no longer be clearly categorized and thereby threaten established categories and established social order.

Chronic pain, says Jackson, similarly turns people in pain into liminal creatures, whose "uncertain ontological status provokes stigmatizing reactions."[13] Disturbed by the confusion people in pain create, others (including healthcare professionals) attribute all kinds of "explanations" for our condition that force us into categories that were developed for other conditions and that are not relevant to our lives in pain, categories that distort and trivialize instead.

Jackson's article struck a raw nerve. I recognized myself in it, in how others react to me, how ambiguous I appear to them – I look normal but am not well; some hours or days I behave normally but suddenly I am in great pain though seemingly nothing out of the ordinary has happened; I write a book but tell them there are many hours I cannot even think straight because of pain. After not seeing me for a while, even friends who once seemed to realize the seriousness of my situation, will think I am fine again. "Oh, I thought you would be better by now…" a dear friend said to me, after not having seen me for two years. Pain goes away. Chronic pain may last a bit longer but, in the end, it also goes away… except of course when it doesn't. And when it doesn't, doubt about the pain's veracity or about our state of mind sets in.

Being aware I don't fit into existing categories of normal human behavior, and I can't explain the "borderland" I now inhabit, I often end up pretending I am normal when with others. I force mind over bodily pain for as long as I can, and try to leave inconspicuously when I know I have reached the end of my ability to do so. People living with pain do not live within dualities. *We* are never in doubt about our experience. We don't experience ourselves as liminal creatures. We do not have to choose between opposites: Is the pain in my mind or my body? Is what I feel objective or 'only' subjective? Is what I feel real pain or psychogenic pain? None of these oppositional frames echo our experience. They make sense only to outsiders, particularly to the very people who create them in the first place. That professionals create them does not mean they have validity for lives lived in pain – which is far more complex than and cannot be understood within these dualistic frames. We simply experience the simultaneity of physical pain and its emotional and psychological impact, the simultaneous need for social contact and the instinct to withdraw; the awareness of how others only see "external" pain behaviors while we experience a far more complex reality. The problem is not that at times there are specific reasons in pain research to refer to "the body" or "the mind," but that these dualisms have become categories into which we must fit. Categories that are often blindly superimposed onto us and which do not reflect our lives.

Liminality as a stigmatizing process does not apply to those who have acute pain. There is no category confusion. No ambiguity. Objective knowledge is applied. For the most part, there is a diagnosis. The patients gets better or may get worse, but there is a measure of clarity about what is happening. There is no space left for stigmatization to develop.

Jackson's work shows how anthropological constructs can illuminate the ways in which living with chronic pain "acquires stigma along the way" to borrow Nielsen's words.[14] To adopt ways of knowing that lie outside of existing explanatory models and that are deeply grounded in the actual contexts of our lives is crucial if processes of stigmatization are to be better understood – and prevented. For stigma is not addressed by those who adhere to the biomedical model. Nor is it addressed by those who adhere to psychological models and who over-psychologize or psychiatrize chronic pain, nor by models that address the role the brain plays in sustaining chronic pain. These explanatory frames in fact can easily contribute to iatrogenic stigmatization to the extent they shift the "cause" of chronic pain solely to the psyche and the mind.

Direct and indirect stigmatization

There is still another way of looking at how stigmatization can be experienced by people living with pain: there is a direct and an indirect way in which we are told that we no longer belong. The direct way in which this occurs typically involves explicit negative judgments: being out for secondary gain, being a whiner, a catastrophizer, a drug seeker, and so forth. Conferring these judgments onto us absolves the labeler of having to deal with our reality. Or of having to deal with us at all.

The indirect way social stigma is experienced is more subtle, and the stigma unintended. Looking at it from the outside, it does not even look like stigma. It may well look like innocence or kindness. It occurs when the other, although knowing we suffer from chronic pain, has no grasp of what it means. Well intended things are said, "What do you do all day?" "Must be nice not to have to work and be able to sleep in!" "Are you going to travel now you don't work any longer?" and so forth. These comments (all said to me among many more) reflect, not a disbelief as such, nor a negative characterization, but the superficial understanding and serious misconstruction of what living with serious chronic pain is like. These words, although not mean spirited or accusing, marks the person in pain as someone who suffers from this mysterious condition that just can't be that serious. As someone who is on some sort of vacation. Who is taking a break from work. One would almost be envious – all that freedom in exchange for a bit of pain.

For the person in pain, an unbridgeable schism is instantly created because there are no accurate words that the other can understand with which to prevent this kind of indirect stigma: We are essentially told, in a very pleasant way, that we may just be exaggerating a little, though the speaker does not quite realize this. This pleasant way of stigmatizing causes an immediate sense of paralysis: Shall I try once more to patiently explain what I actually live with? Explain why I am not sleeping in and am not on vacation. Shall I just gently disagree, and leave it with that? Or shall I just give up and say nothing, thereby quite possibly sending the message that they are right in their minimization of the harshness of my life?

Neither form of stigmatization is easy to take. Disbelievers with their explicit negative judgments, particularly when they are supposed to be sources of support, can ruin your life, keep you from having access to pain care, and force you into poverty. Those who stigmatize from lack of understanding do not know their words have a stigmatizing effect.

In my case, the stigma I have felt has not been the direct form of stigmatizing comments, except as received from the car insurance company. But the indirect stigma arising from a lack of clarity about what my life in pain is like, creates all kinds of expectations of "normalcy" against which I have to defend myself: "Sorry, I can't go on that hike. It is too risky to walk on uneven ground. My neck will go out." "I can't do a movie and dinner in one evening." "That restaurant is too noisy for me. I would get a headache."

The indirect form of stigmatization is difficult in that it often comes from those you are close to, and who you thought would understand, but who in many ways expect you be who you were before – just with a little bit of pain. We are expected to be "normal" in order to be part of the social sphere. If you cannot do so, you find yourself essentially excluded as others rarely adjust to your limitations, in part because they do not understand them. Such isolation is experienced by us as being marked by stigma: We are not fun to be with; we are too "self-involved;" we always seem sad; we should cheer up; should have some fun; we always seem tired. These observations are "true" from the perspective of normal social behavior. As seen through the lens of chronic pain, they simply reflect our pain problems. Our normalcy.

Then there is, of course, the stigmatization associated with taking opioids for pain medicine. The stigmatization related to pain medicine is truly unique: I can't think of any other kind of medicine for any other disease that has that kind of stigma attached to it. In most cases there is not any stigma attached to taking medications for whatever ails you.

Further, there are layers of additional stigmatization based on gender, class, race, ethnicity and appearance. A pain researcher to whom I mentioned these additional forms of stigmatization said, "But pain does not discriminate based on gender or race or anything else!" I agreed. But, I said, society does. People do. Professionals do. Those who assess and treat pain patients do. There is ample evidence for differential access to pain care and for treatment outcomes. Minorities are at risk for problematic access, poor assessment and inferior treatment; women are more likely than men to be under-treated or inappropriately diagnosed for their pain; Women are more likely to be given sedatives for pain while men are more likely to receive pain medication, suggesting that women are more often perceived as anxious rather than in pain; attractive women are seen to be experiencing less pain than unattractive ones.[15] "Patient profiling," says Richard Payne, chief of Pain and Palliative Care Service at the Sloan-Kettering Memorial Cancer Center in New York, is a major problem.[16]

The essence of stigmatization, then, lies in pain's invisibility and un-say-ability, thus creating a blank slate for others to write on. The very moment I try to explain what I live with, or why I cannot join in certain activity, or why I cannot hold a job anymore, or travel by myself, I freeze. I feel excluded the moment I try to speak. I do not know how to reach the person. I always hear myself stumble. In a sense then, the stigma toward us starts the moment we utter the first word trying to say something about our lives. For immediately we know, that the words we say can not convey the reality we live.

Many give up. "I just smile and say "I'm fine…" says a woman I befriend-ed whose horse had stumbled and fallen on top of her fifteen years earlier, breaking many of her bones, resulting in chronic pain ever since. "I don't care any more," says another person I met, "No one gets it. So I just joke around."

When stigmatization is explicit and guided by crude calculations, e.g. when insurers engage in denial while they know better, the person in pain knows what he or she is dealing with and the stigmatizer may know that the person in pain knows what is happening, but can't do anything about it. With the well-intended indirect forms of stigmatization, the person in pain knows what they are dealing with (ignorance), but the stigmatizer is simply igno-rant. Hence, they often encourage you still more strongly to "have some fun," or to join activities you can no longer do…

All forms of stigmatizing readily bring about isolation, psychologically, emotionally, and physically. The relationship between stigmatization and isolation can be complex. Not all isolation is caused by stigmatization and ex-clusionary attitudes. Chronic pain is a hard physical fact. The actual pain one experiences *itself* brings on isolation. Anyone living with serious pain will tell you that the actual pain keeps one home bound, keeps you in a world that has shrunk to one's living room or bedroom, or to the chair in which you wither away in front of the TV. Being social –the talking, the chatter, the shifting topics, the back and forward of conversing– can be just too much for a brain in pain. When pain is intense and ongoing the person in pain may not be able to tolerate even the presence of another. For the presence of another implies attending, talking, listening, responding. Then, only absolute stillness is needed to keep one's sanity. The need to withdraw can feel total and is a coping mechanism, not a rejection of the other.

On the other hand, when in acute pain, the presence of others is typically desired as it represents the likelihood of help and support. The other is responsive to moans and cries and can get you to a doctor. Most people would not want to be alone when in acute pain. Stigmatization and isolation do not routinely happen when in acute pain.

Ironically, another avenue for stigmatization can be in the writings on the social and cultural processes in relation to chronic pain, however crucially important these views are. But they can give the impression that social and cultural meanings given to chronic pain are the most important features to understand. The physical reality of pain, already invisible and not measurable, is then conceptually ignored, and stigmatization easily slips in. Care needs to be taken when writing about culture, language, and psychological aspects of the lived experience of chronic pain, that our physical agony is neither ignored nor trivialized and that the danger of stigmatization is minimized.

11 *How do we know that we know.... let me count the ways*

What we observe is not nature itself, but nature exposed to our method of questioning.

Werner Heisenberg, *Physics and Philosophy*

I have come to know something simple. Each sentence realized or dreamed jumps like a pulse with history and takes a side.

Dionne Brand, *No Language is Neutral*

There is a beautiful story told by the great astrophysicist Eddington. He said that there was once a fisherman who was a keen observer of nature... and after 20 years he suddenly realized that he had discovered a new law of nature. The law of nature was that all fish are longer than four inches, but the reason was, of course, that his net was a four-inch net.

Chen Ning Yang, in *The Aesthetic Dimension of Science. The Sixteenth Nobel Conference*

My observations here emerge foremost from having lived with pain for many years. My academic background in educational and social science research also comes into play. But I would not have been able to make these observations based on my academic background alone. I would have not understood how particular ways of knowing shape understandings –or lack thereof– of lives lived in pain. But neither could I have made these observations based solely on living with pain. I would not have understood the assumptions and systems of belief about how one is allowed to claim knowledge –and how one is not– that are embedded in theories and research methodologies used in much of pain research.

Nothing I say here refers to research designed to address physiological processes. That is not my area of expertise. My comments are exclusively about research that purports to address the experience of chronic pain which, unfortunately, is my area of expertise.

Also, none of what I say is meant to critique individual researchers who carry out research on the experience of chronic pain. I cast no doubt on their concern for our well being. I do, however, cast doubt on the habit of thought by which many approach their research agenda. And that is a different matter. It is habit of thought that must be re-examined.

As is, that habit of thought is 'the tyranny of method.' The 'tyranny of method' refers to the belief that the use of a prescriptive methodology, based on the demand to quantify, keep under control, and statistically analyze the phenomena of interest, is the sine qua non of research. This privileged methodological foundation, borrowed from the natural sciences a few centuries ago, frequently stands in the way of gaining insight into how chronic pain works in a person's real life. It allows researchers *not* to have to imagine our real lives, *not* to have to genuinely listen to us, *not* to get to know the particular conditions of our lives. Their measurement instruments function as a shield. Researchers do not even have to be present or get to know us. Research assistants can "run" the study.

As we have understood the story of research for the last few hundreds of years, it has been a story of distancing and counting. Of separating researchers from what or whom they study by adherence to a predetermined methodology. This story holds that in order to come to know something, the researcher has to be in control of the phenomena of interest – of the research question, the research design, and the analysis of the data. It is the story of the *idea* of control.

The idea of control as a necessary condition for making knowledge claims emerged as a new value with the development of the 17th century scientific revolution which gave us, among other things, the scientific method. The idea of control is not the same as the exercise of control. Animals, children, and adults all exercise control when carrying out many functions in life. On the other hand, when control for the sake of control is seen as the starting ground for inquiry, control itself comes to be seen as more important than the nature and content of what the control actually attempts to control.[1]

As early as 1928, science writer J. W. N. Sullivan, in his book "Gallio or The Tyranny of Science," lamented the narrowness of slavishly following the scientific method –so successful in the natural sciences– for domains for which it was not developed, such as the study of human behavior.[2] A good deal of what passes for scientific work, including in psychology, he said, consists of "attempts to match things which are qualitatively different." The bias towards measurability is very strong, and typically we really have no clear idea at all as to what is being measured. This essentially sums up my earlier critiques of the over-psychologizing and psychiatrizing of chronic pain. Sullivan then adds,

> The methods found so successful in physics are applied to everything under the sun…In their eagerness to "measure" something our researchers seem to lose their ordinary common sense…

Science, Sullivan goes on to say, was undertaken as an intellectual adventure: an attempt to find out how far nature could be described in mathematical terms. But scientists made the mistake of casting their scientific nets too wide.

When I read articles that are largely devoted to methodological issues, while claiming to research our lives, I feel the lack of life. The lack of meaning. Indeed, the often total lack of common sense. It is never about me or about the many people living with persistent pain I have come to know. I read instead mostly about research methodology.

Tellingly, Fishbain et al. for instance, in their review of studies on secondary gain as it relates to marital reinforcement of pain behavior, at least recognize that studies that took place in an experimentally controlled setting may not apply to "real life."[3] The phrase "real life" is put between quotation marks, as if real life is an abstraction, a foreign construct which cannot be directly engaged. "Real life" is too messy, it cannot be brought under a researcher's control.

When real life is seen as a phenomenon that research cannot directly engage, the notion of "ameaningful thinking" becomes directly relevant. Back in 1981, psychologist Sigmund Koch sharply critiqued what he referred to as "a syndrome of ameaningful thinking" that characterized, he said, much of modern scholarship, especially the psychological sciences.[4]

> A meaningful thought regards knowledge as an almost automatic result of a self-corrective rule structure… a methodology – rather than a discovery. In consequence, much of psychological history can be seen as a form of scientistic role playing which, however sophisticated, entails the trivialization, and even evasion of significant problems.

Ludwig von Bertalanffy, father of General System Theory, uses the word "scientism", which he sees as "the intrusion of scientific, or rather pseudo-scientific ways of thinking into fields of human experience where they do not belong."[5] While research that relies on the idea of control has, of course, done wonders for the hard sciences and for technology, what it has done for the "soft" sciences has not been so successful. From the 1980's on, many voices have objected to the limitations of borrowing methods from the hard sciences for the study of human behavior.[6] The following sections outlines some of these limitations.

Knowledge of lives lived in pain: The "merely objective"

Cultural historian Morris Berman observed that the word "merely" in English never precedes the word "objective."[7] "Merely," he points out, is always used in connection with the word "subjective" or "anecdotal" and assigns an inferior status. The anecdotal and subjective are interesting perhaps, adding a human touch, but they do not constitute real knowledge. The first time I read Berman's rephrasing from "merely subjective" to "merely objective" it struck a nerve. It reminded me of the feeling I had sitting through many research methodology courses when pursuing graduate studies in education: I couldn't find the connection to real life. It was all, indeed, "merely objective." I was taught that, as a researcher, I did not have to listen to what students and learners needed to tell me. I was the privileged one to ask questions to further my own research agenda as long as I used the prescriptive methodologies we were taught. It didn't matter what the "subjects" might have wanted me to know. Or how they lived their real lives in schools. The notion that one can posses 'objectivity,' says Corradi-Fiumara, "claims the 'right' not to listen."[8] It establishes an alienating mode of consciousness.

I did not feel pulled toward that type of consciousness. I knew that there were other ways of knowing, influenced as I was by courses I had elected to take which had exposed me to the work by Ludwig von Bertalanffy, and the work by Barney Glaser and Anselm Strauss on grounded theory methodology, a qualitative approach to gathering and organizing descriptive data from real life settings.[9] And so I ended up conducting a qualitative research dissertation using ethnographic research methods.[10]

I now read pain research and I often want to say to the researchers: You don't have a clue about our real lives. You may have never had a real conversation with us. You may have never genuinely listened to us. The data you have obtained are "merely objective," extracted from what you have forced into measurable form. Your questions are not based on the reality of our lives, but are "merely" generated by methodological dictates. Most of our lives cannot be so understood.

If lives lived in chronic pain are to be understood, there is an urgent need for approaches to knowledge that rely on closeness, rather than distance; on participation rather than separation; on listening rather than measuring; on understanding and imagining rather than on exerting control.

Knowledge of lives lived in pain: aggregates of variables

Some time ago I looked at dozens of abstracts of studies that addressed the relationship between chronic pain and suicide, chronic pain and anger and trauma, and chronic pain and depression. I knew, more or less, the kinds of methodological studies I was going to read, and yet, I was taken aback by the repetitive and mechanical nature that characterized them. After reading a couple of dozen abstracts, I did not want to go on. My mind started to blur. I felt I was reading the same study over and over again.

I looked for my life in these studies. I couldn't find it. I felt shredded into a collection of variables to be brought under methodological control. The list of variables tried out on us is essentially endless. A lot of hairsplitting is going on. Why, for instance, do we need to develop a variable called "mental defeat" given there is already "helplessness"?[11] I can imagine psychologists somewhere bent over their desks, thinking of still another variable closely related yet different enough, or so they decide, from both "mental defeat" and from "helplessness" for which they can develop still another measurement instrument. Perhaps "mental fatigue"? Or, "emotional fatigue?" Perhaps "spiritual defeat?" Or, "emotional defeat?" Or, "spiritual fatigue?" Or, "spiritual helplessness?" This seemingly unending search for additional variables that can be correlated with chronic pain does not resonate with the complex *patterns* that shape our lives, involving not only individual, but also social and societal events, processes, and meanings.

This is not to say that interesting correlations couldn't be one possible starting point for research. But there are many other possible starting points. As is, "variables," large numbers of them, are pictured to be the essential building blocks to "understanding" our lives. They are imagined as solid units of reality that can be separated, brought under control, quantified, measured, and separately "intervened" upon. The research subjects, however, will have an entirely different web of concerns.

I am further struck by the disproportionate relation between the efforts that go into these studies and results rendered, results which typically seem thin and do not resonate with our real lives. Take for instance, again, Tang and Crane's often quoted review of 12 research studies on the relation between chronic pain and suicidality, which is an intensely important topic for us.[12] All of these studies presumably emerge from the question: Why do people in pain end their lives so often? But the question that is actually asked is, "What are the variables that correlate with suicidality in chronic pain patients?" And that is a different question.

The rephrasing is crucial. The first phrasing, "Why do people in pain end their lives so often?" would be the question for which one would need to directly be in contact with family and friends of those pain patients who have ended their lives, and be involved with pain patients who have suicidal thoughts, or have attempted suicide, and listen to the specifics of their situation, witness, and try to understand, from a real life perspective, what might go into that final decision.[13] All kinds of methodologies could be used: living with us for a while to observe first hand the intense and wide ranging difficulties in our lives; in-depth unstructured interviewing; looking at art we might engage in; letters or dairies we may be writing; talking with our family members and friends.

The question, "What are the variables that correlate with suicide?" does not require any of that. It is a question that leads to the use of a number of typically already available psychological variables and their related measurement instruments. Researchers do not have to get to know anyone of us. Someone else in fact can "run" the study. No need to witness our lives. To listen with attentiveness (that is, without a priori variables in mind) to a person in pain who is suicidal.

But our problems are not research design problems. Not laboratory problems. Our problems are concrete, big, complex, terribly difficult, and are embedded and embodied within webs of social and societal practices and institutions. What it takes for many of us to end our lives, is not a high score on a measure of the variable of hopelessness, catastrophizing, or problem solving deficits, as Tang and Crane would have it (and who would "target" these specific constructs for intervention). Rather, it is a specific trigger which can be anything that throws a system already in serious disequilibrium, over the edge.

I feel a sense of paralysis as a person who lives with pain: If help to prevent us from ending our lives would have to come from studies such as those reviewed by Tang and Crane that see us as aggregates of variables, we'll be waiting in vain. By insisting that inquiry into lives lived in pain has to use methods borrowed from the hard sciences, the pendulum is about as far away from human experience as it can get.

The search for linear causes

The question, "Does chronic pain lead to depression or does depression lead to chronic pain?" is one of the linearly phrased questions often asked in pain research. The very phrasing of the question tells the story of seeing reality as sets of linearly related variables.

Ask a person living with persistent pain if the pain has led to depression or the depression to the pain, you may well get a strange look: "Don't you already know? Take the pain away and my depression will disappear!" If this seems to imply a linear answer, that is only so because the question is asked in linear phrasing. What we are actually saying is that our constant pain and depression *co-emerge within* the relational web of pain and all its consequences. Once the pain has started to gnaw its way into our lives, this web of relentless pain and its many consequences has started to weave itself. This cannot be unwoven into neatly delineated variables by superimposing simple questions of linear relationships. One has to enter the web and look within, while realizing that no two webs are the same, and that they are being re-spun continuously with changing individual, social and societal forces and with changing pain levels.

When researchers say that there is abundant clinical evidence that depression occurs with high frequency among chronic pain patients, we already knew that.[14] Of course. But when they then add, "The fundamental reason for this association is unknown," we say, "Are you kidding?" "Who did you ask?" "Why didn't you ever ask us directly?" Why haven't you studied our real lives?" And when researchers speak of "the enigma of pain and depression," I want to refer them to the many "voices of pain" on web sites of pain organizations.[15] And to the work by Elaine Scarry and David Morris, to journalistic work by Marni Jackson and Roger Rosenblat, and say, "Here, read this. There is no enigma. The 'enigma' you think exists is an artifact of your chosen methodology." I want to say, "Go and live with someone who is in severe pain for a month, even just for a week, day and night. And you must get up in the midst of night when pain tortures her or his sleep. You can ask thoughtful questions if you don't understand what you observe or hear. But leave your variables at home. Listen carefully and respectfully instead. And you will see and hear contextual answers to your research question about the web of relations in which pain and depression occur."

Within standard research approaches that ask the question whether pain leads to depression or the other way around, our immensely difficult lives in pain which are embedded in multiple social and societal forces, are flattened and reduced to "common pathological mechanisms that are related and involved in the co-morbid presentation of chronic pain and depression" – a typical way of phrasing what is seen to be at the heart of our problems: pathology.[16]

This language always gets me. "Pathological." "Co-morbid." Definitions of "morbid" are all, well, morbid. They include "an unhealthy mental state or attitude," "gruesome," "corrupted," "vitiated," "caused by disease."[17] Depression, brought on by physical pain and by the social and societal barriers and affronts we encounter on a daily basis, collapses unfairly and incorrectly into individual pathology.

Most of us are in no position to fight this game. Ironically, our depression shows normal mental functioning: It would be *ab*normal if our terribly difficult lives did not bring on bouts of depression. As I described in a previous chapter, take the pain away, and with it its consequences, and Poof! – depression is gone. There is no such magic for true clinical depression.

Says a college student,

> I battle not only chronic pain but also depression…the depression seems to be in equal proportion to the amount of pain I am experiencing. I definitely notice that on my good days –days in which my pain is at a relative minimum– my mood drastically improves. The world just seems like a much better place…the sky seems bluer, the air smells sweeter…But it never lasts (for the pain returns).[18]

As my daughter said to me, "Mom, you are not a depressed person. You just have very depressing times." Pain and depression are linked in the immediate concrete embodied experience of the actual pain and the depressive array of consequences living with chronic pain brings on. The problem is that researchers ignore the embedded and embodied nature of our lives as lived.[19]

Fishbain et al. reviewed 191 studies that related to the pain-depression association and concluded that depression is more common in chronic pain patients than in healthy controls as a consequence of the presence of CP (chronic pain)."[20] "Surprise, surprise," I thought. "Do we really need 191 studies to tell us that? Fishbain et al. found greater support for the consequence and scar hypotheses than the antecedent hypothesis. That is, depression does not bring on pain. Pain brings on depression. We could have enlightened the research community on that as well. Except that the *co-emergent* nature of pain and depression within complex webs of social and societal relations would still have been missed. Because of how these research questions are asked, only a narrow, linear answer can be elicited.

To get at the question of how depression functions in the presence of chronic pain, a range of approaches can be used: narrative research, the use of diaries (or for those who do not like writing, the use of audio tapes), focus groups, in-depth non-structured interviews or conversations, at the person's home if that is more comfortable, or in small group gathering. The use of artistic expressions can be incorporated. The loyalty is to the phenomena of interest, not to a prescribed methodology. Methodological decisions are adjusted to keep the integrity of the phenomena of interest in tact.

One may even put the formulation of the research question into the research participants' hands. One might further ask them to extend their findings or to provide after thoughts. One might ask them to be involved in the organization of the data. Imagine our excitement if a pain researcher would knock on our door and say, "Help us do our research. What do you think is important to find out? Help us to ask questions that are important to your life and help us to think through how we might conduct the research so it stays true to your experience." How it would humanize the construction of knowledge. How much more relevant the outcomes would be.

From lab to life?

Referring to laboratory experiments in which a controlled pain-producing stimulus is given, such as heat, cold, pressure, or electricity, in the hope to learn how people deal with pain, Patrick Wall has this to say:

> First, it is obvious that the experimenter and the subject are certain that the stimulus will not produce any prolonged injury or pain. This is a necessary restriction but makes it an artificial pain outside normal experience, where pain comes together with a packet of worry and doubt. Second, the subjects are assured by the scientist that they are able to stop the pain at any instant when they decide it is not tolerable. What is being measured is pain without suffering that can be instantly abolished. We should all be so lucky if that was the type of pain we wish to understand.[21]

Despite these problems, says Wall, these kinds of experiments have been carried out in thousands of trials which address "pain liberated from perception and meanings." And I would add, liberated from the many stress inducing and pain intensifying social and societal forces that impinge on our lives. The sterility of the laboratory setting is blinding. I have been amazed, and frankly appalled, at how often findings from short experiments in the artificiality of the laboratory are unproblematically generalized to our lives.

How, possibly, can putting your hand in ice water on a Tuesday afternoon at 3 p.m., always able to retract, causing just a bit of pain, be compared to living with constant pain for many years, and encountering the "nightmare of losses" that goes with it. Indeed, how would I wish to be a volunteer in such experiment instead of leading the life I lead. A brief hand dip into ice water is no match for living with chronic pain, losing your job, the disappearance of your social life, isolation, and impoverishment.

Not infrequently, healthy volunteers are used, often university students, who often receive course credit or are paid for their participation. For instance, Williams et al., who use healthy university students without pain to develop a 39 item questionnaire to assess preferences regarding pain-related support, "acknowledge" that their initial validation of the questionnaire was done with a "nonclinical" sample.[22] Williams et al. suggest that "the most appropriate next step" would be to bring in a "chronic pain sample."

Should I be happy that a "chronic pain sample" may be brought in at some point? Even if that were to happen, validation has already been completed using people who have not the slightest idea what living with chronic pain is like. The logic is only understandable within the context of the demands inherent in the tyranny of method. As Sigmund Koch aptly noted, the methodology comes to be seen as so rule-regulated as to make the role of the cognizer superfluous.[23] It no longer really matters that we actually *live* with pain.

Other ways of knowing

> Our vision of nature is undergoing a radical change toward the multiple, the temporal, and the complex.
>
> Ilya Prigogine and Isabelle Stengers, *Order Out of Chaos*

> A story can tangle you up so badly you start to think differently.
>
> Rudy Wiebe, *A Discovery of Strangers*

Research subjects have been allowed to react, not to act. "Researchers have seldom invited patients with chronic pain to describe their lived experience," says researcher Sandra Thomas.[24] Research subjects *react* to what the researcher wants them to do. On the other hand, within other ways of knowing, "subjects" *act* and hence become *research participants*. As actors, they are full-fledged human beings, bringing their own meanings, intentionality, and the complexity of their real lives to the research table. Their stories are at stake. That is, their lives are at stake. "Stories enable humans to *be*," says Arthur Frank.[25]

In many fields within the social sciences, there has been a turn to qualitative and interpretive research, to the humanities and the arts, to ethnography, narrative inquiry, and in-depth qualitative interviewing. For many of these approaches to knowledge construction one has to have the courage to imagine oneself in the other's shoes. One needs to know how to be respectfully silent and listen genuinely. One needs to engage in descriptions of the complexity of real lives gathered in real life settings and over time. These crucial ways of knowing are not yet part of mainstream methodologies in pain research.

The turn to other ways of knowing has typically occurred because of discontent with what the standard quantitative and experimental measurement frameworks have accomplished. Social psychologists Kenneth Gergen and Mary Gergen spoke in this regard of "the family of discontent" back in 1982, a family which has since grown to be a very large family.[26] In pain research, Daniel Carr makes a passionate argument for qualitative research as he acknowledges the limited relevance for practice of quantitative research and its inability to help him with the individual pain patient before him.[27] His discomfort with the inadequacy of quantitative research, he says, stems from the fact that important, even essential, signals, feelings, and messages never make it into numbers on psychometric instruments. Helping to organize the 2002 World Congress on Pain, he was asked to identify possible omissions in the program. The absence of qualitative research, he says, was obvious.

Different ways of knowing entail an entirely different understanding of the relationship between researcher and research participant, and relatedly, a different understanding of the function of method. They see the individual not as an aggregate of variables to be brought under control, but as an intentional agent in her/his own right who lives within intricate patterns of social and societal relations. Other ways of knowing do not apply fixed and prescribed methodologies, but strive to stay true to the phenomena of interest as they occur in their natural settings. Methodological decisions are made accordingly.[28]

When a woman living with considerable pain reads my memoir and tells me: "This is astonishingly accurate," and when someone else says "My picture could be on the front of your book," I know that narrative, qualitative work can have high "reliability." (I prefer terms such as 'trustworthiness' so as to not identify with the standard methodological meanings of 'reliability.') When someone writes to me, "Between my mother and myself we have experienced everything you write," I know that my experiences were not unique, not "merely" subjective, not "merely anecdotal," but reflective of the *patterns of experience* people in persistent pain live with. When pain specialist Scott Fishman and Will Rowe, past CEO of the APF, tell me that my story could have been told by thousands of other pain patients if only they were writers, and when still another pain specialist writes to me that he has heard hundreds of stories like mine, I know that there is no inherent problem with the trustworthiness of qualitative, narrative knowledge.[29] Of course, it is possible to obtain flimsy qualitative information, but for every flimsy qualitative study there surely is a flimsy quantitative study.

There are publications about the lives of people in pain that engage different ways of knowing – by journalists, by those working in the humanities, by poets, cultural studies scholars, and artists. But these publications are rarely referenced by pain researchers. In the pain research community, there continues to be a sharp separation between scientific methodologies and other ways of knowing.

The very *ownership* of over the research process, and who is qualified to carry it out, has become contentious. For instance, certain aspects of the Maori community in New Zealand have formally refused to be researched and insist on having control over all aspects of research that affect Maori people.[30] Similarly, many groups within the disabled community have taken ownership over research on disability.[31] Male researchers once routinely did research "on" women. No longer. Many deaf people refuse to be studied by hearing researchers. White researchers once routinely studied "the Black experience." That has ended. These voices have claimed their right to their own epistemological and methodological story. We are seeing a kind of epistemological and methodological civil rights movement.

It is telling, that "African American studies," "women studies," "post-colonial studies," "queer studies," "deaf studies," "disability studies," all have set aside the word "research." I was one of the founding mothers of the "disability studies in education" field (which focuses, not on measuring and ranking disability, but on problematizing the construct of "ability" on which "disability" is always based). I remember about ten of us sitting around the table, some disabled themselves, some parents of disabled children. When we had to decide on a name for what we were about, not one of us suggested a phrase containing the word "research."

People who have been endlessly researched by traditional research methodologies that are under the control of others know that such research all too easily, even routinely, distorts their lives. It is a narrative they resist. If people living with pain had the stamina to do so, we too could organize a field of "chronic pain studies," which would address those matters related to *living* with chronic pain we would deem important. We would take ownership and control over the narrative and the methods used to address our lives. We would replace the inadequate and the plainly wrong stories now told about us. But we are too incapacitated by pain to do so.

Other ways of knowing in pain research

Pain research has started to engage a range of qualitative ways of knowing. Typically, qualitative research involves face-to-face interaction that is mostly unstructured and of a relatively prolonged nature. But what exactly is deemed "qualitative" varies across researchers and has to do with degrees of control, or absence thereof, over various aspects of research design. Sara Hurst for example, used semi-structured telephone interviews to discuss with those living with pain the circumstances leading up to a suicide attempt.[32]

Carrie Norman et al. used semi-structured interviews of approximately 60-90 minutes in length, conducted by researchers trained in qualitative interviewing, to explore questions that individuals with traumatic spinal cord injury had regarding their chronic pain and their preferred methods of acquiring answers to their questions.[33] The researchers used a "low-inference" form of interpretation, aiming to stay with the "every-day terms" of what they were told. Data analysis proceeded according to the approach taken by many qualitative researchers: coding the data line by line, labeling words and passages using codes that most closely capture what was said. Based on similarities and differences, codes were then sorted into categories. This process is circular and recoding often occurs as new insights emerge. Codes are then combined to form categories.

A. L. Dewar et al. also used semi-structured interviews to gather qualitative data on how people living with chronic pain experienced the healthcare system.[34]

Sandra Thomas interviewed thirteen individuals to explore "the deeper meaning of what it is like to live with chronic pain."[35] "In-depth, nondirective" interviews lasted one to two hours each. Interviews were audio-taped and transcribed verbatim by a professional transcriptionist. Transcripts were coded by the researcher as well as by an interdisciplinary research group for themes, and patterns. Any proffered interpretation had to be supported by a citation of specific lines in the text. Amanda Nielson used "narrative interviews" with twenty adults living with pain who were asked to "tell the story of their pain in whatever way made sense to them."[36] Transcripts were similarly coded.

Lennard Voogt situated his study within the parameters of phenomenology, which is characterized by an openness on the part of the interviewer whose attentiveness is focused on the thoughts, meanings, feelings, and emotions that constitute the experience –here, of living with chronic pain– of the participants.[37] Voogt listened to 15 pain patients, for a total of 25 interviews, each lasting an average of 90 minutes. Transcriptions of all interviews were shared with the participants for clarification as needed. The essential themes of the structure of the chronic pain experience are then isolated and discussed within a theoretical framework.

Physician Ruth Dubin used her own professional setting to carry out a retrospective review of the life-trajectories of six of her pain patients who had been with her between 6 and 22 years.[38] Reviewing the complete medical files of her patients, and listening to their stories, Dubin constructed their case histories.

Most qualitative research then, uses interviews that are semi-structured with some venturing into a more unstructured format – "venturing" because many researchers hold on to relatively structured formats which still provide a measure of control. To engage in truly unstructured interviewing requires an ability to let go off the need for control and instead develop genuine listening abilities and participatory ways of interacting.

Such change is not easy. As philosopher and linguist Gemma Corradi-Fiumara notes, our present systems of knowledge production ignore the relational listening processes that once characterized language.[39] Fiumary traces the meanings that define language – both *logos* (to know) and *legein* (to say, but also the relational meanings of to 'gather,' 'keep,' 'receive,' and 'shelter'). She notes how in the tradition of western thought the relational propensities of the word *legein* have disappeared entirely. We have a "reduced-by-half concept of language," she concludes.[40] We engage a saying without a listening. We have been left with only an assertive construct of language. Fiumara points out that while there is a lot of research in our culture that focuses on expressive language activity (such as initiating, interrupting, and turn taking), there are hardly any studies on the nature and practice of listening understood as 'gathering' and 'harking' and 'receiving.' Listening in our cultural and research habits is typically understood to mean only a hearing-in-order-to-assert, while an absorbing, attentive listening (for the sake of listening for something we do not yet know), has "fallen out of language." When I read studies in which researchers give a population of chronic pain patients questionnaires that are "quick" to administer, which supposedly can "detect" a wide range of disorders, I know, had I been one of the subjects, I would be imprisoned by an exclusively assertive language. Reading these studies, I feel, to borrow Fiumara's words, a "crushing deafness produced by an assertive culture intoxicated by the effectiveness of its own 'saying' and increasingly incapable of paying 'heed.'[41] I feel confronted with professional blindness. I feel that I am not being listened to or understood in even the most basic truths of my pained life.

The online "Pain-Is-Not-Invisible" project by Chronic Pain Australia, is perhaps the most extensive qualitative research project in pain research to date.[42] Unstructured qualitative data (as well as some descriptive quantitative data) were gathered from 747 people living with pain throughout Australia, asking them to tell in their own words the issues and experiences they encounter, how they impact their lives, and what support they need. Likely, the worst cases were not represented given that a person had to be able to use a computer and be capable of telling their story.[43] The stories show clear patterns of experience and needs across these hundreds of people. Most stories are also heart-breaking.

Visual art offers another way into understanding chronic pain. The on-line "Pain Exhibit" must be the most extensive art exhibit about chronic pain.[44] When I first saw the painting when the web site opens, the tormented face in pain with iron rods going through its skull, I burst into tears. Unexpectedly. From one moment to the next. My own pain problems are all neck and head related. The painting captured my years in suicidal pain from 1998 to 2004 – in a flash. It is stunning how a work of art can go, instantly, to the deeper truths and meanings that not even the most sophisticated statistical analysis ever could dream of reaching. If that picture doesn't move the heart of its viewers, I don't know what will. Several of the paintings also effectively show the social isolation experienced by people in pain, and some tell of the experience of chronic pain as causing a sense that one is slowly dying.

Addressing chronic pain, physician David Biro in his work on language and metaphor, includes various references to art, including the work by Frida Kahlo. Kahlo, the Mexican artist, was in a horrendous bus accident at fifteen, in which she fractured her spinal column, her collarbone, several ribs, and bones in her foot.[45] She underwent over thirty surgeries and still ended up in great pain for the rest of her life. Her paintings, too, go straight to the essences of what lives lived in pain are like. Biro further mentions the work by photographer Deborah Padfield, herself also a person living with pain, who, in collaboration with patients at a pain clinic, produced striking photographs that capture the "increasingly distant and lonely worlds" inhabited by people living in pain.[46]

Artistic expression can go where unimaginative prescriptive methodologies and statistics cannot. Hard data rarely move people to greater moral sensibilities, to empathy, or to action. If they did, the world would be a very different place. Pain specialist Daniel Carr similarly notes that quantitative evidence by itself "does not inspire conviction or action in the beholder with anything close to the effectiveness of emotional appeals to compassion, meaning, or purpose."[47] Through the arts, says Stanford professor Eliot Eisner, we learn to see what we had not noticed, to feel what we had not felt… These experiences are consequential, for through them we engage in a process through which the self is remade.[48]

The book "`Narrative, Pain and Suffering" is an interesting publication, both heartening and confusing.[49] It is confusing because all ways of knowing seem to be referred to as narrative, although the book includes chapters that belong well within mainstream quantitative research.[50] If every form of writing or research is seen as a "narrative," then the word "narrative" no longer has any discerning power. The book offers no actual narratives by people living with pain, although most contributors described "narrative" as a story-form through which to tell about one's life. The book then largely is about the need for narrative work.

I was moved and surprised to come across the poem already cited in Chapter 3 called, "The silent woman who sits and breathes." It is on the first page of a 2012 issue of the journal "Pain Research & Management" by a poet who lived for 30 years with pain."[51] The very few times when personal stories, poems, or writings on art and pain have been included in professional journals they typically appear on the last page, or in some corner.[52] A personal touch. But not quite real knowledge. This poem was presented as a real source of information. Physician Peter Watson, who submitted the poem, notes how the poem presents the question whether the pain research community can be more sensitive to non-verbal artistic expression in its attempts to understand pain. I believe Watson's question echoes my argument that every way of knowing offers unique information that cannot be obtained in other ways. What this poem tells us about living with pain cannot be grasped by variable analysis or experimentation, but instead points to the limits of variable analysis and experimentation. Things go astray when we single out one way of knowing as the only correct one to render trustworthy knowledge.

Peter Kramer, clinical professor of psychiatry, sets out a rational for the use of narrative: Readers recognize themselves in narratives (they don't in reading statistics); narratives retain "the texture of life;" readers feel less alone which gives them support; they feel they belong in a community which gives encouragement.[53] Such has indeed been the reaction to my memoir about living with pain. Data are, of course, important, Kramer says, but numbers can imply an order that can be misleading and thus narrative acts as a counter balance to a "straightened understanding of evidence."

The pull of the familiar

Even for those who feel the need for other ways of knowing, the authority of statistical models can still get the best of them. The problems caused by mainstream methodologies are recognized, but the solution offered is more of the same, only better. For example, John Ware, notes many problems that exist with established research methodologies.[54] Borrowing the term "aporia" from Quinter et al., Ware wants to find a way "to understand what it is patients are trying to tell us from their aporia of pain." ("Aporia" as the word is used by Quintner et al. refers to "a space and presence that defies us access to its secrets," the Greek meaning being "without a path, a passage or a way." [55]).

Great, I thought, Ware now will turn to alternative ways of knowing, to narrative, in depth listening, art – but all Ware suggests is the need to develop better classification systems and better measurement instruments. Ware wants to be "rational" with the implied necessity for statistical analysis. But one cannot enter or share the aporia of pain by what is considered the standard, rational method.

Similarly, Giordano wants to be inclusive and bring together science and the humanities to address the intersection of "external *and* internal, body *and* mind, brain *and* mind, physiological *and* phenomenological, and ultimately the self *and* others(s)."[56] Yet, Giordano struggles with the "subjective nature" of pain, and still wants to be "developing metrics that can accurately measure these complex factors in some objective way." The Cartesian dualism of objectivity vs. subjectivity continues to dominate. To welcome the humanities and the arts (as Giordano does) on equal terms (which he does not) one needs to find a way out of these imposed dualisms.

From the perspective of those living with serious pain, there is an urgent need for ways of knowing that result in an increase in moral sensibilities, in the ability to listen in ways that the "aporia" of pain can be accessed, and in a willingness to actually help people living with pain with the many concrete social and societal problems in their lives. The tyranny of method, based as it is within an alienating and objectifying mode of consciousness, cannot accomplish this, but instead keeps the doors to the "aporia" of pain firmly closed.

As long as traditional research as applied to the study of our lived experience maintains its privileged status, as long as "to measure" is considered the same as "to know," many important questions about our pain experience cannot be asked. For questions that cannot be formulated in the form dictated by the methodological demands, and there are many such questions, then they cannot be asked. And that is the tragedy.

One way to understand how institutions do or don't work in an adequate manner, is to study the institutional practices that emerge to contain their failure. In research, the tyranny of method is one such institutional practice. Its privileged status allows ignoring its many limitations and failures – there is always "more research needed." Which means more of the same kind, only better executed. This reflects the belief in a self-correcting methodology. That process is self perpetuating: It has no end. There are always more methodological problems to improve upon. "Have we unintentionally accelerated the dehumanization of healthcare by defining experience exclusively, in practical terms, as numbers?" asks Daniel Carr.[57] We, people in pain, want to say to researchers, "Even after all that research, all those data, you still hardly understand anything about our lives." Reading through the pain literature, I too, often feel that I am ghost. I am not there. I am forgotten. And my thoughts go to Alice in Wonderland where Alice asks the Queen,

> How can you possibly award prizes when everybody misses the target? Well, said the Queen, some missed by more than others and we have a fine normal distribution of misses, which means, we can forget about the target....

I beg the pain research community to not forget about the target: our real, actual day-to-day embodied lives lived in webs of social and societal relations. I beg them to broaden the research enterprise. To become participatory. To invite us into all aspects of the research. To look at publications about chronic pain that emerged from other ways of knowing for personal and scholarly inspiration. To engage in participant observation, spending time with us in our natural settings, respectfully listening and observing and conversing. Telling our stories. Have us tell our stories. Sometimes we need standard approaches to research, but don't look through that lens at what cannot be so represented – which is most of our lives. And do turn your attention to the multiple social and societal forces that stand in the way of obtaining pain relief. *Describe* them. Show how our stories are "caught up in other stories" as Arthur Frank comments on the function of narrative inquiry.[58] *Confront* the other stories. Help us to *improve* them.

12 Anger and pain management: anger's context

In one of the pain management programs I attended, we received the following handout:

> Anger can affect your relationships because hostile exchanges leave scars. The people you love become wary and less open. The people you work with withdraw, backbite, or counterattack... Anger robs you of a sense of connectedness and belonging to the universe... Instead of feeling inner strength and peace, it leaves you helpless and bitter. Anger is about trying to change others... (But) the more you try to change them, the more they resist... You can change the helplessness at the root of anger by using two simple mantras: *I cannot control others. Others do what they want.* And *I am responsible for coping with my own pain. If what I'm doing is not working, I need to try something else.* Accepting that others will not change allows you to focus attention on the one person you can control and change–yourself.

The central message was, "Thou must never be angry." No matter what others do to you. No matter what goes on in the systems you have to deal with that justifiably make you angry. Do not upset others.

Here, a purely psychological interpretation of anger, one *not* grounded in an understanding of lives lived in pain, ignores all adversarial societal contexts – as if these have nothing to do with the anger people living with pain justifiably develop. Also note how anger is unproblematically equated with hostility, an incorrect and harmful equation to which I will return later.

The message in this handout silences us in one of the worst ways possible. What we are really told is: shut up; stop complaining; be nice; don't bother us with all the injustices you are experiencing. We don't want to deal with any of it. Just take the blame for your anger yourself.

This kind of "help" is supposed to pacify us, to keep us silent, and to protect the healthcare professional. In another pain management program

I attended I was cut off when I brought up the injustices inflicted on us by insurance companies, and was told, "We don't deal with that here." How can we work with our anger if those who say they can help us won't even listen to experiences that are related to the pain we live with, experiences that make us justifiably angry?

Sandra LeFort and Lisa Cardas, in their widely used pain management self help program, note in a brief introductory statement of a section on anger, that there are "valid reasons" why people with chronic pain "at times" feel angry.[1] Reasons mentioned are inadequate medical care, "conflicting" medical information, "many unsuccessful treatments," and "insensitive" employers and insurance systems. "However," LeFort and Cardas then state, anger can "block effective management of pain," it can result in "lack of motivation and inactivity," it may result in being "hostile towards others," in "acting out" behavior which can "alienate those who can help you most." Thus, within no time, "the "valid reasons" for our anger magically disappear. Anger is now located squarely inside the individual. A psychological trait. An emotional problem.

We should only use "I" messages, we are told, rather than blame the person we are angry at and who we should not offend. We are further encouraged to use a problem solving approach consisting of seven steps: identify, list, select, assess, substitute, utilize resources, and accept.[2] ("Accept" meaning, to accept that the problem "may not be able to be solved at this time." Note that solving the problem is considered entirely to be our burden.) Concrete examples accompanying the listing of these steps all have to do with "everyday problems," such as getting dressed, bed making, cleaning the house, sleeping, working in the kitchen. There is not one single example of how to use these problem solving steps in relation to the injustices mentioned even by the authors as "valid reasons" for our anger. As they indeed are "valid reasons," one would think that, in a problem solving approach, the contexts that gave rise to our anger would be central. But the discussion digresses instead to house cleaning and cooking. Anger is now no more than an individual "communication and emotional" problem that can even be approached with "humor and laughter."[3]

Humor and laughter about the anger we feel toward insurers who tell us we lie and malinger? Toward doctors who often don't listen, some even who do not believe us and who would rather not deal with us? Laughter as a way to deal with anger toward uncooperative employers? Humor about many unsuccessful treatments? I am pretty sure that the "valid reasons" for our anger noted by the authors in their introductory statement disappeared from their minds the moment they were written down. Their mention a mere obligatory nod to our reality, to be forgotten immediately, so all anger could be seen as an individual "communication and emotional" problem which can be dealt with by using psychological strategies already on hand – much easier for the professional.

Ellen Mohr Catalano and Kimeron Harden provide similar suggestions to handle anger, also without incorporating the contexts that give rise to it.[4] They refer to "anger" and " hostility" interchangeably, as does Margaret Caudill in her pain management book.[5] Caudill, in the end, sees the solution to "anger" and "hostility" as the ability to forgive. These routine psychological anger management approaches imply the problem of anger is purely ours: *It matters no longer what the anger is about.* All defaults to psychology.

Looking through different lenses, such as those of anthropology, sociology, ethnography, narrative inquiry, autobiography, the humanities, and qualitative and phenomenological inquiries, all methodologies that honor meaning and context, *it would matter crucially what the anger is about, and who or what gave rise to it.* Understanding anger and figuring out what to do about it would greatly depend on the contexts that gave rise to it.

How is it that pain management programs unproblematically use "anger" and "hostility" interchangeably? Before you realize it, our justified anger is equated with being hostile, which, as everyone knows, is a bad personality characteristic. Anger is *about* something, something specific, while hostility refers to a particular kind of person. Not making this crucial distinction absolves others who are at the core of our justified anger from any responsibility and places us, again, into the realm of pathology.

Without attention to the contexts of our anger, generic pain management strategies make us resentful at a deeper level, for we know that something is wrong when the contexts of our anger are ignored. But most of us do not know how to articulate that knowledge, for the discourse of "anger management" is presented to us so pleasantly, so understandingly ("Being angry about an unfair situation is normal" we are kindly told[6]), so patronizingly that we are thrown off guard. We are spoken to as if we are third graders. We do not have the words to object on the spot. Hence, we let ourselves be silenced and blamed, once again. Tobias Smit, a man living with a lot of pain who I befriended on line, read this essay on anger and wrote to me:

You are so right on that I got pissed! It absolutely describes my feelings. On top of the fact that we are injured human beings to begin
with, they make it sound as if it is OUR fault! None of these people
(in pain management programs) have the guts to even look at the
next levels of emotions we as pain sufferers get to eventually: decep-
tion (I am fine... so f@#k of), depression, desperation, and suicidal
thoughts...[7]

Smit further told me he had shared some of what I said in the essay
with two other men living with pain, and it had set off their anger at certain
professionals as well.

Thus, instead of examining the real reasons for our anger, our anger is
psychologized and correlated with an array of negative personality and mood
disorders. I have not seen any studies that correlate anger in people living
with pain with positive personality characteristics, such as a sense of justice,
courage, social awareness, insight, and analytic ability. And there is plenty
of that among us. But correlates of strength and perseverance do not interest psychologically oriented pain researchers who instead obsess about the
negative as described in earlier chapters, and who attribute everything to the
"individual."

The psychologizing of anger can lead to studies that are so far removed
from real life that one shakes one's head. John Burns, Phillip Quartana, and
Stephen Bruehl for instance, state the purpose of their research as follows:

To determine whether (a) trait anger-out and/or trait anger-in
moderate effects of Emotion-Induction (anger, anxiety) x Emotion
Suppression (non-suppression, experiential, expressive) manipula-
tions during mental arithmetic on pain intensity and cardiovascular
responses during and following a cold pressor pain task, such that
"mismatch" relationships emerge (preferred anger management style
is discrepant from situation demands); and (b) general emotional
expressivity accounts for these effects.[8]

Statisticians may love this. People living with constant pain think they
are reading some sort of strange science fiction. And they are. Something
completely unrelated to their lives in pain. The subjects for this study were
"healthy nonpatients." Yet, the conclusion section suggests that the results,
whatever they were, would be "essential for the development of interventions
to relieve suffering among those afflicted with chronic, painful conditions."[9]

Thus, the results of this fragmented and unrelated-to-real-life laboratory experiment, carried out using healthy non-patients, are unproblematically generalized, as is so often the case, to the day-to-day lives of those living with chronic pain. As if the statistical and methodological control in the research design is a divine power, that overrides the experience of actually *living* with pain.

In these kinds of studies, of which there are too many, it does not matter what the anger is about. The researcher might say, it does matter: We created a frustrating task so we know the anger is about the task we ask the subjects to do. The point is that a frustrating laboratory task is no substitute for the ongoing multiple, interacting, personal, social, and societal difficulties we face, day after day, on top of and as a result of ongoing physical pain – for unfortunately, we are not "healthy non-patients." We are not angry because someone tells us to do a frustrating arithmetic problem.

I am not an angry pain patient. But I do feel anger for very specific reasons. "Substantive anger" I call it. Correct anger. At the inadequate knowledge of the world of medicine. At insurers who outright accuse us of lying and deny valid claims. At the fact that there are not nearly enough pain doctors for us. At doctors who do not listen. At insurers who pay for what surgeons do with no questions asked, but not for effective alternative procedures. At the pharmaceutical industry for making false claims about the medicines I take. At the serious side effects of the many pain medicines tried out on me and the seemingly nonchalant manner in which at least some doctors reacted when I told them about those effects. At having had to navigate, largely on my own but for a few helpful doctors, an enormously complex system of medical care that often fails to address chronic pain. At the fragmentation of the system. At the professions of psychology and psychiatry for throwing an endless list of negative personality traits at us. At the ignorance of society at large. It makes me angry when I am told I should not be angry.

Will Rowe recalls a movie where people all over the country open their windows shouting out, "I'm mad as hell and I'm not going to take this anymore."[10] That's the sentiment, says Rowe, that should bubble up in the world of people affected by chronic pain. Writing about all this is my way to express, indeed, how mad I really am.

I beg all those who think they have the knowledge and the means to address the "problem" of our anger, which in most cases is not a problem but a justified state of being: Do not psychologize and psychiatrize our anger by wiping away the contexts that gave rise to it. Do not try to teach us some generic "anger management" strategies that strip away our justified reasons for being angry, placing the responsibility for anger and its solution only on us. Stop letting those responsible for our anger off the hook by attributing our anger to our personhood. Stop equating our rightful anger with hostility. It is inflicting insult upon injury. Listen instead. That, in itself, will help. Then assist us in thinking through, and where possible help us deal with the actual situations that gave rise to the anger that we so rightfully live with.

13   *Suicide: the end of pain*

"I didn't get anything accomplished! Anne, I am going
backwards! I am more suicidal than ever!"
"No. You are in transition."

Participant in a Self help program, and group leader

The above exchange occurred during a self help pain management program I attended in 2010. We had been asked by the group leader, Anne (not her real name), to report on whether or not we had accomplished the goals we had set for the week that had just passed, when a woman who was always in obvious pain responded as quoted above.

What followed astonished me. Anne's response was a blank, paralyzed, second-long stare. Then, "No. You are in transition." After that, she went right on to the next person who reported that she had met her goal for the week: walking her dog twice a day.

"Great," said Anne, clapping her hands as would a third grade teacher, "well done!"

The group leader's script did not allow for suicidal thoughts, going backwards, or anything else "negative." I froze. I wished I had said something. Perhaps, "Anne, I think you should take our suicidal thoughts more seriously." Or I should have gotten up, inviting the woman for a cup of coffee, leaving Anne and her distortions behind. But it all went too fast. It is unconscionable that a self help pain management program denies its most vulnerable participants their truth.

I talked to the woman during the break. Having lost her job, she had to move into a basement apartment, living on less then $800 a month in disability income. She had had to give up her beloved German Shepherd as she could no longer afford to take care of him. "But thankfully, I have visiting rights," she added, tearing up.

Of course, the group leader knew nothing of any of this. "In transition." What, for Pete's sake, did this psychological mumbo-jumbo mean?

It would be easy to attribute this unconscionable behavior to the fact that the group leaders were "just" volunteers. But I think much more is involved. After all, given the very high rate of suicide among chronic pain patients (two to three times that of the general population), one would assume that training people to lead pain management sessions would involve, at the minimum, teaching them *not* to trivialize suicidal thoughts. What should be taught, of course, is how to react in a professional manner, which, at the minimum, means the legitimization of our experience. What was involved here, I believe, is the relentless emphasis on "the positive" as the bedrock of self help pain management programs. Only optimism, cheerfulness, steady progress, and returning to a "normal" and "satisfying life" is allowed.

When people living with severe pain end their lives, it is seen as a suicide. Suicide, however, is not the accurate word to use. We do not want to die. We want to live. But the *pain needs to end*. And that is an entirely different matter. Unfortunately, when nothing has helped, in order to end the pain one might think of ending their life. "Who will end the pain?" journalist Sharon Kirkey asks in her series on chronic pain.[1] That is the question. When no one can, when unrelenting pain has ruined our days and nights for years, there comes a point when it has to stop. It simply has to stop. Ending our lives then has not to do with being mentally ill as pain researchers so often declare, suggest, or imply. It has to do foremost with *Pain*. Take the pain away and suicidal ideations are gone. Life can get back to normal.

As Ilgen et al. also observe, efforts to identify patients at-risk for suicide focus routinely on the presence of psychiatric symptoms or recent suicide attempts.[2] Not on the actual difficulties of our daily lives.

Carol Levy relates how two decades of terrible pain from severe trigeminal neuralgia had made her deeply suicidal.[3] Then, she became one of the lucky ones: At the stroke of an implant, her pain disappeared – and so did her suicidal thoughts.

> I walked into the bathroom. I took out every pill, capsule and liquid I had saved. One by one…they went into the toilet. For the first time –I didn't know how long– I wasn't thinking of suicide. Death was the last thing I wanted.

Wanting to die, and needing the pain to stop, are two different states of being. Unfortunately, they can become connected in practice. When I would think of ending my life, which during the worst years was daily, it was because I couldn't bear the prospect that sharp pain would wake me, typically in the midst of darkness, for the 2000th or 3000th time. It was not that I wanted to die. I wanted to live. But the relentless pain had made a mockery of living.

There would be an overwhelming need to REST – the desire to lie down, underneath a warm blanket, hug a pillow, and never be woken up again by pain. The concept of killing was not present. Just of ending pain. Of resting. Of knowing, "I have done my best and can do no more." The desire to stop the pain and the intense need to rest have no violence in them, do not have to do with killing, and are not brought on by mental illness, by too much "catastrophizing," or by a lack of problem solving skills as the psychological and psychiatric literature that hijacks chronic pain would have it. They are the outcome of a body and a mind crushed beyond the capacity to absorb the deadening force of years of relentless pain.

"I don't think I'm going to keep myself alive much longer" says a pain patient.[4] "You wonder whether you want to go on…" says another.[5] A research participant told Thomas and Johnson, "(I) really don't fear death because one day I won't hurt."[6] This participant, say Thomas and Johnson, expressed the feelings of so many. Another person admitted trying to imagine how his suicide could be made to look like an accident or a natural death. I can personally attest that such plotting and planning is very much alive among us.

Studies show a higher suicide rate for chronic pain than for any other illness except bi-polar.[7] A recent report by *NeurologyNow* cites that 50% of chronic pain patients consider suicide to escape unbearable and relentless pain.[8] Over the years, I have read figures as high as 80% of us thinking of suicide frequently.

How do these figures impact our health care? What is being *done* about it? How do these facts change the attitude, listening ability, the words said to us, or not said to us, on the part of healthcare professionals?

Sadly, our experiences show that healthcare professionals at large keep trying to ignore these facts. The literature that contains our own stories, including my own work, shows over and over how doctors and other healthcare professionals go out of their way *not* to respond to the death wishes we express. The response I received from six health care professionals to whom I tried to talk about my suicidal ideation during the worst years, in the hope of getting some sort of support, was "let's not go there."[9]

In 2004 I moved to Victoria, B.C., and after a long and hard search, I found a very attentive doctor and an equally attentive masseuse. Both initiated a conversation about suicide. I couldn't believe it. Particularly because by

then my suicidal thoughts had become much less intense given the pain relief
I had experienced from prolotherapy. I can only wish that my doctors earlier
on, who I nearly begged to listen to me, had done so.

Carol Levy describes how she tried to talk about her suicidal intent with
several healthcare professionals.[10] For her too, no one wanted to go there.
Finally she was sent to a thanatologist (a specialist in death, particularly in its
social and psychological aspects) who listened respectfully. Finally, someone
acknowledged the reasonableness of her desperate need to get rid of the pain.
He did not try to contradict her. He did not tell her she was "in transition."
He did not judge. He saw her as a reasonable person, not a crazy one. Not
one who, by definition, had a "mental disorder" just because she wanted to
end her life. She knew, that if she went ahead, he would not think any less of
her. *That* is important to us. Extremely important. The issue here is neither
to condone nor to negatively judge our suicidal intentions. We are not asking
for either. We simply want to be understood, and seen as sane for wanting to
die given how we have to live. Healthcare professionals who deal with those
living with severe chronic pain should all receive an education in thanatology.

I had the same beneficial experience with my therapist, Dr. Brian Grady,
a clinical psychologist whose approach to therapy with me I write extensively
about in my book.[11] In his presence I could give full expression to any fear,
any terror that lived in my mind. Not once did he contradict me. "Let's not
go there," was not in his repertoire. Not once did he make me feel that he
thought of me as mentally disturbed. Not once did he try an intervening
general strategy such as positive self talk or problem solving skills – the only
two approaches suggested by Nicole Tang and Catherine Crane after their
lengthy review of the literature on risk factors for suicide.[12] Few of us find
such a person in pain management. I was lucky. Dr. Grady's attentiveness
helped greatly in dealing with the pain and with my suicidal ideations. Don't
ask me for a variable analysis explanation of that. Or for a cognitive behavioral explanation. There are none. What I am referring to is not accessible to
these research and psychological methods. Instead he left me whole. His keen
attentiveness and his desire to understand what I was experiencing told me
that my life was worthy to be known exactly as it was, including my desire
to end the pain by ending my life. It was the biggest gift he could have given
me. The huge burden of intense isolation had lifted a bit.

Pain research offers many studies correlating our suicidality with family
history of substance abuse, with pain beliefs, and with constructs like hope-

lessness, catastrophizing, mental defeat, depression, passive coping, active coping, problem solving deficits, and other negatives psychology and psychiatry bestows on us.[13] These correlations are invariably contradicted by other studies. The few that hold up across studies are so obvious (high pain intensity and sleep deprivation) that I must wonder why it needed to be studied at all.

This is from my journal:

> It is almost midnight, home alone, New Year's Eve, 2003 (before prolotherapy brought considerable relief). The pain is fierce and constant. I count pills. If I didn't have my cats, tonight I might go. One of my cats licked my face earlier on. She cuddled up, trusting that my tears are just part of life and not harmful to her. I want to get drunk. A form of temporary death. I don't want to be there at midnight. It is only a day on the calendar I keep telling myself. The real anniversaries, someone wrote, are "the anniversaries of the heart." Thankfully I have some of those. Yet, calendar anniversaries spent alone, when everyone is supposed to be celebrating with family and friends, do me in. They symbolize everything lost since the accident.

I have not seen "New-Year's-Eve-spent-alone" as a risk factor for suicide anywhere in the pain research literature. Nor any of the other specific embodied events related to living with pain that can be suicide triggers, such as receiving a rejection letter from the insurance, being let go from a job you can no longer handle, the sudden realization that your marriage is falling apart, or having to give up your beloved German Shepherd.

A woman who I befriended because of our shared pain experiences has several horses and adores them. We have freely expressed our preoccupations with death to each other and are glad we have each other to do so. She wrote me, "One thing is for sure, if I ever lose those horses, I will only last a week before the end will be upon me."[14] I myself may not have lasted if I would have had to give up my cats during those horrible years of intense pain. Losing your beloved animal is a risk factor in suicide. Has any researcher ever thought about that? No – because mainstream research on chronic pain and suicide does not start with our actual embodied lives. If it did, the loss of a beloved animal might have been observed to be a risk factor. Helping people in pain to keep their animals might then be the proper "intervention."

It bears repeating, that mainstream research on chronic pain and suicide *routinely* starts and ends with general psychological and psychiatric constructs which are then correlated with chronic pain. Researchers operating in this mode will never learn what real life triggers for suicide can be. They are so preoccupied with having to measure something that our real lives pass by them. Under what specific conditions did the person decide that enough was enough? If researchers want to shed any light on the nature of our suicidality, they must find out directly from us.

Most importantly, almost all of us would score high on hopelessness or depression scales, but do *not* end our lives. We tell ourselves as playwright Samuel Becket famously wrote, "I can't go on. I go on." What needs attention are the particular, unique, concrete, and qualitative details of the person's thoughts, the particular stresses in her/his life, the particular fears and values the person holds and which have been shaken. Sadly, one could make an argument that knowing "the literature," knowing the data about psychiatric correlations between chronic pain and suicide, can easily stand in the way of carefully listening to the qualitative and embodied details of a particular pain patient's life that might, in fact, contain real warning signs.

A therapist told me that in the pain clinic where he had worked for several years, suicide was never addressed. Nor was grief, unless a pain patient brought it up. Then general strategies to overcome grief were offered, rather than dealing with the specifics of the person's grief. In the four self help pain management programs I have attended, suicide was never brought up. Worse, the one time a participant brought it up, the validity of her emotion was completely denied: "No, you are in transition." Sadly, the woman was indeed "in transition" – from wanting to live to feeling she wanted to die so the pain would stop. But that was not what the program leader meant – she probably didn't know herself what she meant. I would not be surprised if the training session this volunteer had gone through did not address suicide. Suicide does not suit these programs' characteristically uplifting and cheerful tone. None of the self help books and materials I have read nor the programs I attended referred in any way to the desire to end one's life.

Responsiveness to our suicidal triggers is not facilitated by knowing correlational data. Such research does not engender the courage to open oneself up to a face to face interaction with a person in pain about wanting to end their life. There is nothing in knowing such data that necessarily appeals to empathy and moral sensibilities. Nothing that engenders the willingness to engage the imagination about what our lives are like, and respond accordingly. The six healthcare professionals whose only response to my attempts to talk about my preoccupation with ending my life was silence or a variation of "let's not go there," surely were aware of the data, but failed (did not want to, did not know how to, were too insecure, were afraid) to respond.

Cultural historian Morris Berman sets out to show that the concept of "data" is the most disembodied construct there is.[15] Pain specialist Daniel Carr similarly notes that there are important, even essential signals, messages, and feelings that never make it into numbers on psychometric instruments.[16] He speaks of the inadequacy of quantitative medicine to capture the nuanced and non-mathematical realities of illness, pain, and suffering. Quantitative evidence by itself, he notes, does not inspire conviction or action in the beholder with anything close to the effectiveness of emotional appeals to compassion, meaning, or purpose.

Given that pain is invisible, not much will change without the willingness to imagine our lives, for to understand the invisible one has to imagine it. For that to happen one has to listen. Not just for diagnostic "material," but really listen. When I think of the many health care professionals who refuse to be responsive when their pain patients bring up suicidal intentions, I think of the words by a character in Michael Cunningham's novel "By Nightfall,"

> You have failed in the most base and human ways – you have not imagined the lives of others.

Until healthcare professionals who work with us dare to "go there" by carefully listening to us and engaging their empathy and imagination, we cannot expect to find the kind of professional support that might help us to sustain our lives. In my own case, I didn't even get a referral to a good therapist from any of the six healthcare professionals I tried to talk to about my death wishes. I had to find one myself.

Very few studies have approached suicidality and chronic pain in more embodied ways. Sara Hirst conducted qualitative semi-structured telephone interviews with women living with severe pain who had attempted suicide.[17] They discussed the circumstances preceding and leading up to suicide attempts, their experience of the attempts, and the meanings they ascribed to the attempts over time. The attempts had often occurred at the interface of an "acute stress" and their chronic pain experience. Suicide, Hirst concludes, is fundamentally an unpredictable phenomenon. An individual's experience with suicide, she notes, can only be thoroughly understood by careful, nuanced exploration of each person's unique experience.

As a person living with pain, I connected with this study. I felt I had participated in it. I never feel that way when reading correlational studies about chronic pain and suicide. For instance, when I read, "Because of a lack of clear control groups in much of the prior research, it has been difficult to determine the extent to which pain is a unique risk factor for suicidal thoughts and behaviors,"[18] I write impulsively and irritatedly in the margins: "Not difficult at all! Why didn't you *ask us?*" Ask our families. Live in our homes for a while. Listen. When I read, "Although pain and suicidality both occurred... the extent to which pain occurred before, during, or after periods of suicidal thoughts or behaviors is unknown," I scribble, "Don't assume linear relations – ask us, and we will tell you a far more complex story!"[19] I often write things like that in the margins.

What is needed for suicide prevention to be more effective, is close attention to our embodied lives which includes our actual specific social and societal circumstances. These can differ greatly in each case and confront us with a wide range of "acute stresses" that can trigger suicide.

What is needed in framing the complexity and unpredictability of suicidality and chronic pain are constructs from the new sciences as described, for instance, by Illya Prigogine and Stengers.[20] Constructs from complexity theory, such as dynamic relations, non-linearity, and far-from-equilibrium states resonate with the unstable and unpredictable phenomenon of suicide in the context of chronic pain. The sciences, as they emerged from 17th century scientific revolution, stress stability, linear relations, predictability and causality–constructs still dominant in mainstream approaches in pain research. In contrast, the new sciences of complexity theory propose dynamic, emerging and mutually shaping relations that emphasize the temporal, non-linearity, the unpredictable, uncertainty, and the specific local events that can trigger major changes in open systems. In pain research, Daniel Carr too has stressed the importance of the developments in today's sciences –from physics to biology to mathematics– toward uncertainty, complexity, unpredictability, and non-linearity as offering constructs relevant to pain research.[21]

Of course, that means giving up on the *idea* of control in how we make knowledge claims. Researchers may counter that science demands a certain rigor that only the application of the scientific method can meet. None what has been said here denies the importance of rigor. But there are different views within different epistemologies on what constitute rigor and how to engage it.

Correlations, which assume stable associations, would be good predictors if our lives were always in equilibrium. When things go well, when our lives seem stable, when no major problems are occurring, then correlations might have some measure of predictability – for as long as such stable situation lasts. For then, the system cannot be easily perturbed. Small inputs have little or no effect – they can be easily absorbed. Stability allows a certain degree of predictability.

However, as complexity theory tells us, when a system is in "far from equilibrium" states, to use Prigogine and Stenger's phrase, where non-linear relations prevail, it becomes extremely sensitive to external influences.[22] It has become so unstable that a small input can trigger major consequences. The instability that characterizes a system in far-from-equilibrium states amplifies the effect of a seemingly small input in complex and unpredictable ways, resulting in consequences that, from the traditional perspective would seem completely out of proportion to the size of the input and therefore not accurate. In traditional models a small input is an input that will result in an output that is more or less similar in size. But when a system is no longer in equilibrium, when it is "in far from equilibrium states," it is intensely dynamic, reacting internally to any kind of input in ways that can not be predicted from external measurements or observations, and that seem to bear no direct relation to the size of the input.

Thinking about chronic pain and suicide, I immediately thought of complexity theory. I know first hand, the far-from-equilibrium state within which suicide ideations surface and within which the desire to end one's life can come up at the most unexpected moments. With unexpected intensity. You actually *feel* yourself to be an unstable yet open system, vulnerable to inputs of which you do not know where they will take you.

Lives of those living with severe pain do not resemble stable systems that cannot be easily perturbed. They are systems in turmoil. They are "far from equilibrium states" in which even a small input can work itself into a major output. All it may take is to lose your German Shepherd, your cat, or have to spend New Year's eve alone (events that in pain free lives would not trigger the desire to end one's life). Clearly, suicide is such a major output. It is not hard for me, at all, as I have lived in that land for several years, to understand that an unkind word said at the wrong time, a rejection letter from the insurance, losing your job, a friendship, moments of intense isolation, a look in the mirror which reflects a haggard and ghostly face – all these, and more, could be the input, the embodied and therefore unique detail, that triggers the ending of a life that has been lived at the edge of chaos and in turmoil for too long.

Correlational studies cannot go there. Regression analysis cannot go there. Structured surveys cannot go there. By themselves, these research methodologies can only point to a possible general direction that has no predictive value in any given case. They are not embodied and specific enough to help to prevent the ending of a particular life in pain. What might?

This is tough. There are no magic solutions except taking the pain away. And for most, unfortunately, that does not happen. Too many of us could end our lives regardless what any professional does. But what one can say for sure is that *being in tune with* the person in pain is crucial. Being in tune demands an embodied attentiveness that can absorb particulars, that is welcoming of personal truth, no matter what that truth is. This is an alternate state of attention, away from prescribed methodologies, away from "intervening" with generic strategies. It involves a non-judgmental listening, believing, and attentiveness. It is a mode of consciousness. Not a role. Not a task. Not a particular time commitment. Modes of consciousness manifest themselves in spite of roles and tasks and time commitments.

Research opportunities can be created including by bringing together those who live with serious pain and for researchers to listen and be fully attentive to what we have to say about our pained lives. For researchers to do so is not easy: He or she can no longer hide behind prescribed methodology–one needs to engage human methodology, so to speak. Human engagement. The engagement of one's self. I venture to say, doing so is far more demanding and rigorous than engaging prescribed methodologies, as it offers no protection, no place to hide from the truths of lives lived in pain. It demands a profound personal kind of rigor. The demanding rigor of attentiveness and true listening.

As long as researchers and physicians have only a correlational and variable analysis understanding of suicidality and chronic pain, the chance they will notice that a patient might be in a state in which a particular trigger could end their life, is practically non-existent. During my suicidal years I have walked out of offices of doctors, specialists, and other healthcare professionals and realized that I was close to ending my life and this person wouldn't have had a clue. Doctor D who we met in the preface, who was surprised that his pain patient went from smiling to crying within minutes, would not likely pick up signs of suicidality given he couldn't even understand his patient's sudden shift in emotions. Correlations may at best be a starting point for trying to understand the nature of our suicidality – though they could also easily be a hindrance. An attentive doctor who understands the embodied nature of human life, and a researcher who functions from within a participatory mode of knowing, wouldn't need them.

Importantly, apart from sensing a patient might be close to ending her/his life, this kind of attentiveness further helps to prevent suicide because it tells us that our experiences are valued. That we are still welcome in this world just as we are. We would experience ourselves again as still belonging somewhere. Our nervous system would have a chance to calm down.

A statistical, distancing mode of consciousness, involved in nearly all pain research, cannot accomplish this. Such research is not designed to directly help us. Telling us to say positive things to ourselves based on a correlation does not draw us into any human community. Mainstream research on chronic pain and suicide such as reviewed by Tang and Crane for example, continue on the same methodological path, calling for research that identify "new short-and-long-term predictors of suicide, and for the development of "routine management of suicidal risk in pain clinics optimizing staffs capacity to effectively detect and handle acute suicidal risk."[23] How suicidal risks will ever be "routinely" managed is beyond me. What would clinicians actually do or say or ask? Tang and Crane have nothing at all to say about this. Could there be anything "routine" about talking with a pain patient who is suicidal? Attentiveness and true listening can never be "routine." I don't mean to keep hammering away at Tang's and Crane's work. Theirs is simply a representative example of how privileged research methods that purport to study our lives render data that have near nothing to say about our lives. What is needed foremost for suicide prevention are fundamentally human interactions.

We do not end our lives because of a generic hopelessness or generic kind of anxiety. Most of us who would score very high on scales that measure these variables do not end our lives. We end our lives, first of all, because of relentless pain.

> There comes the point that the need to end the relentless pain is absolute. The need becomes so intense that the connection between ending pain and dying as a result is no longer in one's awareness. When pain stabs you front, back, and center, day after day, month

after month, and no one can stop it, you yourself must stop it. *Stop it.* What happens after that is not your problem.[24]

Interrelated with the relentlessness of persistent pain are the social and societal adversarial forces that come into play when chronic pain takes over a life. We may be ending our lives because of all of it – woven together into a web of relations the specifics of which will differ across different people. The question is, what can trigger this web to completely break and lose all coherence? What specific events or aspects of living for any particular person might make suicide an act more coherent than life? The only way others might find out is to open oneself up and enter our web. Then, the acute stresses that can trigger the breakdown of coherence might perhaps be prevented or circumvented.

SOCIETY AND SELF

14   *The self in pain and others*

"Are you better now?"
"No – I still suffer from chronic pain. It's actually pretty bad."
"Yah, I know what you mean. I had a tennis elbow for two weeks
last year and it was horrible!"

Me, and someone I ran into

This "tennis elbow" incident took place eight years after the accident
when I ran into someone I had met a year or so earlier and who knew I had
been living with a lot of pain for many years. We engaged the usual greetings.
After a few minutes he asked if I was better… I told him the truth. "I know
what you mean."

I looked straight at him and said, "No, you don't." He didn't respond but
just stared at me. I offered him no explanation for my disagreement.

"Well, I better move on and get my shopping done," I said. I said good
bye, and calmly walked away.

I felt good. For once, I had not given into others' ignorance about chronic
pain by staying silent, which is the typical scenario, because we are lost for
words when trying to counter ignorance. But we think: "There it is again.
This person has no clue." Staying silent in the face of others' ignorance that
trivializes our lives leaves us feeling marginalized, angry, alienated, and alone.

I had no illusion that my response changed anything in him, or improved
his understanding. That was not my purpose for saying what I said although
I would certainly be glad if it did. My response was for me. It left me my
dignity. I spoke my truth. I had pushed him back into his place of ignorance,
rather than letting him override and rewrite my life. I felt calm, not angry,
not alienated. A very good feeling. I had kept my place in the world. My
response was entirely different from what we are typically told to do in pain
management self help programs, such as, to only use "I" messages as to not
offend anyone, and to never promote defensiveness. As we will see in the
next chapter, the "be nice" and "don't be angry" messages permeate self help

programs. When I told this incident in a pain awareness meeting, another person living with pain said, "Yes, we do have the right to keep our place in the world."

Many things have been said to me that reflect ignorance about chronic pain and trivialize our extremely difficult lives. Here are some recorded in my journal notes:

But you look good!

But you are coping well!

But you have gone on with your life!

What do you do all day? (In *Inside Chronic Pain* I devote several pages to being endlessly questioned about 'what I do all day.')

Can't you take some pain killers for that? (I do.)

Have you seen a specialist? (Yes, more than twenty of them.)

But you look so healthy!

Have you tried massage?

You need to go on a vacation. You don't have to work now so you could go anytime. You need to enjoy yourself for a while.

Now you don't work, are you going to travel?

At least you have a lovely home.

At least you have lovely grandchildren.

At least you didn't die in the accident.

Could it be stress?

Well, always think it could be worse.

Oh, a sore neck – I get that from gardening.

Be well. Stay well. Trust you are well.

I thought you would be better by now.

You'll beat this. I just know it.

You got to keep positive.

You need to go out more. Have some fun!

Hope you will get better – I am sure you will.

It's still a pretty neck...

The last phrase was a stunner. I was at the airport standing in line for the security check to go on the last work-related trip I would make, just at the start of the worst stretch of years that would soon end my career. That morning the pain was nagging. Every few minutes the line I am in inches forward. The middle aged man in front of me turns to say something. I keep my attention on my posture to keep my neck straight. I am nervous about a possible major pain attack. We trade a few niceties. He is an insurance agent.

"Oh," I say, "don't make me think about insurance."

"Why?" he asks.

I briefly tell him about the accident and recite my horrible experiences with my car insurance company. He asks where I was injured. For a moment I thought I sensed some sympathy. I tell him my neck was badly mangled: pain here, and here, and there. And terrible headaches. His eyes, an unde-fined blue, from behind heavy glasses that blurred the exact meaning of his glances, had followed the movement of my hand. His eyes focus for a very long second on my neck and he says,

"It's still a pretty neck…"

Had I been able to walk away, I probably would have said something. Something to the point. But I couldn't get away. I stood there silently with as much dignity as I could muster. Would this man have said what he said, had I told him I had a cancerous tumor in my neck? That is the point. Cancer would have been real. Pain was not real…not really anyway. You can make of it what you want.

The "but you look good" message in its various forms has a different meaning when said to a person living with serious pain versus a person living with, say, cancer or heart problems. In the latter case it carries the meaning of a compliment: In spite of the disease you have which everyone knows is real, you still manage to look good. When said to a person in chronic pain, it can easily send a message of doubt that the pain is serious, or even real, because he or she just looks too good. The "But…" and "At least…" statements often said in a reflexive, hasty manner, reflect the tension between the person in pain's claim to pain and the other person's claim to doubting it. Tobias Smit, who has lived with severe pain for many years, having received too many "But…" and "At least…" statements, told me, "I just don't want to commu-nicate anymore. It is a defense mechanism, because what I live with gets impossible to explain."[1] He speaks for many of us.

Messages about "peace" and "joy" are also hard to take and infringe on the truth of a life lived in pain. A distant relative who read my memoir, wrote for my birthday,

> My wish and hope for you is that this day… is blessed with joy, fam-
> ily, friends, and peace… I believe we all have so much to be grateful
> for but that gratitude is at times fogged over by harsh reality and

dreams that need to be adjusted…I hope your days are full of great moments.

The words jarred. The need to not let this person push my harsh 24/7 reality aside, was so strong that I responded instantly,

> Frankly, severe physical pain, as my story shows, puts a limit on why one would still know what joy means… In other words, pain pulls you into its very presence to strongly that other possibilities of being disappear. So, it is not surprising that our suicide rate is roughly 3x higher than of the general population, and 80% of us think about it every day. It is not just a matter of adjusting dreams… Sorry to be so harsh, but the major problem we have is that others do not want to see how terrible it is to live with constant pain. There is so much denial going on.

In an interview by Polly Young-Eisendrath, Dan, a who became a quadriplegic, notes how hurtful it can be when others *try* to say helpful things, such as those said to him, "I'm glad your arms are still working;" or, "Aren't you lucky to still have a career;" or, "You are lucky to be alive;" or, "But at least you have a nice home!" Of course, says Dan, all I wanted to do was die."[2]

What does help, is when others show they have reflected on the intense difficulties of our lives, and react accordingly, rather than utter clichés. My wonderful masseuse, when my eyes flooded with tears telling her how bad it had been, simply stated, "Even a lovely grandchild doesn't make up for it, does it." All I said was, "No, it doesn't." I relaxed. I could let go of the tension that is always there as I prepare myself for sugar coating or denial.

A to-the-point and practical booklet, "But You Look Good! A Guide to Understanding and Encouraging People Living with Chronic Illness and Pain," by an organization called "The Invisible Disabilities Advocate," notes a similar set of utterances as those said to me, as well as suggestions for what to say instead.[3] As the authors, Wayne Connell and Sherri Connell also note, there are of course reasons for these evasions and denials. First of all, the invisibility of the disease and our normal appearance make recognizing its severity near impossible. In the words of a friend who read my memoir,

> I have just finished your book … and to put it mildly, am completely stunned. One simply can have no idea what chronic pain really means outside of experiencing it…but your words and descriptions

certainly give the reader a fragment of appreciation, which, at least for me, was quite overwhelming."

Said another friend,

> Reading somebody's account of such an intimate experience as pain inevitably drags the reader into unknown territory that resonates with where he is afraid to go… One does not finish with that lecture unbruised… We do not suffer like chronic pain patients with that "relentless" aspect that you mentioned, but we all experience that fall into some abyss that we recognize in your writing. We are humbled to realize that our fall could go so much deeper and darker than what we endure.

Both friends, who I would see for coffee perhaps once a month during my good hours, are highly empathetic people. Yet, without the intense exposure to my life through reading my book, they did not understand what my life in chronic pain was like. "The problem," one told me, "is that when I see you, you look normal, and after a few minutes I forget that you live with pain." He also forgot that I see him only in the afternoon, only during my good hours.

And here we see again the problem of "normality" as it relates to invisible and unmeasurable diseases. Had I had cancer or any other major but known disease, my "normal" appearance would not make the other to forget it. What confounds this even more, is that people imagine chronic pain to manifest as does acute pain – the only point of reference to pain they have. When I met a colleague of my daughter for the first time he afterwards said to her, "Is that your mom? I had imagined someone very different! Someone bent over in pain."

Then there are the truly empathetic folks who try to imagine your life. During the worst stretch of years, a friend in the Netherlands told me in our yearly phone conversation, upon hearing my pain problems had continued: "I had a toothache for five days. It drove me crazy. I could not find pleasure in anything! I thought of you…" Another friend said during that time stretch in disbelief: "I had back pain for a couple of weeks – How do you do it year after year?" I don't do 'it.' It does me. I go crazy. I sob. I think of death. I can't go on. I go on. You only see me going-on.

Other reasons Connell and Connell mention for saying things that end up trivializing our lives include that others truly do care: They badly want to fix you and give advice, often endlessly. But cheering us up in ways that do not match our reality, never helps. Or others are intimidated. A very good friend of mine who had stopped contacting me for a long time told me after we re-united that she realized she had been "in denial of the reality you face." She had been "intimidated" by my "torment." How do others become unintimidated so they might be truly helpful?

What does help those in pain, Connell and Connell say, and I fully agree, is to acknowledge the seriousness of their situation and their losses. To respect their boundaries and limitations. To offer *actual* help. And to stay with specifics, such as in "I'm glad you could meet today," or, "I'm sorry you had to cancel." Avoid clichés and generalizations.[4]

It is that bad

The voice of denial jars our existence every time we encounter it, which is almost on a daily basis in one form or another. This does not happen with visible and measurable diseases. This denial and ignorance stand in stark contrast to the seriousness of chronic pain. In the words of Mary Lynch, President of the Canadian Pain Society, "Chronic pain is associated with the worst quality of life compared with other chronic diseases such as chronic lung disease or heart disease…"[5]

People living with severe pain will often say they wished they could trade in their pain for another major disease, or that they had died instead. Particularly during the worst few years, I wished the accident had killed me, or I had ended up in a wheelchair instead of with constant pain. Says a person who became a paraplegic after a car accident, "It was easier for me to accept loss of the use of my legs than the ongoing extreme pain I have to endure."[6] Another spinal cord injury patient tells pain researcher Allan Basbaum, "I don't care if I ever walk again if you can get rid of my pain."[7] Physicians Angela Mailis-Gagnon and David Israelson tell of a patient whose leg had become numb from his foot to just above the knee.[8] For eighteen years he walked with the help of a brace. Then he fell and ended up with knee pain that got worse and worse while the numbness went away completely. He pleads with his doctors to take away his pain and give him back the numbness and paralysis. Robert Teasell reports on a study that found that over one-third of those who stopped working after a spinal cord injury said it was because of their pain and not their paralysis.[9] Pain was regarded as a significant cause of work disability, even when they had a more "acceptable" explanation, i.e. paralysis.

A physician named Dave, whose words are already quoted in chapter 3, words so indicative of the devastating nature of severe chronic pain, that I like to repeat them here, says,

> I'd survived the traumas of a major motor car accident, the ignominy of a prostatectomy, and the despair and exasperation of three separate cancers and their harsh therapies, but nothing had prepared me for the greatest challenge of my life, dealing with chronic pain.[10]

He thought that he had understood pain, spending his career caring for the sick and injured, but he found out he didn't.

> Chronic pain proved to be different, it's continuous and unremitting nature challenged my psyche, mocked my considered strengths, and upended my confidence. The realization that each morning pain will be the first experience on awakening and the last experience at the end of the day dominated my thoughts, imposed on all plans and restricted all activities.

Tell this person, But you look good! At least you have a nice home! Could it be stress? What do you do all day now you don't work?

Some years ago when the pain was still severe I spoke with a friend who had been diagnosed with breast cancer. Thankfully, chemotherapy and the removal of her breast were very successful. She did not have to go for a check up for ten years. She had no pain. She never had to stop any activity except during recuperation from surgery and from chemotherapy. She continued to do what she loves to do: travel, study art history, visit museums. She knew how it was for me. Waking up every night from intense pain. Not being able to function until late in the day, and even then, pain flaring up unpredictably. Having lost my job, income, the ability to travel.

"It must be horrible to have pain all the time," she told me. "I have thought about it, but I wouldn't have wanted your life instead of mine."

"To be perfectly honest," I said, "I would rather have your life than mine." She understood. Here we were. She having come down with an awful disease, but living, for all practical purposes, a normal life. I, having my normal life destroyed by an invisible disease that many in society do not even think is real, and for which for many of us there is no effective treatment.

It may well come as a shock to many readers: rather cancer than living with severe constant pain. Even my wonderful therapist seemed puzzled,

"You would rather have your breast removed?" I needed no time for reflection.

"In a heartbeat."

Edward Covington, who directs the chronic pain program at the Cleveland Clinic, has had at least two patients in his career who came down with terminal cancer and were pleased.[11] Now others would know that they had a real disease, they told Covington. Most people who do not live with pain would not understand this. Everyone living for years with severe pain will. No longer would they be seen as exaggerators or catastrophizers. Friends would believe them. Employers would believe them. Insurers would believe them. Their terminal cancer could not be psychologized or psychiatrized away. And now there was an end in sight. The desire for death on the part of his patients' suffering from severe constant pain, says Scott Fishman, becomes like a "primitive drive."[12] They will do anything, says Fishman, to end the relentless pain, including risking paralysis or death – and that can include wanting to come down with a terminal illness.

This from Nancy Klimas of the Institute for Neuro Immune Medicine, who specializes in auto-immune illnesses:

> My H.I.V. patients for the most part are hale and hearty thanks to three decades of intense research and billions of dollars invested. Many of my C.F.S. (chronic fatigue syndrome, often accompanied by pain) patients, on the other hand, are terribly ill and unable to work or participate in the care of their families. I split my clinical time between the two illnesses, and I can tell you, if I had to choose... I would rather have H.I.V.[13]

Having said all this, there are illnesses of course, including terrible cancers, that are so horrible that people living with severe pain would not want them in exchange for their pain. To draw comparisons, which I wished I did not have to do, is ultimately an act of *descriptive desperation*: The impossibility of showing the world what living with severe pain is like forces us to draw comparisons to other illnesses that the world does understand.

There is an abyss between our own experience of chronic pain on the one hand, and the sugar coating of it by too many in society on the other. How to cross that abyss is the question.

Exposure

The crossing of that abyss must involve extensive and intimate exposure to our lives and our voices. I say that because of the difference in how several people changed in their relationship with me toward much greater realism after they read my memoir. These included two physicians. Although they had "known" me before, they really did not know my life, seeing me only briefly during an afternoon visit or appointment. It is the very nature of chronic pain that allows others to be protected from its reality. The "proof" of pain is always on us, and there is nothing available for us to provide such proof.

Equally important, when pain is intense, you do not see anyone. You hide by necessity. You don't make any commitments involving activities or settings that can trigger pain or make it worse. And when pain flares up while with others, you hide it for as long as you can, then excuse yourself and leave. To partake in at least some semblance of normal life, suppressing pain, which often comes at a cost, is almost always necessary.

The relation between the self in pain and others then is a very lopsided one: Others almost always profoundly underestimate our pain and do not adjust to us. We, on the other hand, cannot prove nor adequately describe the pain we live with, and therefore must try to adjust to the pain free life of others. When people have cancer or any other measurable and knowable disease, they are commended for taking part in social life regardless and no one takes their participation as a sign that they are not really ill. With us, the mere fact of taking part in normal life can result in others believing the validity of our pain even less. Ironically, to the extent we hide our pain and force ourselves to pretend we may well be increasing society's ignorance.

Yet, we must do our best to partake in social life to avoid complete isolation, which is a killer. But it is difficult, because we never have reliable control over the pain. With, say, cancer, it is not the case that we can have cancer one hour but not the next. With chronic pain that is the case for many of us. And we never know with certainty which hour lies ahead. Clearly, this presents a huge problem for socializing. The need to have an "exit" plan is always foremost in our mind and an integral part of any social commitment.

"When I socialize," says a 51 year old woman, "I don't feel as if I'm among the living...I'm experiencing everything through the hazy, heavy filter of pain."[14] Says another person, "Getting out and doing things does not always make me feel better, and can often make me seriously worse...Sometimes participating in an activity can cause more pain than you ever (can) imagine."[15]

Last summer, when I still lived in Victoria, B.C., two friends visited from out of town. They took a day to see Vancouver: Granville Island, Stanley park, the museum, a nice dinner.

"Come along," they urged. "It will do you some good."

Coming along with the pain free life. Driving half an hour to the ferry, conversing, my neck strained by the movement of the car (being a passenger is far harder on my neck than driving myself), then the busy ferry for one and a half hour's drive, then an hour's drive to downtown, then the museum, then... Neither my neck nor my brain would be able to handle the multiple stimuli around me, the noise, the talking, the fast pace of city life. I probably wouldn't make it further than the ferry. And although the worst years are over, there is no way I can handle a day like that even today. Pain would inexorably intensify. Unless we would spread these activities out over several days, drive slowly, find a quiet place on the ferry, not talk too much in the car, and be willing to change plans if needed. In other words, having others come along with me. How can I expect others to do so? Who understands what I live with so well that they understand the need for them to adjust?

My daughters do. They have spent enough time with me to know my limitations. They even work preventively – carrying my purse (relieving pressure on my shoulder which can cause flare-ups), making sure we have a quiet place on the ferry, finding a quiet restaurant, dragging pillows along to support my neck. A rare friend does. But I have given up to expect others to do so. If it happens, I am grateful. For the most part, even those who seem to understand and initially adjust, will soon fall back into their own patterns and treat me as if I am normal. They forget. We can never forget.

Says physician Eric Cassell, social life and the rules for social participation normally override the inner needs of the individual.[16] The acutely ill are relieved from these rules, observes Cassell, but the chronically ill rarely are. Yet they are not able to sustain the behaviors demanded for social life except at great cost. The conflict between the demands of social interaction and the pained person, says Cassell, is intensified even to the point where it threatens to tear the person apart.

People living with pain then, are caught in paralyzing traps in their relations with others: Pretend your are better than you are in order to be "normal" and people will underestimate your pain problems even more; be frank about your pain problems and people will think you are exaggerating because they cannot see anything.

A four day series of full page articles on chronic pain, published by Postmedia News in newspapers across Canada, with pictures and videos that vividly tell our stories is a fine example of the extensive exposure that is needed to bring our realities to the regular public.[17] Nothing was sugar coated. The exposure was extensive. And it was in regular newspapers. Front page. Not just a few comments about chronic pain and short interviews with medical professionals somewhere tucked away in a health section. Not in a publication read mainly by the medical world. Not in a pain-awareness pamphlet read mainly by people who live with pain and by their families. But in regular newspapers. The feedback received by Postmedia News on this series was overwhelming. I myself received many phone calls within hours of publication. My best friend said, "Wow, I didn't know it could be that bad." She had never seen me early in the morning when intense pain wakes me, as shown in one of the pictures in the article.

My therapist who read my memoir told me that although he had heard many of my experiences over the years I visited him, and although he had heard many of the same kind of stories from other pain patients, to see it told "all in once place" had hit him hard. That's why we need extensive exposure, told "in one place," a place of considerable concentration, using various media, to get our reality across. Without reducing the abyss of ignorance, not much will change for us, barring an unlikely medical breakthrough.

Coralie Wales, President of Chronic Pain Australia, hands representatives of pharmaceutical and insurance industries and of the medical profession copies of the stories gathered by her organization from people across Australia who live with pain, essentially telling them: "Here, read these stories."[18] Data by themselves, will not readily move society to empathy, understanding, and helpful action. The abyss that now exists between our lives and society's understanding of them must be crossed foremost with exposure to our voices, to our lives.

15 Self help pain management programs: helping and hurting

The reason to address self help pain management (SHPM) programs within a framework of a societal model, is that considerable parts of these programs reinforce the separation of the person in pain from the societal web of forces that impact their pain.

SHPM programs are difficult to look at realistically and critically. For when the world of medicine deals inadequately with chronic pain, who could possibly have anything critical to say of the self help movement in pain management? However, the self help movement is not as straightforward as it may sound. What kind of 'self' is being helped? On whose terms is this 'self' defined? How is the self-in-pain told to behave? During the 20 years of living with pain, I have attended four SHPM programs, read seven SHPM books, read piles of articles on SHPM, and followed various pain management web sites. I have also spoken about SHPM programs with many others who live with pain and who I met in these programs or in pain clinics.

My comments here arise foremost from these experiences. SHPM programs and materials are typically developed by healthcare professionals (psychologists of various orientations, nurses, therapists, doctors) who by the clout of their profession carry a certain authority. These professionals do not advocate for us. Instead, they place themselves in a formal position in which they are assumed to have greater knowledge of pain management than we do, often providing advice based on trends and theories that guide their own profession. I have had to conclude that their advice is sometimes helpful, but too often it is not. And not infrequently, SHPM programs and materials ignore the lives of those who live with severe pain, or unintentionally trivialize those lives by offering cheerful and superficial strategies. Too often, the advice does not reflect an in-depth knowledge of our actual lives. The main point of this chapter is that in-depth knowledge of our actual day-to-day lives as the basis for developing these programs is crucial to their success.

The first SHPM program I attended in 1998 was a physical therapy/ exercise program, offering the same content for everyone, with a minimum of counseling. That's about all that needs to be said here. Except that it followed a no-pain-no-gain philosophy which I found torturous. The second program in 2002 was a private ten day residential program, exclusively invested in alternative treatments (acupuncture, massage, biofeedback) and counseling sessions, based on humanistic psychology –group hugs and all– which reminded me of the 1960 and 70's. The third program I attended in 2008 was connected to a pain clinic, and consisted of a wide array of activities. The program was new and the group leader, a professional person, told me they had "grabbed" activities from "everywhere" to get ready. The fourth program I attended in 2010 was extremely scripted, also consisting of many kinds of activities, and was part of a movement to increase the number of SHPM programs in Canada. The program followed the standardized format developed by Sandra LeFort and Lisa Cardas.[1] The group leaders were two "peer volunteers." One had suffered from pain in the past; the other suffered from "minimal" pain compared, he said, to what most of us lived with.

The purpose of my comments here is to describe a set of concerns that have arisen from my own and others' experiences with SHPM programs and materials in the hope that articulating them suggest ways to render these programs more relevant and more helpful. I will focus in particular on the 2008 and 2010 programs in that they reflect a trend to develop increasingly standardized programs to be "delivered" to people living with pain. Standardization would seem the obvious way to go given the millions of people who need help. But in the end I believe scripted programs may well defy the purpose of helping us to help ourselves: Our selves are complex, and there is a great diversity among us in terms of our needs.

The seven SHPM books I have read ranged from Margaret Caudill's book written with a seriousness that reflects a desire to understand our lives and makes at least an attempt to differentiate pain levels, to books that are essentially descriptions of cognitive and behavioral psychological theories superimposed onto our lives, and books that offer quick and all too simple solutions.[2] When I see the title "10 simple Solutions to Chronic Pain," or a sub title, "Back pain can be stopped for ever," I am immediately suspicious.[3]

A healthcare professional who works with pain patients told me, referring to SHPM materials, "They are well below average if you ask me." I had to agree. A physical therapist told me his pain patients pick up a SHPM book from a pile on his table, look at it, and within seconds throw it back on the table. No interest. Pages filled with lists, questions to answer, and worksheets to fill out. There is something about them that we find patronizing – yet missing the mark. We rarely see or feel ourselves in these materials. We feel being talked down to. There is so much cheerfulness.

What follows is what has stood out to me and to others as helpful or not so helpful, as honoring our lives or as being disconnected from our lives.

The good

For the most part, SHPM programs have no problems attracting us. We are desperate. For company as much as for potentially helpful information. We need a place where we can gather and know we will understand each other. SHPM programs offer such a place almost regardless of the kind and quality of program they offer. We are thankful to be with others who live lives like ours: We instantly understand each other. Even if the leaders of the program may not. We have such similar stories to tell. We tell them to each other during the break and before and after the often scripted meetings. There is suddenly a sense of belonging that has disappeared from our lives. A woman in pain who has become a good friend, wrote me,

> It's funny how it always seems like no time has passed when I do get to see you again. Even though our lives are so different this pain binds us together in such an intimate way. I take comfort that you are out there in the world and know my pain as well as I do.

This sense of finding kinship was the main reason why I continue to attend even the one program I found inexcusably flawed. Some professionals acknowledge this central kinship function. Physician Ruth Dubin says about her SHPM program, "We interviewed clients and found that the important thing was the group interaction....Chronic pain patients tend to be isolated. They made friends, they didn't feel so alone, they really blossomed."[4]

Then there is always the possibility of learning something helpful. That happened in the 2008 SHPM group where a lot of attention was paid to the plasticity of the brain, which was new information for most participants. As well, the group leader guided us through some good mindfulness meditation sessions, which was also new to most participants, and people really took to it.

SHPM programs provide a social outing. Going out "to be social" is for many who live with serious pain no longer a part of life. Going to a SHPM group has none of the pressures of regular socializing: Not knowing what to do when the pain flares up; pretending nothing is the matter; dealing with too much noise; not knowing what to do when people say ignorant or insensitive things. You don't have to worry that your posture or your facial expressions show pain: No one will misinterpret or stigmatize you. If you have to leave that is fine. If you are late that is fine. You can be social on your own terms because all participants live by the same kind of terms. You will have a couple of hours in which you can be authentic.

Further, the meetings provide a structure to your week. There is a day you know you will go somewhere. You dress decently. As many of us walk around at home in old stuff, dressing decently and going somewhere where your pain is welcome, brings back a sense of normalcy. SHPM programs then provide an immensely important function just by providing meeting places. From the perspective of the lived experience however, there are also problematic aspects.

Fragmentation and mismatches

"Grabbing" activities from "everywhere" is not a good basis upon which to build a coherent SHPM program. It represents a piecemeal, additive model of thinking which becomes equated with "covering" a list of things: a bit about nutrition, a few exercises, a few yoga stretches, something about one's posture, about sleep, about stress, a minimum overview of drugs, rules for "non-violent communication," a suggestion or two for dealing with your doctor, affirmations to say to oneself, a bit about relaxation, an exercise in positive self-talk, advice about distracting oneself, a handout on self-esteem, another one on feeling peaceful, something else about anger management, about time management, about problem solving, an emphasis on goal setting, on pacing oneself – *all* these were present in the 2008 and 2010 programs combined. The risk is of course that few topics are dealt with in any depth, and that the real life problems we need help with are not addressed.

Topics are all too often taken from areas that were designed for purposes other than dealing with chronic pain. This can even increase pain. In the 2008 program I attended, we were asked to play a game which was supposed to make us laugh and thus would increase our endorphins which would in turn help our pain. We all got a spoon, but I can't remember how the game went for I freaked out the moment I realized that everyone was going to bang their spoon on the table. When the noise hit, I instinctively got up fast and left – and so did the person next to me who suffered from closed head injuries similar to mine. Both of us felt an immediate sharp headache coming on. Neither of us can tolerate loud noises. "I don't need this," he said as we walked quickly down the hall.

The literature shows that head and neck injuries can make people extraordinarily sensitive to noise – as I have become. We informed the group leader afterwards why we had left. She had never thought of noise leading to an increase in pain. I can only hope that participants in SHPM programs educate the leaders in what they do not know, but need to know.

In the 2010 program, we were asked, "Where does your time go? What activities do you do in the normal course of a day?"[5] (Note: The assumption is that our days have a "normal" course.) We were encouraged to keep a time diary of both activity and rest periods. Of course, to balance activity with rest is very important. But then we are asked to do the following:

> Make sure *all* the time periods in the day are filled with activities and rest breaks. Every hour of the day should be accounted for. This encourages you to be time-oriented rather than pain-oriented. You tend to concentrate on your activity, rather than on your discomfort....[6]

When ever I read the word "discomfort" to refer to chronic pain my brain already leaves the page. What I and others who live with severe pain feel is not discomfort. It is *pain*. Just replace "discomfort" with "severe pain" in the above quote, and the advice doesn't work so well anymore.

"People of the Western world, particularly Americans, tend to think of time as something fixed in nature, something...from which we cannot escape ..." anthropologist Edward Hall noted.[7] So did this pain management book. But living with pain creates an ambiguous construct of time. It can slow time down. It can speed up time. "Pain - expands the Time - Pain contracts -the Time-" says Emily Dickinson. When pain is severe, time collapses into itself. Severe pain draws one's attention so powerfully into the present that the boundaries between past and future, between this hour and the next hour, become vague. And when the pain gets really bad, time disappears altogether.[8] Then we don't even 'have' hours to account for. Also, relaxation and meditation, activities often advised for chronic pain patients, can only be done if one *forgets* clock time altogether.

I would have a full blown anxiety attack if I forced myself to account for every clock hour. As much as possible, I arrange my days so that for long periods of time (especially in the morning when my neck and head pain is the worst) I do *not* have to pay attention to clock time so I can stay quiet and let my wound up nervous system settle down.

The same linear and rational approach is offered for "problem solving."[9] Seven steps are suggested but only one step ("identifying the problem") provides an example of how that would work in a life lived in pain (the other six steps are illustrated with examples from other areas of life). We are told to identify "*specifically*" what causes the pain. For example, "preparing dinner" might increase pain. But is it "peeling vegetables," or "standing over the sink," or "bending to put things in the oven," or "opening jars"? That is rarely how chronic pain works, except in the case of arthritic or other localized pain problems. But for many of us, such a specific part of an activity as the cause of chronic pain cannot easily or consistently be identified. Often pain flares up minutes after an activity and there is no way of knowing exactly what part of the activity triggered it. Perhaps the entire thing brought it on. At times a certain specific movement brings on pain while at other times the same movement does not. What is assumed by the "preparing dinner" example is a stability of conditions that is just not present.

This linear 7-step progression looks good on paper, and might work in other areas in life under narrowly and well-defined and stable conditions. But my eyes in pain glance over it. We must plan of course. But more so than in pain-free lives, we must plan for contingencies. For unavoidable chaos. As journalist Marni Jackson observes, "[T]he random power [of pain] to strike makes you feel temporary as a sand castle."[10] We must learn to plan with great flexibility. You cannot experiment in 7 linear steps with a sand castle as waves and winds are not under your control.

These all too-rational pieces of advice are "grabbed" from areas of theory or practice (here, time management and problem solving models) that did not consider the nature of chronic pain when originally formulated. The only way to organize a coherent SHPM program is *to start*, not with a collection of things taken from everywhere, but with a deep understanding of the lived experience of our lives, an understanding against which every activity or piece of advice must be compared for its relevance.

Then, a SHPM work book would not show a section of twelve pages on the benefits of walking taken directly from a "Guide to healthy active living" for older adults, showing pictures of older people happily walking, fit and smiling.[11] No pain to be found. Nothing wrong of course with suggesting that walking might be a good idea. But when I read, "Are you wondering where you can fit walking into your busy schedule?" and "… everyone has a busy schedule," I know they are not talking about us. People living with severe pain typically have lost their busy schedule. Again, the deeper message is: be normal, be happy, be social. The section even ends with the mandate to "Enjoy and have fun!"

Be positive! Smile more! Don't worry! Let's be cheerful! Get on with your life!

At the start of the 2010 SHPM program, we were asked to respond to the question, " What has chronic pain meant to you?" There were twelve participants. I wrote down word by word what everyone said. Going around the circle, these were their responses: "It has destroyed my life." "I can't meet people's expectations anymore." "Loss of friendships." "Depression." "Pain is a constant demand on my attention." "Everything has changed." "I fear the future." "I can no longer work." "I am now poor." "I feel I live in a prison." "My spouse left me." "No one understands what I live with." One person cried when she tried to speak of how chronic pain had ruined her life: "…and you go to a doctor and nothing happens…." Everyone nodded.

That first round was the only time we were allowed, for just a minute, to speak freely about the immense difficulties caused by chronic pain. From there on, anything "negative" we expressed was countered with an attempt by the group leaders at a positive make over. Relentlessly.

Pain management books and programs are on the whole so *cheerful*. The difficulty of living with pain is acknowledged at the start in a sentence or two, but from there on the message is typically a cheerful one. Lack of differentiation of pain levels is important here: Cheerfulness may be fine when someone suffers from occasional light pain problems. Being cheerful toward that person could perhaps serve as a distraction. But it is worse than inappropriate for people who live with severe pain, have lost their job, their social life, are often housebound, and may well be suicidal. From my 2010 journal,

> The pain has gotten much worse again. Always the fear it means a permanent worsening.[12] Fourteen years of this is enough. I cannot be doing this when I am 90. How can someone live this way till the age of 90 or 95?

That evening I read through the workbook I had just received from the 2010 SHPM program. I see the phrase "a satisfying and fulfilling life," repeated three times.[13] The phrase, along with other pleasantries in the workbook, turns me off. Had I not wanted to be in the company of others who live my kind of life I would not have gone back.

Dahl and Lundgren in their SHPM book mix acceptance theory with cognitive behavior modification, with denial, and with ignorance about the lived experience of chronic pain.[14] On virtually every page we read that the pain itself is not a hindrance to anything: only our thoughts about the pain are. "You just decide that you're going to do what *you* need to do."[15] You just take your pain "along for the ride."[16] If only we do the many worksheets and exercises and practice the uplifting cheerful self talk strategies they offer, we will then be free "to do exactly what you want to do."[17] It blows the mind.

It is characteristic of these kinds of publications that there are no references to any biographical or autobiographical writings about living with chronic pain. Dahl and Lundgren cite none. Nor do they cite any of the qualitative research studies where our voices and our lives are represented. Nor any of the thoughtful writings by pain specialists, journalists and scholars in the humanities and in cultural studies who write about lives lived in pain. Their sources, apart from citations of epidemiological data on pain and some studies on biofeedback, are publications from the same trends in psychology their work is based on. That's it.

I am always flabbergasted when I am cheerfully told to "get on" with life ("get on with living," or "get your life back"[18]). Which life are we to get on with? The life we had before the pain erupted? The life in pain we have now? What do these words *mean*? I think of the man who sits next to me in the pain management program who has great difficulty walking and is visibly in pain. He makes many humorous/cynical comments. I marvel at his ability to do so. After years of pain, he has only one friend left he tells me – his partner. He has two cats that give him comfort and an aquarium full of fish. He hardly goes out anymore.

We are asked to do an exercise in which we have to ask the person next to us to put a name on a "difficult emotion" and then report back to the group. He says his "difficult emotion" is "I don't care." At first I didn't know what he was referring to. Then it became clear that he was referring to "I don't care" *as* a difficult emotion. I was intrigued: We don't usually see the "I don't care" attitude mentioned as an emotion (other people came up with the usual: anger, frustration, sadness, despair). I probed for what he meant. He didn't care anymore because "there was nothing to be done about it anyway."

I asked him what happened to the emotions we all have: the sadness, the despair, the darkness.

"I don't care because that is a way to avoid those," he said. I suddenly got it. There was no point to having those emotions, but since they keep cropping up, one had to step above them, so to speak, and look at them with a "I don't care" sense of self and the world. For him, "getting on with life" meant to no longer care much about anything. What, actually, could the "satisfying and fulfilling" life be like that he was supposed to be creating by following the program? *Why* all these clichés, the meaningless promises?

We went from merely mentioning our "difficult emotion" to the next exercise: What could we *do* about these "difficult emotions?" We all understood the desired answer: Distract ourselves.

I wrote down the distractions the group came up with: sit in the sun, cook a meal, call a friend, go to the mall, watch television, have happy thoughts. They were all accepted by the group leaders and dutifully written down on the flip chart. I think *anything* cheerful and pleasant would have been happily accepted. This separating emotions from their contexts, turns you into a kind of robot. I feel deeply disturbed when I am asked to replace my "difficult emotion" with a distraction without any further talk about why I feel this difficult emotion. I am being de-souled. And I become suspicious: For whose benefit is this superficial treatment of our "difficult emotions?"

One participant, hesitantly, for it didn't fit the format, said, "Maybe you think this is strange, but someone told me to go in the shower and cry." Stunning. It is what we all do, but in this pain management session she had to gather her courage to say so, because it was not "positive." Not the right distraction.

I thanked her for saying that, because, I added, "we all have our crying places, but it is hard to say that in a society and a medical system that isn't even acknowledging the horror of chronic pain." I was aware I was not looking at the group leaders but directly talking to the woman and the rest of the group. Something in me decided to bypass the group leaders – who did not say a word. This was intimate information only for ourselves. Information they had no natural right to considering their many denials of the difficulties of our lives.

In the residential program I attended we had to draw a picture. Then everyone had to say what they saw in each others' pictures. Needless to say, everyone had only nice and cheerful things to say about everyone else. In still another activity we had to say something affirmative about ourselves, such as "I accept myself." "I am a lovable person." Then there were the group hugs. A woman sitting next to me whispered: "I don't need this. I need someone who can help me to get on disability."

It's amazing to me that to find validation of my life I have to turn to journalism (Arthur Rosenfelt, Marni Jackson, Sharon Kirkey), the humanities (David Morris, Elaine Scarry, Alphonse Daudet, Arthur Frank) and to autobiography.[19] Even Time magazine in its 2012 March special issue on chronic pain, let me see myself realistically. When an openness to our real lives is missing, no amount of cheering up will fill that gap. It will register as denial. Cheering me up without being open to my story is silencing me.

Even the Mayo Clinic takes part in this,

> panic, grief and anger…like the pain that spawns them, can linger and transform you into a different person. A person you don't like. A person no one likes…Your pain and unhappiness also may trigger cycles of difficult emotions and dysfunctional behavior in those around you.[20]

Now we are blamed not only for our own grief and justified anger, all of which, we are told, is really inappropriate and dysfunctional, but we are also blamed for the unhappiness and even "dysfunctional" behavior of those around us! Clearly, our pain should never, ever, make anyone else uncomfortable.

The Mayo Clinic does acknowledge some of the reasons for our anger (mentioned are unrelenting pain, interrupted sleep, unsuccessful treatments, job woes and insurance battles) but does not expand on any of them and we are told instead, "It's unhealthy to stay angry."[21] We must recognize, we are told, that we are really "catastrophizing," "polarizing," "filtering," "emotionalizing" and then we must learn to change these unpleasant ways of thinking into positive thoughts.[22]

A handout we received even in the best of the four programs I attended cheerfully told us, "Don't worry. Worrying doesn't help… (we must be) confident that what we want and need will come." Worrying is only a thought, the group leader added in the discussion that followed. It instantly reminded me of the "Don't worry, be happy" slogan of the 80s. And of the pain specialist in Vancouver who told me, "Don't worry dear. Don't worry. Let's not worry." This was years after the accident and after multiple treatments had not worked. "General reassurances of the "don't worry" type are worse than useless," says well known physician Eric Cassell.[23]

Anthony Guarino, a Director of Pain Management, Washington University in St. Louis, also sees worrying as "only" a thought.[24]

> Watch a funny movie or share a joke with a friend. Talk yourself out of feeling bad. After all, it's only a thought and a thought can always change.

Note how pain has now been replaced with "feeling bad." Within certain trends in cognitive and behavioral psychology, physical pain magically disappears and is reframed as no more than a psychological or cognitive event.

Worrying is indeed a thought, but it is not "only" a thought. When you have lost your job, your income, and most of your social life, when doctors can do no more than prescribe pills that do not work well and have nasty side effects, when it has become clear that your spouse may not hang in there with you much longer – these worries are distinctly not "only" a thought. They are facts or real possibilities with enormous consequences. Presumably, the message on the handout was based on Buddhism. But Buddhist traditions never said: "Don't worry – a worry is only a thought." Buddhist traditions involve closely observing one's thoughts precisely because they *are* so consequential. The goal is *not* not to worry about them. The goal is to observe them closely, become intimately familiar with them, and see them in action. Then, one might be able to deal with them with a certain degree of wisdom. And that is extraordinarily difficult to do when living an extraordinarily difficult life. The handout was really an insult. I got angry. I said something close to: "I *know* I will be woken up by freakin' pain in the middle of the night as I have been for years. No one knows why or what to do. I may have to live with this for the rest of my life. I lost my job. I lost my social life – and you tell me not to worry?" The staff member got it. She looked a bit startled, and said: "Are you saying this trivializes you?"

"Of course."

Afterwards I thought about how other participants may also have felt an unease. It has been my professional job to look critically at theories and models. I knew that in Buddhism thoughts are a hugely important aspect of human functioning. If you don't have these things in your background, it would be hard to articulate a feeling of unease or anger on the spot.

This example illustrates what can happen when activities are borrowed from elsewhere (here: from the worry-free 60s, or from a cheap version of

Buddhism which is just as bad as a cheap anything) and superimposed on the chronic pain experience without carefully considering its appropriateness. The staff member afterwards apologetically explained that they were a relatively new program and had "grabbed" activities from everywhere. That is exactly the problem.

In critiquing the ubiquitous cheerfulness in SHPM programs, I am not advocating being negative all the time, or talking endlessly about our problems. I object to forcing our behavior into the simplistic dualistic framework of "the positive" and "the negative." Within this binary frame, the "negative" perceptions we have of the conditions of our lives are seen as "distortions." According to Ellen Catalano and Kimeron Harding, we engage in eight "distortions"(several of which are also noted in other SHPM materials): we "filter," we "blame," we "catastrophize," we "emotionalize," we "polarize," we "have control fallacies," we "engage in emotional reasoning" (that is, thinking that what we feel is true), and we "have entitlement fallacies."[25] One can see here how SHPM programs and materials are grounded in the pathologizing and psychiatrizing theories I discussed in earlier chapters.

Caudill as well lists ten similar "cognitive distortions" people in general engage in and asks us to consider if some "sound familiar" to us.[26] To my pleasant surprise, Caudill at the same time observes that, "There may be too much psychological labeling of chronic pain patients who do not get better. This only increases everyone's frustration and devalues patients' experience."[27] She then notes the following "common psychological labels" that are "incorrect" or are "misapplied": depression, hysteria, hypochondriasis, malingering, and post traumatic stress disorder.[28]

Social critic Barbara Ehrenreich discusses what she sees as the American obsession with positive thinking as a "dominant, almost mandatory, cultural attitude" which leads to a "morbid preoccupation with stamping out negative thoughts."[29] Much of SHPM suffers from just such morbid preoccupation.

When our thoughts about so many of our real problems are *not* allowed on the table, because they are seen as "negative," space is created for trivialities instead. In the 2010 program, one man who had set himself the weekly goal of cooking three healthy meals, reported on how his asparagus had gone bad. This engendered a lively discussion, lasting at least five minutes, on how to cook asparagus. Suicide –no. Insurance problems– no. Difficult doctors – barely. Asparagus, now, that is worthy of a five minute conversation. Had the serious topics been allowed, a cooking discussion would have been fine as a diversion. But now it took the place of talking about our real difficulties.

In the 2008 SHPM program I attended we were told to say affirmations several times a day, choosing from a handout we were given of more than 140 of them (yes, 140). It contained niceties such as, "I am a balanced person," "I am a capable person," "I am a lovable person," "I am a cheerful, adorable, independent, optimistic, light-hearted, elegant, dynamic, and 130-more-of-them-person." Tellingly, I then could have walked across the street to see a psychiatrist and hear that I have a personality disorder, or that I am a "high catastrophizer." Our "self" is easily exalted in the "positive psychology" movement that colors much of SHPM programs. It is just as easily pathologized within the psychiatric approach that colors much of pain research and clinical practice.

My wonderful Buddhist therapist said to me a few times, "You are welcome here with all your pain." He left me whole and real. Had ever he said anything about needing to be positive, or any of such messages, it would have been the last session. The very few times someone has had the courage to say something straightforwardly true, as did my masseuse who said, "Even a lovely grandchild doesn't make up for this, does it," the burden of pretense dissolves. "It's tragic," another person said, learning about my life. Again, truth and relief. Our conversations could continue unhindered by the slippery slopes of denial, niceties, clichés, and avoidances.

One could in fact argue that "negative thinking" is characteristic of the mindset of many who write SHPM. For in order to tell us to be "positive" we, of course, need to be first seen as being negative, otherwise all this emphasis on the positive would not make sense. There is a long list of negatives already ascribed to us before we arrive: We engage in many distorted ways of thinking; our attitude is bad; we don't know how to solve problems; we are self involved; our "pain behaviors" are exaggerated; we don't know how to communicate; we are fixated on our pain, we are too angry, we catastrophize, and all the rest of it. But, not to worry. All we have to do it replace these "negative" states with cheerful, positive thoughts and distractions. What I do not see reflected in these SHPM books and materials, is any reference to how many of us still manage our lives well. How inventive and patient many of us can be in dealing with the professionals who do not understand our lives. In dealing with our spouses, children, and friends. How strong we must be to keep our families together. How many of us courageously deal with institutions that harass us. How we learn to endure. In none of the programs I attended was time provided to focus on how, in real life, we actually *do* deal with terribly difficult conditions. I do not remember *ever* hearing: "How did you approach that problem?" Or, "Tell us what you did about that, perhaps others can learn from it."

You must socialize! You must act normal!

You need to develop a strong support system, the Mayo Clinic advises us:

> Answer phone calls and letters. Accept invitations to events, even if it feels awkward and difficult at first…Take the initiative and call someone…Take part in community organizations, neighborhood events or family get-togethers. Strike up a conversation with the person next to you at a local gathering. Talk about things that interest other people.[30]

Note, that we are advised to engage in these social activities *while* we are living with pain that drains our energy (no pain level is specified – supposedly, it doesn't matter). This from a person living with constant pain,

> When I do socialize, I usually don't feel as if I am among the living. I often feel like I'm experiencing everything through the hazy, heavy filter of pain. It is as if I am seeing everything around me in a fun house mirror, distorted and harrowing…[31]

From my own journal, November 2010.

> When I read that I should maintain my social life, I feel that another burden is placed on me: On top of this horrible pain, the exhaustion– *I* am the one who has the obligation to keep in contact with friends. Somehow, miraculously, I am to continue with normal socializing though the pain that prevented me from doing so in the first place has not gone away. What are these people thinking?

Another professional suggests we have fun and go "ice climbing" or "skiing," or camping, and live a "full and productive life."[32] Perhaps people living with light pain levels can do all that. I can't think of anyone I know who lives with considerable daily pain who could go ice climbing. Or attend noisy community events. Even accepting invitations for low key events demand forethought. There always needs to be an exit plan if the pain flares up beyond control. You may have to leave midway. As a woman wrote to me, "I always have an exit strategy." Mine include always driving my own car, so I can leave if needed without inconveniencing others. Also, my mind, exhausted from so many years of pain, has really no space left to talk about something just because it interests other people and constitutes proper socializing. I don't care about "proper" socializing anymore. As Hildur Kalman and Naomi Scheman aptly ask,

> At what point does the ignoring of one's own pain (to please someone else) turn into self-estrangement? If you never let on how you feel, it is more than possible that the habit of this creates a distance from your own feelings…[33]

Striking up a conversation with someone who happens to sit next to me, as the Mayo Clinic tells me I should do, something I used to do easily (for once I was an outgoing person), I now avoid. Suffering from pain and the sleep deprivation that inevitably comes with it, it would be using up energy I do *not* have the luxury to waste. Our brains are trying to *preserve* energy.

The reality is that we need to carefully pick and choose: places, people, time of day, kind of activity, noise levels. For, as one of the 10,000 voices in pain of the former American Pain Foundation project said so correctly, "I fear to participate in social activities for they often make the pain worse." That has happened to me many times. Says another person living with pain, "Getting out and doing things does not always make me feel better, and can often make me seriously worse."[34] Talking about traveling, a man suffering from severe daily pain says,

> I cannot travel far because the accumulated vibrations in a car or plane after 20-30 minutes leave me exhausted because you are always anticipating a bigger bump or side-way shift.[35]

I completely identify. Numerous times my neck has "gone out" just from being a passenger in someone's car, the side-way shifts or the sudden movements of breaks can cause pain attacks that last for hours.

This from a woman in her twenties,

> The hardest thing I find is having to say no to things that I would love to do…Other people say they understand but then expect you to perform as everyone else in society does.[36]

We need to try to maintain some form of social life, but it has to be according to our knowledge of how the pain functions in our lives. Not according to some theory about "socializing." The suggestions the Mayo Clinic and others offer are so contra-indicated for many who live with considerable daily pain, that they seem taken from a handbook written for shy people, and then willy-nilly applied to us. Says Eric Cassell,

> The conflict between the desire to live in society and the need to retreat continues even in the privacy of the person's thought. The more intransigent the conflict between these competing needs the more the conflict becomes a source of suffering ... Family, friends, and acquaintances reinforce the conflict by continually urging the ill person to "try and be like everyone else."[37]

It is impossible for us to be like everyone else, Cassell goes on to say. I wished Cassell would have written SHPM books. I am sure they would be realistic and fair.

For there is a deep unfairness and injustice about all this "live normal - have a social life" advice to those who live with serious pain. Rarely do I come across advice for the non-pain community as to what *they* can do to keep us in their midst. What are the ingredients for social events that do not set off pain or make the pain worse? What preparations are needed to have us there without increasing our pain? Places to lie down? Soft music? Easy chairs? Low keyed conversation? Not too many people? People talking slower? Being absolved from having to bring food? We need a responsive societal model of how those living with serious pain can stay part of the community.

Distraction

The group leader, reading from her instruction sheet, says,

> Ok, what is your pain level? Write it down. Now distract yourself. Think of something nice, like a sunny beach. Now write down your pain level again. For whom did the pain level go down?

She did not take her eyes of the sheet while reading these instructions in one breath. I didn't have enough time to do what she told us to. Of course a few participants raised their hands: Their pain had gone down. But that is neither here nor there. Perhaps it did, perhaps it didn't. The pressure of the moment alone can get people to raise their hand. Perhaps some people felt that their pain should have gone down – after all, group leaders are supposed to have some level of expertise.

A common explanation for why distraction can help in pain management is that one cannot hold two things at the same time in one's head. One has to choose. Just decide to think of something else instead of the pain and the brain won't feel the pain, or at least the pain will diminish.

There are several problems with this. Pain is not just a thought. Pain, while influenced by thought, does not equate thought, although this equation is dangerously implied both in traditional pain theory when pain is seen as psychogenic and in more recent theories that rely largely on various trends in cognitive psychology. Whether or not a distraction can override physical pain depends not in the least on how intense the pain is. We know that severe pain wipes out the ability to attend, and no amount of chatting on the phone or going to the mall will help: In fact, when in severe pain one cannot even do these things.[38] As Elaine Scarry observes, "In serious pain the claims of the body utterly nullify the claims of the world."[39] And as a person living with severe pain aptly said, "It (the pain) crowds every other thought out of your brain."[40] When pain is severe, it pushes away thought. Not the other way around. In fact, when pain is severe, distractions, when forced onto the person in pain can make the pain worse. This has happened to me a number of times. When in intense pain, a well-intended friend started to tell me funny stories or tried to distract me with gossip, I had to gesture her to stop as hearing her voice ramble on heightened the pain to the point where my head seemed about to burst.

The ubiquitous emphasis on distraction in pain management as though it were effective for all pain levels, shows again how differences in pain levels are rarely taken into consideration. One pain specialists does: "Distraction is the first line of defense against pain. (But) You can't distract yourself when you're suffering 10 out of 10 overwhelming pain."[41] When my own pain is light, I can distract myself and it helps, although the pain will often force its way back once the distraction is over – after all, one can only chat on the phone or think of sunny beaches for so long.

Further, mindfulness meditation, now increasingly suggested in pain management, asks for deep attentiveness to things-as-they-are *in* the moment. You bring full attention *to* the pain, the breath, the body, not away from it. This stands in contrast to the strong emphasis in SHPM on distraction. A far more nuanced discussion about the place of distraction in SHPM is called for.

The basis for suggesting distraction to diminish pain is based on controlled laboratory studies, where pain, in the form of a pain probe (a quick heat probe, putting a hand in ice water) is inflicted. When research subjects are distracted less pain is perceived. The distraction could be anything, from images of being on a sunny beach (often used in SHPM materials) to smelling a "pleasant odor."[42] These experiments are interesting by showing us how perception of momentary acute pain can be changed by distraction. But invariably, it is implied, and often explicitly noted, that such distractions work for chronic pain, presumably at any level. Ignored is the problem of generalization from the experiment to our real lives: two completely different sets of circumstances.

The "just think of something else" advice becomes even more irritating when health care professionals give "personal examples" of how they override a bit of pain by changing their thoughts about it. For instance, a neuroscientist states, "I'm periodically trying to get into shape…I go to the gym and work out way too much and my muscles are really sore, but I interpret that as a positive. I'm thinking, I've really worked hard."[43] We just shake our heads. The emphasis on distraction can lead healthcare professionals to think that if it is that easy to chase pain away then those who complain about chronic pain must indeed be exaggerating. I don't even want to think of how insurers must be welcoming the distraction proposition.

And finally, and most significantly, distraction refuses deep meaning. Chatting on the phone, seeing a fun movie, watching tv, shopping – in the SHPM programs it didn't matter *what* distraction we came up with. I saw myself at 92, still in pain, walking with a cane in the shopping mall buying stuff, chatting on the phone, or sitting numb in front of my television.

Instead I listen to Victor Frankl,

> "Whoever has a reason for living endures almost any mode of life," says Nietzsche. The conviction that one has a task before him has enormous psychotherapeutic and psychohygienic value. We venture to say that nothing is more likely to help a person overcome or endure objective difficulties or subjective troubles than the consciousness of having a task in life. That is all the more so when the task seems to be personally cut to suit… Our aim must be to help our patient to achieve the highest possible activation of his life, to lead him, so to speak, from the state of a "*patiens*" to that of an "*agens*."[44]

During my worst years of constant severe pain when the ultimate pain killer almost became suicide, I set myself two purposes to accomplish while being essentially homebound. As I have always valued writing, I scribbled numerous journal notes on what the pain was doing in my life, which later became my memoir, and I tamed two feral kittens and a severely abused, aggressive cat (not all at the same time). I don't know how I managed to do the-taming-of-the-cats because that is a task requiring great devotion and self restraint (though I could also ignore them during the worst of the pain). Doing what were for me highly meaningful tasks may well have saved my life. Tasks of consequence and responsibility, that I could work on "around" my pain attacks, gave me a reason to be. Temporary distractions are something most people do in the face of difficulties. And that is fine, of course, as far as that goes. But emphasizing distraction in the absence of a larger framework of meaning leaves one empty in the end. Good SHPM programs, in my view, must lower the current obsession with distraction and explore with us the larger meanings that our lives still might engage.

The "self-without-a-world" in SHPM programs

The exclusive focus on the "self" in SHPM programs allows others to put all responsibility for pain relief onto us. We are our own healer, we are told. "You are in control. You are the *only one* who can control your pain."[45] A lonely and desperate existence it is indeed, when no one else is expected to take responsibility for the impact they have on your pain. This is of course unfair and misleading. We are *not* the only one who can control our pain. When people living in pain talk among themselves about what makes the pain worse, the "self" is not the narrow self SHPM programs portray it to be. Then, the contextual reasons that can make pain worse are obvious. Yet, all SHPM programs and materials I have become familiar with are constructed around a "self" that supposedly stands in the world all alone, separate from everything and everyone around it. Everything becomes *our* angry psyche, *our* faulty cognition, *our* difficult emotions, *our* lack of problem solving skills, *our* communication problems, and whatever else that is wrong with us. Actual social and societal forces that impact our lives in pain, if noted, are at best briefly acknowledged, but mostly ignored by immediately transposing them to our psyche where they become our problem. The focus then is on how *we*, people in pain, should "not be angry," speak only in "I messages" as to not offend anyone, "forgive," use "non-aggressive language," practice "positive self talk," and deal with the "difficult emotions" by distracting ourselves, emotions often caused by social and societal neglect or abuse. This, of course, allows the helping professions to stay as far away as possible from our real life problems.

A Self help program that refuses to listen to our suicidal thoughts, our problems with employers, with insurers, and with our difficult doctors – problems which, as physician Ruth Dubin notes, "could be driving the presenting symptoms [of pain]," problems we cannot possibly deal with on our own – what kind of Self help program is that?[46]

One with a very restricted, narrow, and psychologized notion of "self." One that, however unintentionally and unconsciously, engages the blaming-the-victim attitude by turning every possible problem we encounter into a problem of our psyche, our cognition, our emotions. As others have also noted, this implicit "morality of responsibility," these "blame focused" explanatory models, stigmatize and further victimize the person in pain.[47] As Dubin also stresses, for healthcare professionals to facilitate "[T]he resolution of patients' insurance, occupational, financial and mood issues should also be an important component of the primary care plan." These words may raise eyebrows among healthcare professionals, and Dubin does not explain what would be involved, but it is provocative nevertheless to hear a physician express a view which inches closer to a societal model of chronic pain.

Pain levels: for whom are the SHPM programs?

SHPM programs are typically advertised as helping anyone living with "chronic pain." In some aspects, that may well be so: some gentle yoga, some gentle exercises, nutritional information, relaxation – all that can be helpful even to those living with severe pain. But a closer look shows it is not that straightforward.

In the SHPM programs I attended, those who clearly were in great pain, did not return for the second or subsequent sessions. In terms of program evaluation, *that* would be immensely important to evaluate in depth: Why did those in great pain not come back? After all, it is those with severe pain who often end their lives. They really do need help. What can SHPM do differently to keep people in severe pain from dropping out?

As is, SHPM programs seem to be moving toward a one-size-fit-all format, which means they become geared to the lowest common denominator. "I'll do my nails and forget about this baloney," Catalano and Hardin suggest we tell ourselves to get away from stress brought on by pain.[48] Or we can say to ourselves, "This is just a wave of pain, it never lasts more than an hour."[49] These suggestions may be fine for those who live with light pain but give them to those in serious 24/7 pain and on the brink of suicide. Who, exactly, are the authors talking to? Catalano and Hardin further think it would be great if we could get rid of all negative thoughts (also referred to as "distortions"), but feel that the most we can expect is to reduce them "by 50, 60, or even 80 percent."[50] The rest of the negative thinking, they say, is probably unconscious. To fight that, we need to engage stress-inoculation procedures, such as doing your nails. "Don't let negative thoughts creep in," they admonish.

In the 2008 program I attended with a good professional group leader, who knew how to be flexible, and how to genuinely listen to our comments, the lack of clear differentiation between pain levels was a bit less of a problem because our input was welcomed and therefore different problems for different pain levels came to the fore more easily. However, in this program too, two people, clearly in great pain, who came to the first class did not come back. In the 2010 scripted program we started with twelve people. Three of them, clearly in great pain, did not return after the first meeting. Three others dropped out later. Those in severe pain who drop out are the ones we really should be worrying about. However, I am not aware of any study that has followed up with those who have dropped out of SHPM programs.

Some voices do understand what severe pain is like. Albert Schweitzer thought of pain as a "more terrible lord of mankind" than death, and added,

> The Fellowship of those who bear the Mark of Pain...Who are the members of this fellowship? Those who have learned by experience what physical pain and bodily anguish mean, belong together all the world over; they are united by a secret bond. One and all they know the horrors of suffering to which man can be exposed, and one and all they know the longing to be free from pain.[51]

It would serve SHPM programs well if those who develop them would first listen to the Victor Frankls and the Albert Schweitzers of the world. To the Elaine Scarrys and the Alfonso Daudets. And to us. To our lives.

I feel absolutely certain that the SHPM movement leaves those of us living with severe pain out in the cold. As I am writing this, June 2014, I have just had another major pain attack: four days of cutting pain, all over the back of my skull, in the muscles on the left side of my neck, shoulder and upper back, and an excruciating headache. Today I could think clearly enough again to type this paragraph to try to capture the contrast between these days of intense pain and what I have been reading in the SHPM materials that speak of "discomfort," "aches," "feeling bad," or "flare ups." What I had the last four days is not "discomfort." Not an "ache." Not a little "flare up." It is days of deadening pain. How we use language is highly consequential.

A way has to be found to reach those who live at the edge of life, rather than exclude them either procedurally (see below) or by making them invisible behind cheerful pictures and other pleasantries.

How are these programs evaluated?

After the last session of the 2010 program I found so badly flawed, I walked out with two other people, one of whom the woman who had had to give up her German Shepherd and who had not been allowed to have suicidal thoughts. As we left the building, she said, "This was really abysmal." The other person and myself agreed. Had we been asked to fill out an evaluation (for whatever reason we had not been asked to do so), I suspect we would not have mentioned the word "abysmal." I myself probably would have given it a bit below average rating rather than a terrible one. I would have thought, they did the best they knew how and at least I got some social time with others like me.

Validity problems with quantitative evaluation scales have long been recognized in the social sciences. Most people want to please. Most people are rarely bluntly honest. Lefort et al. conducted a quantitative ranking evaluation study with a randomized treatment design, using a wait-list as the control group.[52] The treatment was the standardized program LeFort developed herself. The 2010 program I myself attended was the exact same program. LeFort et al. report short term "modest" positive trends (from 9% to 47%) in pain reduction, vitality, life satisfaction and in self efficacy and resourcefulness and less dependency on others.[53] These short term positive results make immediate sense in that SHPM programs provide a meeting place that facilitate a sense of belonging and social contact, which lifts one up, something the control group did not experience.

A few observations are important that make the modest gains actually less than modest. Program drop outs (7%) were not included. When initially assessed, they had higher pain quality scores, were more depressed, had poorer general mental health, less vitality, poorer social functioning, less self-efficacy, and poorer social functioning.[54] Unfortunately, their feedback on the program is absent. LeFort et al. attribute the dropping out to the possibility that the pain patients may not have had "enough motivation."[55] However, they were motivated enough to start the program. What is not considered is that they might have dropped out because they found the program ignoring or trivializing the severity of their pain. Attributing dropping out to "lack of motivation" while not considering other reasons, including the possibility that the program was not meeting their needs, is another example of the over-psychologizing of chronic pain, of attributing everything "negative" to the psychological make up of the person in pain.

Also, several potential participants were excluded based on a judgment of "ineligibility." Reasons for "ineligibility" included not being able to read or speak English and suffering from "major cognitive or psychiatric disorders."[56] Some who were unable to sit for a long time, likely meaning that their pain problems were severe, also did not participate. Combining the ineligible pain patients, the drop-outs, and those who could not sit long enough, it is fair to conclude that the percentage of severe chronic pain sufferers who were procedurally or programmatically excluded was not insignificant.

Physician Ruth Dubin in her SHPM program, which combines the LeFort's program with a program of exercises, procedurally excludes the frail and elderly, patients with addiction problems, those with spinal cord injuries and neuropathic pain (because exercise doesn't help), "and anyone who's not well enough to do the exercises."[57] Thus those excluded highly likely suffered from more severe forms of chronic pain. None of this is to say that these programs did not help those who participated, but it is to stress how easy it is to exclude from SHPM programs, and therefore from the program evaluation process, those who suffer most.

Further, and what LeFort et al. recognize about their own study, is the confounding aspect of leadership. All evaluation sessions were led by LeFort herself, who is a professor of nursing, and thus well experienced in leading groups. The use of a single facilitator is noted as a limitation of the study. It is hypothesized that had there been multiple facilitators it might have been possible to show that the content and process of the program made the difference, not the personal attributes of the facilitator.[58] LeFort et al. clearly want a standardized program that can be reliably delivered irrespective of who the group leader is.

But one cannot take the human element out of facilitating groups. I believe the question rather should focus *on* the human element: who the facilitator is; what kind of background does he or she need to have; what training does he or she need to do this kind of work; what kind of personality works best for a SHPM group; how good a listener he or she is; what kind of flexibility in leading a group is desired, and so forth. Leadership makes all the difference. Let's imagine that the two "peer volunteers" of the 2010 "abysmal" program I attended had conducted the sessions for the evaluation study instead of LeFort herself. We may be sure it would have rendered a different set of evaluations, and quite possibly an even higher drop-out rate.

The advocacy group Chronic Pain Australia, having tried volunteer peer led programs without success, looked to the "Scottish Model" for inspiration.[59] In Scotland the volunteer model had also first been used without much success.[60] Now professionals who are trained to lead groups, deliver SHPM programs throughout Scotland, as well as follow up monthly meetings in which the trainers "tune into the needs of groups ... reviewing whatever topics are important to that group." Clearly, other countries are also struggling with leadership in delivering SHPM groups, and the "peer volunteer" approach does not seem to work out well.

I would wish for self help programs to keep topics real. To not use popular approaches taken from elsewhere, be it from cognitive, behavioral, or humanistic psychology, without carefully considering these choices against the facts, truths, and scope of our lives. To be open to the problems we encounter that are lodged in social and societal forces. That means becoming familiar with the literature that actually describes our lives, and it means learning to genuinely listen to us.

I would wish for group leaders who know how to lead a group. How to listen to us, let us say what we need to say, while skillfully keeping the thread of the discussion in mind. It is not necessary for a group leader to have or have had chronic pain themselves. In fact, the group leader of the 2010 program I attended was so self-referential about her own experiences with pain that precious time was taken away from participants' needs. I wish for group leaders who approach people in pain as intelligent adults who understand their own lives and know the limits brought on by their pain. We need SHPM programs that differentiate pain levels so that lives lived in severe pain are no longer trivialized or ignored or excluded. Those who make administrative decisions must consider if separate programs for those living with severe pain are needed, or that, with the right leadership and flexible programming, those living with severe pain can benefit equally.

More concretely, I can imagine, for instance, speakers who are able to provide from an inside perspective, insight into how insurance companies and workman compensation processes work; who can give tips for applying for disability benefits; a lawyer who has been successful in winning cases for people living with chronic pain; an overview of particular foods that have an anti-inflammatory effect; an open discussion about suicidal thoughts. A spouse could be invited to speak on what living with someone in pain is like and how to arrange a couple's life so that the person in pain does not feel guilty and the spouse or partner does not burn out, and so forth. Real life topics. I realize that these suggestions introduce political tones, but as noted in earlier chapters, political considerations are at play everywhere in any event. Keeping real life out of SHPM programs is surely a decision that carries political impact, whether those who develop these programs are aware of it or not.

Of course my wish list does not consider how all this can be accomplished. I am "merely" a person living with pain. But that makes me and the millions like me the voice of a constituency that should play a vital role in the development and delivery of SHPM programs.

16 *To take a true measure of our days...*

In telling of our experiences of living in pain in this society, I can only hope that I have helped to stir the reader's soul and open people's hearts so that they can take a true measure of our days.

Paraphrasing physicist David Bohm, before the rise of science, "to measure" something, in the sense of therefore knowing it, meant to understand the totality of inner proportions, to understand its "innermost being."[1] A measure was a form of insight, and such insight was gained, not by conforming to external standards, but by creative insight into the deeper meanings of the structures of that which one wished to understand, and then act accordingly. It has been only since the rise of seventeenth-century science that "to measure" something has come to mean comparison to an external standard only.

True insight into lives lived in pain can only be had when the legitimacy and severity of our condition, invisible as it is, is widely acknowledged. As is, we struggle constantly for legitimacy in a society that is hardly interested in us and often doesn't believe us. How to bring fundamental change to this state of affairs?

General improvements people in pain ask for include increasing access to pain care; early interventions to prevent pain from becoming chronic; improving the education of physicians; educating pain specialists to be broadly informed and not beholden to any particular medical or psychological discipline; giving up "the conceit of cure" (the belief that if a doctor cannot cure us there is nothing else s/he can do for us); considering severe chronic pain as a state of illness on its own and finding and helping those who live in deadening isolation; exposing the deeply unjust attitudes and practices by insurance companies and work to change them; educating medical researchers in the use of a broad range of contextually valid research approaches; educating psychologists, psychiatrists, and those involved in self help programs to first learn about our day-to-day lives, to listen, to believe, and to leave us our intelligence and our dignity; educating employers to understand the need for flexible work hours and medical leaves; and educating society about the lives we live so others might adjust to keep us in their midst.

The task is huge. It seems in fact an impossible task because of the invisibility of chronic pain. Elaine Scarry's observation is crucial,

> Given the verbal signs we have for pain are so unstable and cannot portray a certainty of understanding, they can be intentionally enlisted for the opposite purposes, invoked not to coax pain into visibility but to push it further into invisibility.[2]

Following the cultural and scientific beliefs of our times, chronic pain cannot be made visible. It takes no object. It has no external referent. Therefore, we defy existing categories. Our pain, and the difficulties we experience because of the pain, cannot be proven.

But can it not?

To "coax" chronic pain into visibility, profound changes in how one understands what it means to know something must occur. Scarry's words are among the most important ones ever said about chronic pain. They elucidate why pain can so easily be doubted, denied, or misconstrued. Even intentionally misconstrued. And no one can prove that intentional misconstructions are, indeed, intentional as there is no external point of reference by which to draw such a conclusion. We live in a trap.

We need to "coax pain into visibility…" How can that be done?

I have made, I hope, a passionate argument that the field of chronic pain research needs to engage "other ways of knowing" that may have a chance to coax the invisible into the visible. The avenues and methods by which the conditions of chronic pain are claimed to be true must be changed and broadened in fundamental ways to make such coaxing possible. We need autobiography, biography, journalism, art, documentaries, theatre – ways of communicating that can more easily bring about insights into our day-to-day lives. Insights that call forth the compassionate, ethical and moral fortitudes needed for fundamental recognition and action.

The details of our day-to-day lives in all their personal and societal complexities need to be brought to the attention of the larger public as well as to all those in the helping professions who want to help but who, on the whole, do not know much, and are not required to know much, about our lives.

But it may turn out to be far more complex. It has been probably naive on my part to think that exposure of our lives by itself could bring about a major change in people's perceptions and understanding.

In February 2015, I read about a new film out of Hollywood that dealt with chronic pain, called "Cake." I couldn't believe my eyes. A Hollywood film? For the general public? I was both delighted and nervous: How would Hollywood validly portray a life lived in pain? Could it? Of course I had to see it.

To my surprise, I identified with Claire, the main character, played by Jennifer Aniston, who portrays with detailed and persistent clarity the agony of the 24/7 relentless pain in her back and legs which also disturbs her sleep. Claire had a major car accident that killed her young son and left her in relentless pain. She is swallowing pill after pill, preoccupied with counting her pain pills to make sure she has enough of them, stocked (as we all do) in various places.

The film pictures the pain support group's "drippy little exercises" (Claire's words). There is a poster on the wall where the group meets that cheerfully says: "Have a great day!" The film shows a cheerful doctor who doesn't really know what to do. It shows Claire's isolation from the world and her inability to be "social" because of her relentless pain. In the pain support group, participants are asked to come "to closure" over the recent suicide by one of them by sharing how the suicide has affected "your feelings." Images and thoughts of suicide swirl around in Claire's own head throughout much of the film.

I saw the outlines of several aspects of my life in pain accurately portrayed. The film surpassed my expectations and contributed, I thought, considerably to the need to expose the nature of our lives to the general public.

Then I read the reviews. Five of them. Only one report of a screening, where Jennifer Aniston herself was present as well as several high profile pain management professionals, addresses chronic pain as the substantive focus of the film.[3] Two other reviews mention "chronic pain" only once.[4] And one of these (the Variety review) sees the film as a "comedy drama" and as "darkly amusing," descriptions I find extremely disturbing, as there was nothing comical about the film. It appears that the reviewers, blinded by ignorance about chronic pain, could only see Aniston in her usual comedy ways, turning the chronic pain experience into one big joke. This review also rephrases the subject of the film as "a movie about addiction."

A lengthy review by Frank Bruni in the New York Times sees the film as a story about "a devastated woman's uncertain recovery."[5] There is one quote by someone else that has the word "pain" in it. Thus, the review itself never refers to chronic pain as the focus of the film. In the fifth review by Manohla Dargis, the words "chronic pain" only show up in a reference to the "touchy-feely…chronic-pain support group" Claire attends.[6] Nothing else is said about pain.

Thus four reviews, instead of relentless pain, stress as the focus of the film "grief," "loss," "addiction," "suicide," "separation," "depression," "a miasma of moans and true and false notes" and "the spectacle of female suffering."[7] Another major focus of these reviews is Claire's appearance and her psyche: she is "whiny," "pessimistic about her condition," "one hell of a pill," "permanently pissy: short of fuse, forever of headache, no fun." She has a "sallow complexion," she has undergone "uglification," she looks "drained and hideous." We emerge as an unattractive, psychological mess. Reading these reviews felt eerily similar to reading the literature that led me to write the chapters on the over-psychologizing and the psychiatrizing of chronic pain.

My own appraisal of the film and of the main character is quite different.

But that is, of course, because I understand the contexts of this woman's life. Why she acts as she does: not pissyness but ongoing draining pain; not whiny but despondent about her existential challenge; not short of fuse, but at the end of her energy; not 'no fun,' but trying to hold it together; not pessimistic, but realistically fearful of the future; not ugly and hideous, but intensely fatigued and worn out by the relentless pain and by sleep deprivation. Reviewers should stay away from reviewing what they are ignorant about. I cringed several times reading these reviews. The "spectacle of female suffering" eliciting the worst reaction on my part… Several of the published comments by readers of the reviews who live with chronic pain similarly note, some quite angrily so, that the reviewers have no idea what they are talking about.

Reading these reviews of "Cake," it frankly astonished me how easily relentless physical pain, even when so clearly exposed, can be misinterpreted. It is worse than I thought. Grief, addiction, sadness, fear, bitchiness, comedy… almost anything but chronic pain, even when it stares you in the face. It is clear that it is extraordinarily difficult to identify with something that has no external referent and is intensely undesirable to boot. Yet, identification is a fundamental act for insight, empathy and action to occur. I am reminded of Philip Coulter's words: To identify with those who live in pain requires "a conscious ethical act."[8] We can't assume, he says, that there is such a thing as natural empathy.

I now believe that at least two major and fundamentally related constructs need to be revised in our heads before exposure of our lives can have the effect we hope for: the construct of "invisible" and the related construct of "subjective."

Almost every publication about chronic pain, including my own, refers to the problem that chronic pain is "invisible" and therefore "subjective," an "aporia," a "puzzle." I bought into that for a long time. But during working on the chapter on ways of knowing, I started to see the bias in that stance. "Subjective" … "aporia" …"a puzzle" – *from whose perspective*? *Whose voices* are making that claim?

For the millions of those living in pain, there is nothing subjective about it. It is not an aporia. Not a puzzle. The pain that torments us is a hard fact. The consequences are hard facts. There is no doubt involved. To keep referring to chronic pain as "subjective" relegates it to the realm of the unknowable. But for whom is chronic pain subjective and unknowable?

Coming across the project "Pain is Not Invisible" by Chronic Pain Australia, was another occurrence that solidified in my mind the understanding that calling pain "invisible" and "subjective" is a stance that subdues the agency of the person in pain and assigns an unquestioned authority to the tyranny of method, privileging the external view.

To come to understand a life lived in pain one has to dare to imagine it. To imagine a way of life that one does not know oneself, one has to have the courage and the openness to *want to* identify. That is, indeed, an intentional, conscious, and ethical act. Doing so can cross the divide between the invisible and the visible and transcend the assumed dualism of objective vs. subjective knowledge. Once one can let go of this dualism, imagination, identification, and participation become possible. And the invisible can be "coaxed into visibility."

Imagination, identification, and participation leads to empathy and to action far more readily than does the pursuit of objectivity rendering numbers and statistics, however needed they may be for specific purposes. To understand our actual lives as lived in this society we need fundamentally human revisions of knowledge. For those who live with persistent severe pain, whether this happens or not, this can mean the difference between dying or living, between living in isolation or still finding a place of belonging in the human community.

Reference Notes

1 Models of chronic pain–lives lived in chronic pain

1. My life in pain began with a near fatal car accident in 1996. See *Inside Chronic Pain. An Intimate and Critical Account* (Ithaca, N. Y.: Cornell University Press, 2009).

2. I am aware of the question whether chronic pain is, in fact, a disease. Any other condition that disables a person, cause her/him to stop working, interrupts sleeps, causes intense fatigue, causes loss of social life, loss of relationships, would be understood to be a disease of some kind.

3. David Morris, *The Culture of Pain* (Berkeley: University of California Press, 1991), 23.

4. Ibid., Elaine Scarry, *The Body in Pain: The Making and Unmaking of the World* (New York: Oxford University Press, 1985).

5. Keith Wailoo, *Pain. A Political History* (Baltimore: Johns Hopkins University Press, 2014).

6. Ibid., 205, 212.

7. For a discussion of sub-models see John Quintner, Milton Cohen, David Buchanan James Katz & Owen Williamson, "Pain medicine and its models: helping or hindering?" *Pain Medicine*, 9 (7), 2008.

8. How "social" is your biopsychosocial model? http://wp.me/p8EuV-CU posted by adiemusfree, June 14, 2010.

9. John Loeser & Ronald Melzack, "Pain: an overview," *The Lancet*, 353, May 8, 1999, 1607.

10. Ronald Melzack, "From the gate to the neuromatrix," Pain Supplement 6, *International Association for the Study of Pain*, 1999, 121; Ronald Melzack, "Pain and the neuromatrix in the brain," *Journal of Dental Education*, 65 (12), 2001, 1378.

11. Melzack, From the gate to the neuromatrix, 124.

12. Melzack, Pain and the neuromatrix, 1381.

13. JR Rehab Services, British Columbia, "Understanding pain: What to do about it in less than five minutes." November, 2011.

14. Sally Satel and Scott Lilienfeld. *Brainwashed: The Seductive Appeal of Mindless Neuroscience* (N.Y.: Basic Books, 2013).

15. In Melanie Thernstrom, "My pain, my brain." *The New York Times Magazine*, May 14, 2006, 11.

16. Ibid.

17. John Loeser, "Pain, suffering, and the brain: A narrative of meaning," In D. Carr, J. Loeser, and D. Morris (Eds.), *Narrative, Pain, and Suffering* (Seattle: IASP Press, 2005), 17-27, 21.

18. Ibid., 22.

19. Loeser & Melzack, Pain: an overview, 1609.

20. Francisco Varela, *Ethical Know-How. Action, Wisdom, and Cognition* (Stanford CA: Stanford University Press, 1999), 6-7.

21. My own favorite works that trace various aspects of these historical developments include Richard Tarnas, *The Passion of the Western Mind. Understanding the Ideas That Have Shaped Our World View* (New York: Ballantine Books, 1991); Richard Bernstein, *Beyond Objectivism and Relativism. Science, Hermeneutics, and Praxis* (Philadelphia, University of Pennsylvania Press, 1983); Evelyn Fox Keller *Reflections on Gender and Science* (New Haven: Yale University Press, 1985).

22. Francisco J. Varela, Evan Thompson, and Eleanor Rosch, *The embodied mind. Cognitive science and human experience.* Cambridge, MA: MIT Press, 1991.

23. Scarry, The Body in Pain, 12-13.

24. Ibid., 14.

25. Quintner et al., "Pain medicine and its models: Helping or hindering?" *Pain Medicine,* 2008, 9(7), 824-834.

26. Ruth Dublin, "Trajectory of chronic non-cancer pain in six patients: A roller coaster ride." In McKenzie H., Quintner J., & Bendelow, G. *At the Edge of Being: The Aporia of Pain* (Oxford, UK: Inter-Disciplinary Press, 2012), 47, 56.

27. Amanda Nielson, "Journeys with chronic pain: Acquiring stigma along the way." In McKenzie et al. At the Edge of Being, 47-64.

28. Coralie Wales, "Being a rehabilitation professional working with people in pain in compensation systems. A Heideggerian Phenomenological Study." Unpublished Dissertation, The University of Sydney, Australia, 2011.

29. Chronic Pain Australia, Pain-Is-Not-Invisible, Interim Report, 2009, Prepared by Amanda Nielsen, Peter Copleston, & Coralie Wales.

30. Philip Coulter CBC *Ideas,* The Culture of Pain, September 22-26, 2003, 24

31. See Varela et al, The Embodied Mind, particularly pages 72-81, for an explanation why, with regard to neurological networks, the "self" cannot be pinned down but rather is a "never ending stream of experiential arisings" that are in constant coupling with the environment, 80.

32. Lewis Thomas, *The Medusa and the Snail. More Notes of a Biology Watcher* (NY: Viking Press,1979), 2,5. While *se* was also used to indicate something outside and apart (hence "separate" or "segregate"), the original root *se* or *seu* pointed directly to what we now see as "other."

2   Problematic definitions and cheerful representations

1. Harold Merskey & Nikolai Bogduk, *Classifications of Chronic Pain* (Seattle: IASP Press, 1994), 210.

2. Claudia Wallis, "The right (and wrong) way to treat pain," *Time,* February 28, 2005, 37, Canadian edition, 34.

3. Ana-Maria Vranceanu, Arthur Barsky & David Ring, "Psychosocial aspects of disabling musculoskeletal pain," *The Journal of Bone and Joint Surgery,* 91, (2009), 2.

4. Lynne Young, "Editorial redefining pain: Toward a relational definition," *Canadian Nurses' Pain Issues Working Group* Newsletter, February, 2006, 2.

5. David Biro, *The Language of Pain. Finding Words, Compassion, and Relief* (New York: Norton & Company, 2010), 18.

6. Scott Fishman, *The War On Pain,* with Lisa Berger (New York: Quill, 2001), 7.

7. Scott Fishman The Balancing Act Show 885, Nov. 6, 2008, http://www.youtube.cf/watch?v=XYmMnqxWk1o&feature=related

8. American Pain Foundation, "A reporter's guide: Covering pain and it's management," October 2008.

9. David Morris, *The Culture of Pain* (Berkeley: University of California Press, 1991), 73-74.

10. Temple Grandin and Catherine Johnson, *Animals in Translation* (New York: Scribner, 2005), 185-186.

11. Dana Jennings, Pain beyond words, and an impulse just to endure. *The New York Times*, Cases, September 22, 2009.

12. Elaine Scarry, *The Body in Pain: The Making and Unmaking of the World* (New York: Oxford University Press, 1985), 23.

13. Morris, *The Culture of Pain*, 18.

14. Efforts at formulating forever more reductionist definitions of chronic pain continue. For instance, Werner Ceusters, a neuro-psychiatrist with additional degrees in knowledge engineering and information science, is developing a software program that "will allow all pain specialists to express themselves in crystal clear terms...We will create a symptom checklist that can be understood by computers." It will describe data "in uniform and formal ways." As is, given there are no biomarkers or physiological indicators in assessing chronic pain, the pain patient "has to describe what he or she is feeling." And that subjectivity, Ceusters says, "is a serious shortcoming." (ScienceDaily, "To Help Doctors and Patients, Researchers Are Developing a 'Vocabulary of Pain.' July 27, 2011. http://www.sciencedaily.com/releases/2011/07/110726190107,htm) I fear, to borrow David Morris' words, that in the effort to remove all uncertainties, what we end up thinking about will certainly not be pain. It takes a shift in world view, both ontological and epistemological (and hence methodologically), to see subjectivity, not as a "serious shortcoming" but as a facet of human life that simply asks for a different approach to the construction of knowledge.

15. "In their words," Special Section, *Nociception?* Pain Science Division Newsletter, Canadian Physiotherapy Association, 5 (2), 2010.

16. Wikepedia

17. Milton Cohen & John Quintner, "The clinical conversation about pain: Tensions between the lived experience and the biomedical model. In McKenzie H., Quintner J., Bendelow G. (Eds.) *At the Edge of Being: The Aporia of Pain* (Oxford, England: Interdisciplinary Press), 2012, 19-35.

18. Karen Ravn, "When pain becomes chronic," *Los Angeles Times*, July 5, 2011. http://www.latimes.com/news/health/la-he-pain-brain-20100705,0,3556318

19. Will Rowe, Book Review, *Pain Community News*, The Newsletter of the American Pain Foundation, April 2010.

20. Arthur Frank, "Metaphors of pain," *Literature and Medicine*, 29 (1), 2011, 186.

21. Scarry, *The Body in Pain*, 161.

22. American Pain Foundation, "A Reporter's Guide," 8.

23. NBC's *The Today Show* aired a series on chronic pain beginning on March 28, 2005. It noted six defining characteristics, one of which was pain that "appears regularly – meaning three times a month or more."

24. David Morris recalls anecdotal evidence to this extent. David Morris, "Foreword," in Heshusius, *Inside Chronic Pain*, xvi.

25. Ruth Cronje & Owen Williamson, "Is pain ever "normal"? *Clinical Journal of Pain*, 22 (8), 2006, 692.

26. Grandin and Johnson, 186.

27. Scarry, *The Body in Pain*, 33.

28. Simone Weil, *Waiting for God* (New York: Putnam, 1951), 118. Translated by Emma Craufurd.

29. Grandin and Johnson, 185-186.

30. Sharon Kirkey, "Chronic pain sufferers say doctors don't want to treat them." Post-media News. October 13, 2011. http://new.calgaryherald.com/story_print.html?id=5546170

31. Marni Jackson, *Pain: The Science and Culture of Why We Hurt* (Toronto: Vintage Canada, 2002), 34, 39-40.

32 JR Rehab Services, British Columbia, "Understanding pain: What to do about it in less than five minutes." November, 2011. This video quickly appeared at various pain web sites, e.g. http://paintoolkit.org/information and BCPain

33. The Pain Tool Kit. http://paintoolkit.org/information

34. Robert Bazell, "Chronic pain frustrates patients, doctors." *MSNBC* Nightly News with Brian Williams, January 6, 2006, 1.

35. Colin Fernandes, "Coming to know the limits of healing." *The New York Times,* Health, September 8, 2009.

36. American Pain Foundation, PainSafe. Safety & Access for Everyone http://www.painfoundation.org/painsafe/

37. Lawrence LeShan & Henry Margenau, *Einstein's Space and Van Gogh's Sky. Physical Reality and Beyond* (The Harvester Press, 1982). 160.

38. Biro, *The language of Pain,* 123-124, 216-218.

39. Frank "*Metaphors* of pain," 182.

40. Biro, *The Language of Pain,* 173-176.

41. http://www.PainExhibit.com

42. Tara Parker-Pope, "Pain as an art form.". *The New York Times-Well,* April 22, 2008.

43. Biro, *The Language of Pain,* 180.

44. Elaine Scarry, *The Body in Pain,* 9.

45. Sharon Kirkey, "Who will stop the pain?" *Vancouver Sun,* October 2, 2011, 1.

3   Our healthcare: problems and wish-lists

1. Scott M. Fishman, "Clinical Commentary." In Lous Heshusius, *Inside Chronic Pain. An Intimate and Critical Account (*Ithaca, N.Y.: Cornell University, 2009), 131.

2. David Biro, "If Only There Were a Pain Scanner," Listening to Pain Blog, *Psychology Today,* August 31, 2011. http://psychologytoday.com/em/73227

3. Committee on Advancing Pain Research, Care, and Education; Institute of Medicine, "Relieving Pain in America: A Blueprint for Transforming Prevention, Care, Education, and Research." July, 2011.

4. Tara Parker-Pope, "Giving Chronic Pain a Medical Platform of Its Own." *The New York Times-Well,* July 18, 2011.

5. Terri Hayes, personal communication, September, 2010.

6. Media-Newswire, "UC Davis receives grant to develop pain management curriculum." http://media-newswire.com/release_1156314.html

7. Kevin Pho, "Pain management education is key." *USA Today,* The Forum, September 19, 2011, 9A.

8. Newswise, "Pain education in medical schools needs improvement." December 22, 2011.

9. Chronic Pain Association of Canada, "Physician often unarmed against pain." Newsletter, Vol. 14, 1, 2010, 6.

10. See e.g., "Mayday panel report urges revolution in pain care." November 6, 2009, http://updates.pain-topics.org/2009/11/mayday-panel-report-urges-revolution-in.html The Mayday report was written by a 22-member panel and endorsed by more than 30 organizations. See also "Relieving Pain in America," a report mandated by the US Congress and supported by the National Institutes of Health, July 2011.

11. Heshusius, Inside Chronic Pain, pp. 53-59.

12. A. Dewar, K. Gregg, M. White, & J. Lander, "Navigating the health care system: perceptions of patients with chronic pain." Public health Agency of Canada, Chronic Diseases in Canada. Volume 29, 4, October 2009, 5.

13. Scott Fishman, *The War on Pain*, with Lisa Berger (N.Y.: Quill, 2001), 34.

14. ibid., 144.

15. Will Rowe, "The pain care maze." ChronicPainConnection.com. http://www.healthcentral.com/chronic-pain/c/3025/31015/pain-care-maze/pf

16. See Inside Chronic Pain, pp. 62-63.

17. In Elisabeth Rosenthal, "How back pain turned deadly." *The New York Times*, November 17, 2012, 2-3.

18. Ibid., 1.

19. Life is Now Newsletter. "Understanding and Interpreting the NRS and VAS: Part 2, the patient's view."

20. David B. Morris, *The Culture of Pain* (Berkeley: University of California Press, 1991), 72-74.

21. Alan Basbaum, Pain and the Brain video, 2007, http://www.youtube.com/watch?v=gQS0tdIbJ0w It is much easier to think about or imagine love or fear which directly relate to an external referent. You can re-experience it. You can imagine pleasure or fear or anger, because these states are wrapped up in someone or something. But as Elaine Scarry (in *The Body in Pain*) so brilliantly discusses, pain is the only state of being that is not about something or someone: it takes no object. It is therefore impossible to re-experience it.

22. Personal communication, Dr. Gary Lea, December 2011.

23. Coralie Wales, President of Chronic Pain Australia, personal communication, December 4, 2011, printed with permission.

24. Arthur Frank, in Mary Buchinger Bodwell, "How to listen to chronic pain narratives." In *Making Sense of Pain. Critical and Interdisciplinary Perspectives* (Ed. Jane Fernandez), (Oxford, UK: Inter-Disciplinary Press), 2010, 157.

25. See e.g. Richard Payne, "Hurting While Black: Racially Based Disparities in Pain Care," Newsletter of the American Pain Foundation, Summer 2003, 5; American Pain Society, "Racial and Ethnic Identifiers in Pain Management: The Importance to Research, Clinical Practice, and Public Health Policy," October 122, 2004, http://www.ampainsoc.org/advocacy/ethnoracial.htm; Carla Johnson, "Whites More Likely to Get ER Narcotics," Washingtonpost.com, January 1, 2008. Also, women are more likely to be undertreated or inappropriately diagnosed for their pain, their complaints ignored or attributed to emotional unbalance or anxiety. Women are more likely to be given sedatives while men are more likely to receive pain medication, and attractive females are thought to be experiencing less pain than unattractive ones because of the association of beauty with health. See Diane Hoffman and Anita Tarzian, "The Girl Who Cried Pain: A Bias against Women in the Treatment of Pain," *Journal of Law, Medicine and Ethics*, 29, 2001.

26. John D. Loeser, "Pain, Suffering, and the Brain: A narrative of Meanings," In D. Carr, J. Loeser, and D. Morris (Eds.), *Narrative, Pain, and Suffering* (Seattle: IASP Press, 2005), 26.

27. Heshusius, Inside Chronic Pain, 6-7.

28. www.AmericanNurseToday.com Special Report, War on Pain, Sept. 2011,10; Michelle Tan, "Army on brink of new ways to fight pain," *ArmyTimes*, July 11, 2011, 3.

29. Atul Gawande, *Complications: A Surgeon's Notes on an Imperfect Science* (New York: Henry Holt, 2003), 118.

30. Michael Stein, *The Lonely Patient: How We Experience Illness* (New York: William Morrow, 2007), 20.

31. Will Rowe, in Robert Boyd, McClatchy Washington Bureau, "Adequate pain care sorely lacking for patients," October 29, 2008

32. Meghan O'Rourke, "Doctors tell all and it's far worse than you think." *The Atlantic,* November, 2014, 111.

33. Matthew Bair, " Pain management: A look at provider perspectives," *Pain Medicine,* November, 2010, as abstracted in Physician's Weekly. http://www.physiciansweekly.com/Features/11_37/pain_management.html

34. National Institute on Alcohol Abuse and Alcoholism, "Using alcohol to relieve your pain: what are the risks?" www.nih.niaaa.gov

35. Allan Basbaum, Pain and the Brain video, 2007, http://www.youtube.com/watch?v=gQS0tdIbJ0w

36. See e.g. Dirk Johnson, "A $42 million gift aims at improving bedside manner," *The New York Times,* September 22, 2011.

37. John Ware, "What and who is the "difficult" patient?" The role of stress and central sensitization in persistent widespread musculoskeleton pain. Unpublished paper, Spring 2010.

38. Abraham Verghese, "Abraham Verghese on Dialogue." Idaho Public Television, Dec. 5, 2009.

39. Sean Hayes, Genevieve Myhal, John Thorton, Monique Camerlain, Cynthia Jamison, Kayla Cytryn & Suzanne Murray, "Fibromyalgia and the therapeutic relationship: Where uncertainy meets attitude," *Pain Research & Management*, 15 (6), November/December, 2010, 388.

40. Pauline Chen: A Surgeon's Reflection. February 23, 2007. http://paulinechen.typepad.com/ 6.

41. Stephanie J. Davies, Christopher Hayes, & John L. Quintner, "System Plasticity and Integrated Care: Informed Consumers Guide Clinical Reorientation and System Organization," *Pain Medicine,* 12, 2011, 6.

42. Rita Charon, "A narrative medicine for pain," In Carr et all., *Narrative, Pain, and Suffering,* 29, 31.

43. In Pauline W. Chen, "Stories in the service of making a better doctor." *The New York Times,* Health, October 24, 2008, 1.

44. In Melanie Thernstrom, "The writing cure." In Carr et al. (eds.), *Narrative Pain, and Suffering,* 50-51.

45. Heidi Pomm, "Psychological aspects of chronic, nonmalignant pain: Moving from "reality vertigo" to hope," *Northeast Florida Medicine,* Summer 2005. http://www.dcmsonline.org/jax-medicine/2005journals/PainManagement/psychological.pdf

46. Gawande, *Complications,* 118.

47. Teresa Flynn, "Pain Coalition: Academy Unites with Top Pain Organizations to Bridge Communication Gap between Providers and Patients," *The Pain Practitioner,* Fall,16. 2008.

48.   Gina Kolata "When the doctor is in, but you wish he weren't." *The New York Times*, Health, November 30, 2005. http://www.nytimes.com/2005/11/30/health/30patient.html?en=5070&en=Ofc8394987cafded…

49.   In Tara Parker-Pope, "When doctors become patients." *The New York Times*, Well, February 8, 2008.

50.   Dave: Doctor with pain. Chronic Pain Australia, Stories. http://www.painaustralia. org.au/stories/

51.   Liesl Fulton, January 2012, printed with permission.

52.   Peter Watson, "A last poem from Susan," *Pain Research & Management*, 17 (1), 2012, 9.

4   Over-psychologizing chronic pain: stripping context, forgetting the body

1.   In Melanie Thernstrom, *The Pain Chronicles* (N.Y.: Farrar, Straus and Giroux, 2010), 58.

2.   Ellen Mohr Catalano & Kimeron Hardin. *The Chronic Pain Control Workbook* (Oakland, CA: Harbinger Publications, 1996), 91.

3.   Patrick Wall, *Pain: The Science of Suffering* (New York: Columbia University Press. 2000).

4.   Francis Keefe, Meredith Rumble, Cindy Scipio, Louis Giordano, & LisaCaitlin Perri, "Psychological aspects of persistent pain: Current state of the science," *The Journal of Pain*, 5 (4), 2004, 195-211.

5.   Harald Gundel & Thomas Tolle, "How physical pain may interact with psychological pain: Evidence of mutual neurobiological basis of emotions and pain." In D. Carr et al. (Eds.) *Narrative, Pain, and Suffering* (Seatle: IASP Press), 2005, 88-89.

6.   In Sandra P. Thomas and Mary Johnson, "A phenomenological study of chronic pain," *Western Journal of Nursing Research*, 2000, 22, 684.

7.   Gundel & Tolle, 89.

8.   Jingai Cui, Eisuke Matsushima, Katsuko Aso, Akio Masuda, & Koshi Makita. "Psychological features and coping styles in patients with chronic pain," *Psychiatry and Clinical Neurosciences*, 63, 2009, 151.

9.   Richard Chapman & Ernest Volinn, "Narrative as a window on chronic, disabling backpain." In Carr et al., *Narrative*, 82.

10.   Robert Teasell and Harold Merskey, "Chronic pain disability in the workplace," *Pain Research and Management*, 2 (no. 4) 1997. 199-200; Patrick Wall, *Pain*, 155-156.

11.   David Morris, *The Culture of Pain* (Berkeley: University of California Press, 1991), 73-74.

12.   http://www.forgrace.org/women/in/pain_home/ Click on "One's woman's dance with the pain experience."

13.   Such as Sandra Thomas & Mary Johnson, "A phenomenological study of chronic pain," *Western Journal of Nursing Research*, 22, 2000, 683-699; Marni Jackson, *Pain: The Science and Culture of Why We Hurt* (Toronto: Vintage Canada, 2002); Arthur Rosenblat, *The Truth about Chronic Pain* (New York: Basic Books, 2003).

14.   Such as Elaine Scarry, *The Body in Pain: The making and Unmaking of the World* (New York: Alfred A. Knopf, 2002); and David Morris, *The Culture of Pain*.

15.   Alphonse Daudet, *In the Land of Pain*, ed. and trans. Julian Barnes (New York: Alfred A. Knopf, 2002). Virginia Woolf, *On Being Ill* (Ashfield, MA: Paris Press, 2002).

16.   Sociologist Arthur W. Frank, *At the Will of the Body* (Boston: Houghton Mifflin 2002), and *The Wounded Story Teller: Body, Illness, and Ethics* (Chicago: University of Chicago Press, 1995); physician David Biro, *The Language of Pain. Finding Words, Compassion, and Relief* (New York: Norton & Company, 2010).

17. James Giodano, "Pain, depression, brain-mind, and healing: The potential complementarity of process and purpose. *The Pain Practitioner,* 18 (2), 2008, 7.

18. Rachel Wurzman, Wayne Jonas, and James Giodano, "Chronic pain and depression: A spectrum disorder? *The Pain Practitioner,* 18 (2), 2008, 25.

19. In Lennie Duensing, "Working to help others: A prescription for pain and depression," *The Pain Practitioner,* 18 (2), 2008, 63-64.

20. Ibid., 65.

21. Operant conditioning came out of laboratory studies with very unhappy rats and pigeons kept isolated and at a low weight, so they would do anything to get food. That way researchers could establish nearly any behavior by rewarding them with food the moment the animals moved in a way researchers wanted them to, or extinguish behaviors by a punishing response. I personally think, we should always be aware and knowledgeable of how a theory was generated, on what basis and by what kind of assumptions, before we bet on it.

22. Un-authored review of an article by "Pain Focus," published by Centres for Pain Management in Canada. Volume 4, 2008, 2.

23. See Patrick Wall, *Pain,* 156; and Robert Teasell, "The denial of chronic pain." 1997. http://www.pulsus.com/Pain/02_02/teas_ed.htm

24. In Luis Buenaver, Robert Edwards, and Jennifer Haythornthwaite. "Pain-related catastrophizing and perceived social responses: Inter-relationships in the context of chronic pain," *Pain,* 127 (3), 2007, 234-242, 2. http://www.ncbi.nlm.nih.gov/pmc/articles/PMC1866270/

25. Pam Squire, "Chronic pain: The disease." University of British Columbia. www.painbc.ca

26. Keefe et al., "Psychological aspects of persistent pain," 207.

27. A. Dewar, K. Gregg, M. White, & J. Lander, "Navigating the health care system: Perceptions of patients with chronic pain," *Chronic Diseases in Canada,* 29 (4) October, 2009. Public Health Agency of Canada.

28. Joanne Dahl and Tobias Lundgren, *Living Beyond Your Pain. Using Acceptance & Commitment Therapy to Ease Chronic Pain* (Oakland, CA: New Harbinger Publications, 2006).

29. John Cloud, "The third wave of therapy." *Time,* February 5, 2006, 1. http://www.time.com/time/printout/0,8816,1156613,00.html

30. Leroy Sievers, American Cancer Society, as quoted by Rebecca Kirch, "Taking action to control cancer pain." Cancer Action Network, October, 2008.

31. Cynthia, "Dancing an unwanted dance." Voices, The American Pain Foundation. April 16, 2008.

32. No author mentioned. "Chronic pain journal update." February 5, 2004. http://rockhawk.com/chronic_pain_journal_update_02_05_2004.htm

33. Jane Brody, "A new set of knees comes at a price: A whole lot of pain." *The New York Times,* Personal Health, February 8, 2005.

34. Alphonse Daudet, *In the Land of Pain,* 65, 68.

35. Jerome Groopman, *The Measure of Our Days* (New York: Penguin Books, 1997), 189.

36. Elaine Scarry, *The Body in Pain,* 31.

37. David Biro, *The Language of Pain. Finding Words, Compassion, and Relief* (New York: Norton & Company, 2010), 18.

38. Nicole Tang & Catherine Crane, "Suicidality in chronic pain: A review of the prevalence, risk factors and psychological links," *Psychological Medicine,* 36, 2006, 575.

39. Ibid., 582-583.

40. Today Entertainment, msnbc.com, November 25, 2005.

41. Ibid., 582
42. Tang & Crane, 583.
43. Tang & Crane, 583.
44. In Tang and Crane, 578.
45. Tang and Crane, 581.

5   Please don't do this to us: the psychiatrizing of chronic pain

1. Robert Whitaker, *Anatomy of an Epidemic. Magic Bullets, Psychiatric Drugs, and the Astonishing Rise of Mental Illness* (NY: Crown Publisher, 2010), 10.

2. Daniel Carlat, *Unhinged. The Trouble with Psychiatry. A Doctor's Revelations about a Profession in Crisis* (NY: Free Press, 2010), 47.

3. Thomas Insel, "Director's blog: Transforming diagnosis." The National Institute of Mental Health, April 29, 2013.

4. Carlat, *Unhinged*, 53, 54.

5. Daniel Carlat, "Mind over meds," April 19, 2010, www.nytimes.com/2010/04/25/magazine/25Memoir-t.html?ref=general&src=me&pagewanted, 3.

6. Carlat, *Unhinged*, 13.

7. Carlat, Mind over meds, 3.

8. in Gardiner Harris, "Talk doesn't pay, so psychiatry turns to drug therapy," March 5, 2011, www.nytimes.com/2011/03/06/health/policy/06doctors.html?_r=1&nl=todaysheadlines&emc-tha23&pagewanted, 7.

9. Benedict Carey, "Robert Spitzer, psychiatrist who set rigorous standards for diagnosis, dies at 83." *The New York Times*, Dec. 26, 2015, 4.

10. According to Wikipedia, the gathering of statistical information on mental illness – of being seen as 'normal' or 'not normal' – started in 1840 with one single diagnosis: "idiocy/insanity." By 1917 there were 22 diagnoses. The first edition of the DSM in 1952 contained 106 diagnoses and was 130 pages long. The third edition in 1980 listed 265 diagnoses and was 494 pages long. The fourth edition in 1994 contained 297 diagnoses written up in 886 pages.

11. *The New York Times*, "Sunday dialogue: Defining mental illness. Readers discuss criticisms of how conditions are diagnosed." March 23, 2013, 2.

12. Christina Iorio, Constantina Tsirgielis, Elizabeth Pawluk, Monica Vermani, Martin Katzman, "Examining the prevalence of psychiatric features within a chronic pain population," Poster Session, Canadian Pain Society Conference, May 14, 2010; Geralyn Datz, "Psychological assessment for the prevention of misuse in opioid therapy," *The Pain Practitioner* 19, no. 3 (2009).

13. Datz, Psychological assessment, 27, 31.

14. Ibid., 27-31.

15. Ibid., 32.

16. Ibid., 27-28.

17. Marcia Angell, "The Epidemic of Mental Illness: Why?" *The New York Review of Books*, June 23, 2011, 2, 3.

18. Carlat, Mind over meds, 8.

19. Chinua Achebe, *Home and Exile* (NY: Random House, 2001), 24.

20. See my essay about my therapist Dr. Brian Grady, in Lous Heshusius, *Inside Chronic Pain. An Intimate and Critical Account* (NY: Cornell University Press, 2009), 113-115.

21. Other metaphors that point to chaos and vulnerability of lives lived in pain and the unpredictability of pain attacks includes that of a "sandcastle" used by Marni Jackson (*Pain, The Science and Culture of Why We Hurt*. Toronto: Vintage Canada, 2002, 19). Pain as the

"devil" and as the "torturer" are other often used metaphors. For an in-depth discussion on the role of metaphor in communicating about pain see David Biro, *The Language of Pain. Finding Words, Compassion, and Relief* (NY: W.W. Norton, 2010).

22. Viktor Frankl, *Man's Search for Meaning* (NY: Simon and Schuster, 1984), 125.

23. Viktor Frankl, *The Doctor and the Soul. From Psychotherapy to Logotherapy* (NY: Vintage Books, 1986, second edition), 184. Victor Frankl, a psychiatrist survived three years of Auschwitz and Dachau. He became known world wide for his understanding of the crucial role of meaning and purpose in life, no matter how difficult a life it is. Based on that belief, he developed "logotheraphy" – a psychotherapy that rather than focusing on diagnosing pathology, helps a patient find meaning in the midst of and in spite of their suffering.

24. Scott Fishman, "Clinical Commentary." In Heshusius, *Inside Chronic Pain*, 136.c

25. Patrick Wall, *Pain: The Science of Suffering* (NY: Columbia University Press, 2000). 156-157.

26. Polly Young-Eisendrath, *The Gifts of Suffering* (NY: Addison-Wesley, 1997), 40.

27. Harold Merskey and Robert Teasell, "The disparagement of pain: Social influences on medical thinking," *Pain Research and Management*, 5, no.4 (2000), 266.

28. www.eorthopod.com/content/what-is-pain-catastrophizing

29. Francis Keefe, Meredith Rumble, Cindy Scipio, Louis Giordano, Lisa Caitlin Perri, "Psychological aspects of persistent pain: Current state of the science," *The Journal of Pain*, 5, no. 4 (2004), 196.

30. William Simon, George Ehrlich, Arnold Sadwin, *Conquering Chronic Pain After Injury* (NY: Alvery Books, 2002), 86.

31. Ana-Maria Vranceanu, Arthur Barsky, David Ring, "Psychosocial aspects of disabling musculoskeletal pain," *The Journal of Bone and Joint Surgery*, 91 (2009), 2015.

32. Charles Barber, *Comfortably Numb. How Psychiatry is Medicating a Nation* (NY: Pantheon Books, 2008), 142.

33. Irene Tracey, "Taking the narrative out of pain: Objectifying pain through brain imaging," in Carr et al., *Narrative*, 157.

34. Nicole Tang and Catherine Crane, "Suicidality in chronic pain: A review of the prevalence, risk factors and psychological links," *Psychological Medicine*, 36 (2006), 582-583.

35. Dean Tripp, "Catastrophizing and urogenital chronic pelvic pain syndrome: What do we now know?" Conference abstracts, Canadian Pain Society, *Pain Research and Management*, 15, no. 2 (2010), 88.

36. *Neurology Now*, March/April (2009) 24.

37. Michael Sullivan, Scott Bishop, Jayne Pivik, "The pain catastrophizing scale: Development and validation," *Psychological Assessment*, 7, no.4 (1995), 524.

38. Vranceanu et al., 2015.

39. Mark Sullivan and David Zucker, "Becoming mindful of pain narratives," in Carr et al., *Narrative*, 320.

40. Ibid., 320.

41. Sandra Thomas, "A phenomenological study of chronic pain," *Western Journal of Nursing Research*, 22, no. 6 (2000), 689, 693.

42. Carrie Norman, Jacqueline Bender, Jaime Macdonald, Marcia Dunn, Scott Dunn, Bo Siu, Sander Hitzig, Alejandro Jadad & Judith Hunter. "Questions that individuals with spinal cord injury have regarding their chronic pain: A qualitative study," *Disability and Rehabilitation*, 32, no.2 (2010), 119.

43. Sullivan et al., The pain catastrophizing scale, 526.

44. See Francis Keefe, Meredith Rumble, Cindy Scipio, Louis Giordano, & LisaCaitlin Perri, "Psychological aspects of persistent pain: Current state of the science," *The Journal of Pain,* 5 (4), 2004, 195-211.

45. Mark Sullivan, "Exaggerated pain behavior: By what standard?" *Clinical Journal of Pain,* 20, no. 6, (2004), 433.

46. Melanie Thernstrom, *The Pain Chronicles. Cures, Myths, Mysteries, Prayers, Diaries, Brain Scans, Healing, and the Science of Suffering* (NY: Farrar, Straus and Giroux, 2010), 134

47. Thomas, A phenomenolagial study, 691.

48. Ibid., 696.

49. Lennie Duensing, "Working to help others: A prescription for pain and depression," *The Pain Practitioner,* 18, no. 2 (2008), 64.

50. Leslie Broun, personal communication, Sept. 4, 2014, printed with permission.

51. Personal communication, December, 2010.

52. Catherine Berardenucci, in "The Culture of Pain," *IDEAS,* Canadian Broadcast Cooperation, September 22, 2003.

53. Liesl Fulton, personal communication, August, 2009.

54. David Biro, "Book review," *Health: An Interdisciplinary Journal for the Social Study of Health, Illness, and Medicine,* 2011, 15(2), 1.

55. Sullivan, Bishop, Pivik, "The catastrophizing scale," 529.

56. Michael Geisser, Michael Robinson, Francis Keefe, Marni Weiner, "Catastrophizing, depression and the sensory, affective and evaluative aspects of chronic pain," Abstract, *Pain,* 59, no. 1 (1994), 79.

57. Rudy Severeijnsa et al. "Models of pain catastrophizing," http://dolor.blogspot.com/2005/02/models-of-ipain-catastrophizing.html, 2-5.

58. Sullivan et al. cited in Severijnsa et al.; Gracely et al. cited in Harald Gundel and Thomas Tolle , "How physical pain may interact with psychological pain: Evidence for a mutual neurobiological basis of emotions and pain," in Carr et al., *Narrative,* 97.

59. Bonnie O'Connor. "Book review – Inside Chronic Pain." Canadian Pain Society Newsletter, (Winter 2010), 12.

60. James Baldwin, *Nobody Knows My Name* (NY: Dial Press, 1961), 13.

61. In Brian Katz, "James Baldwin talks with Frederick Nietzsche and others." *The Liberator Magazine,* 4.2 no.10, undated, 3., http://weblog.liberatormagazine.com/2011/01/dialogue-across-time-james-baldwin.html

62. In Carlat, *Unhinged,* 195-196.

63. Elaine Scarry, *The Body in Pain: The Making and Unmaking of the World* (NY: Oxford University Press, 1985), 4.

64. David Buchanan, personal communication, December, 2011.

65. Dave Walton, "Research news and views. *Nociception?*" Pain Science Division, Canadian Physiotherapy Association, 2(5), Sept-Oct., 2010.

66. Teasell and Merskey, Chronic pain disability, 201.

67. Merskey and Teasell, The disparagement of pain, 266.

68. Reliable data on malingering or secondary gain seeking among people living with pain is not available. I have come across figures ranging from 1.25% to 50%. Fishbain et al. review 68 studies on the relation between various variations of the construct "malingering" and chronic pain. (D.A. Fishbain, R. Cutler, H.L. Rosooff, R.S. Rosomoff, "Chronic pain disability exaggeration/malingering and submaximal effort rsearch," *The Clinical Journal of Pain,* 15, 4, 1999.) They conclude that prevalence percentages are not reliable due to poor study quality and that no conclusion can be drawn from these data. Mark Sullivan ("Exaggerated pain be-

havior: By what standard?" *The Clinical Journal of Pain*, 20, 6, 2004, 433) summarizes the main problem: pain behavior cannot be validated by matching public pain behavior with private pain experience. The pain experience is not available to scientific investigation due to the highly variable relation between clinical pain and tissue damage.

69. Gary Lea, "Secondary traumatization of work-related rehabilitation clients," *The Canadian Practitioner. A Newsletter for Mental Health Providers*. April 1996, no. 22.

70. Ibid., 5, 6.

71. Personal communication, December 2010.

72. In "Voices in Pain" and "10.000 Voices" which appeared on the former American Pain Foundation web site, and "Pain-Is-Not-Invisible" project on the web site of Chronic Pain Australia.

73. Vranceanu et al., 2014-2015.

74. Teasell and Merskey, "Chronic pain disability," 201

75. In Teasell and Merskey, "Chronic pain disability, 201.

76. Fishman, Book review, 137-138.

77. in Thomas, "A phenomenological study," 692.

6   Health economics: who pays? what is paid? what is not? why?

1. Darlene Field, "Disparities in pain management: An expert interview with Carmen R. Green, MD." http://www.medscape.com/viewarticle/581003

2. See for instance the many similar stories on the web site of the Chronic Pain Association of Australia under "Pain Is Not Invisible Project."

3. Barbara Kivowitz, "How much does living with chronic pain really cost? A patient's perspective," *The Pain Practitioner*, 19 (1), 2009, 31.

4. Scott Fishman, *The War on Pain*, with Lisa Berger (NY: Quill, 2001), 94.

5. Melanie Thernstrom, *The Pain Chronicles* (NY: Farrar, Strauss and Giroux, 2010), 11.

6. Michelle Andrews, "Treating chronic pain and managing the bills." *The New York Times*, Health, February 2, 2011, 2.

7. Jeanne Lazo, "The comorbidity of pain and disability, and tips for pain practitioners," *The Pain Practitioner*, 19 (1), 40.

8. Susan Okie, "Teaching physicians the price of care." *The New York Times*, Health, May 3, 2010.

9. In Holly VanScoy, "Drugs are sometimes abused, but they have great benefits," *Health-Scout*, Oct. 3, 2002, 1.

10. David Morris, *The Culture of Pain* (Berkeley: University of California Press, 1991, 67, 70.

11. Scott Fishman, *The War On Pain*, with Lisa Berger (NY: Quill, 2001), 57.

12. Prolotherapy may be covered now in some areas depending on which professional does it.

13. Scott Fishman, "Clinical commentary." In Heshusius, *Inside Chronic Pain,* 141.

14. Abraham Verghese. The myth of prevention. WSJ.com. June 20, 2009.

7   Drugs: my hate/need affair

1. *The Economist*, "Vioxx Nation." January 29, 2005, 78; Alex Berenson, Gardiner Harris, Barry Meier, Andres Pollack, "In face of warnings, drug giant took long path to Vioxx recall." *The New York Times*, November 14, 2004, 1; Alex Berenson, "Merck agrees to settle Vioxx suits for $4.85 billion, *The New York Times*, November 2, 2007, 1.

2. http://www.healthtalk.ca/misleading_claims_07252004_8290.php, 1,2. The company lied about the increased risk for diabetes caused by Risperdal. Several of the product liability suits resulted from Risperdal causing lactating breasts in boys.

3. Jef Feeley and Janelle Lawrence, "Pfizer agrees to first settlement of a Neurontin-related suicide lawsuit." http://www.bloomberg.com/news/2010-04-02/pfizer-agrees-to-first-settlement-of-a-neurontin-related-suicide-lawsuits.html. See also Ashby Jones, "On trial, starting monday: Does Pfizer drug raise suicide risk?" *Law Blog*, July 27, 2009, 1, http://blogs.wsj.com/law/2009/07/27/on-trial-starting-monday-does-pfizer-drug-raise-suicide-risk/; Alicia Ault, "FDA seeks suicide data for 14 anticonvulsants," *Family Practice News*, June 15, 2005; CBC News, "Anti-seizure drug promotion faces legal fire." February 22, 2010. http://www.cbc.ca/news/health/story/2010/02/22/gabapentin-neurontin-lawsuit.html

4. Ehong, France 24 International News, March 9, 2009. http://www.france24.com/en/print/4832045?

5. Gardiner Harris, "F.D.A. to place new limits on prescription of narcotics," *The New York Times*, February 10, 2009, 2. http://www.nytimes.com/2009/02/10/health/policy/10fda.html?

6. Harriet Ryan, "You want a description of hell? Oxycontin's 12-hour problem." (http://www.latimes.com/la-bio-harriet-ryan-staff.html.), Lisa Girion and Scott Glover, May 5, 2016

7. Gardiner Harris and Duff Wilson "Glaxo to Pay $750 million for sale of bad products." *The New York Times*, October 26, 2010. http://www.nytimes.com/2010/10/27/business/27drug.html See also, Jim Edwards, "Worse than you think: 10 things you don't know about Glaxo's $750M Paxil settlement." CBS Interactive Business Network, October 27, 2010.

8. *USA Newsweek*, "Glaxo to book $2.4 billion to settle legal cases, including Avandia, Paxil." July 15, 2010. http://www.cchrint.org/2010/07/15/glaxo-to-book-2-4-billion-to-settle-legal-cases-including-avandia-paxil/ Lea Yu, "GlaxoSmithKline settles 200 birth defects cases linked to antidepressant." http://www.cchrint.org/2010/06/25/glaxosmithkline-enters-into-confidential-settlement-with-200-families-who-say-paxil-caused-birth-defects/

9. Tom Moylan, "Forest pharmaceuticals pleads guilty, pays $313M for off-label promotion, obstruction." September 16, 2010. http://www.lexisnexis.com/community/litigationresourcecenter/blogs/liti...icals-pleads-guilty-pays-313m-for-off-label-promotion-obstruction.aspx

10. Robert Whitaker, *Anatomy of an Epidemic. Magic Bullets, Psychiatric Drugs, and the Astonishing Rise of Mental Illness* (NY: Crown Publisher, 2010), 284-285. Eli Lilly also pleaded guilty to illegally marketing their anti-psychotic drug Zyprexa, their top seller for years. Lilly developed the drug for schizophrenia and bipolar disorder but also marketed it for dementia and Alzheimer's.

11. http://addictiontreatmenttips.com/first-mirapex-gambling-addiction-trial-results-in-8-2-million-judgment-for-plaintiff/, 2, 3.

12. Thomas Easton & Stephen Herrera, "J&J's dirty little secret." http://torahview.com/bris/html/tylenol.html, 23 May, 2006.

16. Associated Press, "Eli Lilly settles Zyprexa lawsuit for $1.42 billion." January 15, 2009. http://www.msnbc.com/id/28677805/ns/health-health_care/t/eli-lilly-settles-zyprexa-lawsuit-billion/, 1

14. Steve Buist, Luma Muhtadie, Joan Walters, "Worry grows as MDs prescribe drugs for unapproved uses; Blind faith - fourth of a five part series," The Hamilton Spectator, June 29, 2005, 1. In http://www.alancassels.com

15. As Nicholas Kristof reports, the drug industry is getting even greedier by pushing for a First Amendment right to market its drugs for off-label uses. (Drugs, Greed, and a Dead Boy, *The New York Times* Op-Ed, Nov. 5, 2015).

16. Duff Wilson, "Drug maker wrote book under 2 doctors' names, documents say," *The New York Times*, Business Day, November 29, 2010. http://www.nytimes.com/2010/11/30/business/30drug.html? See also Natasha Singer, "Medical papers by ghostwriters pushed therapy," *The New York Times*, August 5, 2009. http://www.nytimes.com/2009/08/05/health/research/05ghost.html?; Stephanie Saul, "Merck wrote drug studies for doctors," *The New York Times*, Business, April 16, 2008. http://www.nytimes.com/2008/04/16/business/16vioxx.html?

17. Stephen Hall, "The drug lords," *The New York Times Book Review*, November 14, 2004, 9; Hall reviews Marcia Angell, *The truth about the drug companies: How they deceive us and what to do about It* (NY: Random House, 2005) and Jerry Avorn, *Powerful medicines: The benefits, risks, and cost of prescription drugs* (NY: Alfred A. Knopf, 2004). See also Marcia Angell "Drug companies & doctors: A story of corruption," *The New York Review of Books*, 56, no. 1, January 15, 2009.

18. Abigail Field, "Johnson & Johnson Subsidiary loses first Levaquin sawsuit," Daily Finance, December 9, 2010. http://www.dailyfinance.com/2010/12/09/johnson-and-johnson-ortho-loses-first-levaquin-lawsuit/

19. Jeremy Pelofsky, "J&J settles U.S., UK bribery, kickback charges," Business & Financial News, Reuters. April 8, 2011. http://www.reuters.com/assets/print?aid=US-TRE7374ZB20110408, 1; Duff Wilson, "Side effects may include lawsuits," *The New York Times*, Business Day, October 2, 2010, 8. http://www.nytimes.com/2010/10/03/business/03psych.html?, 8.

20. Daniel Carlat, *Unhinged. The trouble with Psychiatry. A Doctor's Revelations about a Profession in Crisis* (NY: Free Press, 2010), 97. Whitaker, *An Anatomy of an Epdemic.*

21. Public distrust of pharma: Abandon social media? PRforPharma. http://prforpharma.com/2010/12/10/public-distrust-of-pharma-abandon-social-media/

22. Alan Cassels, "Pfizer eyes Canada. World's biggest drug maker sets it's sights on Canadian healthcare," Common Ground, January 2010, 12-14.

23. J. Lazarou, B.H. Pomeranz, P. Corey, "Incidence of adverse drug reactions in hospitalized patients: a meta-analysis of prospective studies," *Journal of the American Medical Association*, 279, #15, 1200-1205, April 15, 1998.

24. The Chronic Pain Association of Canada Newsletter, 13, no. 3, 2010, 9. See also Tara Parker-Pope "Reasons not to panic over a painkiller." *The New York Times*, Well, July 7, 2009. http://www.nytimes.com/2009/07/07/health/07well.html?pagewanted=print; Stats at George Mason University, "New risks from Tylenol raise question about chronic pain treatment," August 18, 2005. http://www.stats.org/record.jsp?type=logentry&ID=326

25. Alex Berenson, "For widely used drug, question of usefulness lingers." http://nytimes.com/2008/09/02/business/02vytorin.html?th=&adxnnl=1&emc=th&adxnnlx=1, 1.

26. FamilyDoctor,org. "Are herbal health products and supplements safe because they're natural? Undated.

27. The Chronic Pain Association of Canada Newsletter, Volume 14, no.1, 2010, 2.

28. Steven Woloshin and Lisa Schwartz, "Think inside the box." *The New York Times*. The Opinion Pages. July 4, 2011, 1-2.

29. Barry Meier, "Doctors who don't speak out," NYTimes.com, February 15, 2013, 1.

30 Angela Mailis-Gagnon & David Israelson, *Beyond Pain. Making the Mindbody Connection* (Toronto: Viking Canada, 2003), 226.

31. Marcia Angell. "The truth about the drug companies." *The New York Review of Books,* July 15, 2004, 52-55.

32. Patrick Wall, *Pain: The Science of Suffering* (NY: Columbia University Press, 2000), 170-171.

33. Marcia Angell, 55.

34. In Sharon Kirkey, "Canadians in pain: Controls on drugs too tight, editorial says." Postmedia News, August 22, 2011. http://www.timescolonist.com/story_print.html?id=5256812&sponsor=

35. Marcia Angell, The Truth, 58.

8   Don't believe the nice man knocking on your door

1. Harold Merskey & Robert Teasell, "The disparagement of pain: Social influences on medical thinking," *Pain Research and Management,* 5(4), 2000, 259.

2. Ibid., 266.

3. Ulla Bergholm, Bengt H. Johansson & Hakan Johansson, "New diagnostic tools can contribute to better treatment of patients with chronic whiplash disorders," *Journal of Whiplast & Related Disorders,* 3(2), 2004, 7,9.

4. Tobias Smith, personal communication, October 2010.

5. N. R. Kleinfield & Steven Greenhouse, "A world of hurt: For injured workers, a costly legal swamp." *The New York Times,* Mach 31, 2009, 1, 3, 7. http://www.nytimes.com/2009/03/31/nyregion/31comp.html?_r=1&th=&emc=th&pagewanted=pr

6. The National Academies of Sciences, Institute of Medicine, "Relieving Pain in America: A Blueprint for Transforming Prevention, Care, Education, and Research." (Washington, D.C.:. National Academies Press, 2012), 46.

7. Tom Sandborn, "A decade's slide in help for hurt workers." http://thetyee.ca/News/2010/09/29/HurtWorkers, 1.

8. Ruth Dubin & Cheryl King Van Vlack, "Stop this ride. I want to get off! The chronic pain roller-coaster: Fuelled by stress and conflict." Canadian Pain Society Conference, May 14, 2010.

9. Ibid., 2-3.

10. Coralie Wales, "Being a rehabilitation professional working with people in pain in compensation systems." Unpublished Dissertation, The University of Sydney, Australia, 2011.

11. The MayDay Fund, "A Call to Revolutionize Chronic Pain Care in America: An Opportunity in Health Care Reform." November 4, 2009.

12. Relieving Pain, IOM, 148-149, 298-299.

13. Ibid., 46.

14. Stanford School of Medicine, "5 questions: Pizzo on the need for new approaches to pain." July 11, 2011. http://med.standford/edu/ism/2011/july/5q-pizzo-0711.html

15. Melanie Thernstrom, *The Pain Chronicles* (New York: Farrar, Straus and Giroux, 2010), 132.

16. Michael Ricciardelli, "Health insurance company CEOs total compensation in 2008." *Health Reform Watch. A Web Log of Seton Hall Law School's Center for Health & Pharmaceutical Law & Policy.* http://www.healthreformwatch.com/2009/05/20/health-insurance-ceos-total-compensation-in-2008, 3-4.

17. Merskey and Teasell, Disparagement, 267-268.

18. Ruth Dubin, "Trajectory of chronic non-cancer pain in six patients: A roller coaster ride." In McKenzie H., Quintner J., & Bendelow, G. *At the Edge of Being: The Aporia of Pain,* 2012, 47-64.

19. Gary W. Lea, "Secondary traumatization of work-related rehabilitation clients," *The Canadian Practioner. A Newsletter for Mental Health Providers*. April 1996 (22), 3, 6, 8.

20. Jeanne Lazo, "The comorbidity of pain and disability, and tips for pain practioners," *The Pain Practitioner*, 19(1), 2009, 40. (Lazo's book is *Persistence is Power! A Real-World Guide for the Newly Disabled Employee."*)

21. Greg Smith, "Why I am leaving Goldman Sachs." Op-Ed, *The New York Times*, March 14, 2012.

22. Mark Sullivan, "Exaggerated pain behavior: By what standard?" *Clinical Journal of Pain*, 20 (6), 2004, 433.

9   The opioid dilemma as seen through the eyes of pain

1. ScienceDaily, "Chronic pain in homeless people not managed well, study finds; Almost half reported using street drugs to treat their pain." July 21, 2011. http://www.sciencedaily.com/releases/2011/07/110721112613.htm

2. Centers for Disease Control and Prevention, "Prescription pain killer overdoses in the U.S." http://www.cdc.gov/Features/VitalSigns/PainkillerOverdose/index.html; Sanjay Gupta, CNNHealth, "Let's end the prescription drug death epidemic," November 19, 2012. http://www.cnn.com/2012/11/14/health/gupta-accidental-overdose; Centers for Disease Control and Prevention, "Policy impact: Prescription painkiller overdoses." http://www.cdc.gov/homeandrecreationalsafety/rxbrief/

3. Sanjay Gupta, "Let's end the prescription drug death epidemic," CNN Health, November 19, 2012.

4. Caleb Banta-Green, epidemiologist, in Ethan Morris, KCTS 9 Public Television Serving Seattle, Central Washington and British Columbia, "Prescription for abuse: The progression of prescribing opiates in Washington State," January 27, 2012.

5. Harriet Ryan and Soumya Karlamangla, "Opioids are bad medicine for chronic pain, say new federal guidelines." *Los Angeles Times*, March 15, 2016, www.latimes/science/science-now.

6. Tara Parker-Pope, "Reasons not to panic over a painkiller," *The New York Times*, July 7, 2009; *Nutrition Digest*, "Deadly NSAIDs," American Nutrition Association, 35(2), 2010.

7. Nutrition Digest, 5. See also Volume 37, No. 4.

8. Melinda Ammann, "The agony and the ecstasy," Reasononline, www.reason.com, April 2003, 2.

9. http://americannewsreport.com/demise-of-the-american-pain-foundation-can-help-end-the-opioid-lunacy-8814156.htlm p. 5

10. Ibid., p.6.

11. Scott Fishman, *The War on Pain*, with Lisa Berger (N. Y.: Quill, 2001), 94.

12. http://updates.pain-topics.org/2012/08/group-petitions-fda-to-change-opioid.html, p. 29.

13. Ibid.

14. Maginn Mark, Living with pain: I never shilled for pharma." http://americannewsreport.com/i-never-shilled-for-pharma-8814184.html, p. 2, May 11, 2012.

15. http://americannewsreport.com/demise-of-american-pain-foundation-can-help-end-the-opioid-lunacy-8814156.html, p. 14.

16. "Deadly Dose." Sanjay Gupta, CNN, November 18, 2012.

17. Kathleen Meyers, senior researcher for the Treatment Research Institute, in Maxwell Newfield, CNNHealth, "Prescription drug deaths: Two stories." November 19, 2012. http://www.cnn.com/2012/11/15/health/deadly-dose-jackson-rummler

18. Sabrina Tavernise, "F.D.A. toughens warning labels for some opioid painkillers." http://nyti.ms/25jx9bD, March 23, 2016.

19. Deadly Dose.

20. Jan Hoffman, "Patients in pain, and a doctor who must limit drugs." *The New York Times*, March 16, 2016, http://nyti.ms/1UAzsC5

21. http://Americannewsreport, p.13.

22. http://www.abovetopsecret.com/forum/thread784684/pg1

23. Ann M. Martino, "In search of a new ethic for treating patients with chronic pain: What can medical boards do?" *Journal of Law, Medicine & Ethics*, (26), 1998, 334-336.

10 Social stigma

1. In Rick Ruggles, "Stigma makes chronic pain worse," World-Herald, July 2, 2011. Http://www.omaha.com/article/20110702/LIVEWELL01/707029889/1161

2. The mark of Cain refers to Genesis 4 where God curses and put a mark on Cain, the firstborn son of Eve and Adam, for murdering his brother. The mark is often taken to be a physical mark, but has also been understood to be a sign. Throughout history, stigma has referred to in its physical sense to markings cut or burned into the skin of criminals, slaves, or traitors to visibly identify them as morally inferior person, to be avoided or shunned (see Wikipedia).

3. Erving Goffman, *Stigma: Notes on the Management of Spoiled Identity* (Harmondsworth, England: Pelican Books, 1968).

4. Milton Cohen, John Quintner, David Buchanan, Mandy Nielsen & Lynette Guy, Stigmatization of patients with chronic pain: The extinction of empathy. *Pain Medicine*, 2012, 12, 1637-1643.

5. Ibid., 1638.

6. Ibid., 1639.

7. Ibid., 1641.

8. See also John Quintner, Milton Cohen, David Buchanan, James Katz, & Owen Williamson, "Pain medicine and Its models: Helping or hindering?" *Pain Medicine*, 9(7), 2008, 824-834.

9. Amanda Nielsen, "Journeys with chronic pain: Acquiring stigma along the way." In Fernandez J. (Ed.) *Making Sense of Pain. Critical and Interdisciplinary Perspectives* (Oxford, UK: Inter Disciplinary Press), 2010, 43-55

10. Ibid.

11. Ruth Ellen Dubin, "Trajectory of chronic non-cancer pain in six patients: A roller coaster ride." In McKenzie H., Quintner J., & Bendelow, G. *At the Edge of Being: The Aporia of Pain*, 2012, 47-64.

12. Jean Jackson, "Stigma, liminality, and chronic pain: Mind-body borderlands," *American Ethnologist*, 32(3), 2005, 341.

13. Ibid., 340.

14. Nielsen, Journeys.

15. Richard Payne, "Hurting while Black: Racially based disparities in pain care," Newsletter of the American Pain Foundation, Summer 2003, 5; American Pain Society, "Racial and ethnic identifiers in pain management: The importance to research clinical practice, and public health policy," October 22, 2004; Sheri Hall, "The pain gap: Minorities in America are considered under treated for their pain from medical conditions," Asbury Park Press, March 15, 2005; Diane Hoffmann and Anita Tarzian, "The girl who cried pain. A bias against women in the treatment of pain," *The Journal of Law Medicine and Ethics*, 2001, 29.

16. Richard Payne, "Hurting While Black", 5.

11 How do we know that we know… let me count the ways

1. Many volumes have been written about the idea of control and related issues in how we consider what counts as knowledge. My own favorites include Richard J. Bernstein, *Beyond objectivism and relativism. Science, hermeneutics, and praxis.* Philadelphia: University of Pennsylvania Press, 1983; Morris Berman, *Coming to our senses. Body and spirit in the hidden history of the West.* NY: Bantam Books, 1990; Susan R. Bordo, *The flight to objectivity. Essays on Cartesianism and culture.* Albany: State University of New York Press, 1987; Gemma Corradi-Fiumara, *The other side of language. A philosophy of listening.* New York: Routledge, 1990; Gary Gutting, "How reliable are the social sciences?" *The New York Times, Opinionator.* May 17, 2012; Ilya Prigogine and Isabelle Stengers, *Order our of chaos. Man's new dialogue with nature.* New York: Bantam Books, 1984; Evelyn Fox Keller, *Reflections on gender and science.* New Haven: Yale University Press, 1985; Richard Tarnas, *The Passion of the Western mind. Understanding the ideas that have shaped our world view.* NY: Ballantine Books, 1991.

2. J. W. N. Sullivan, *Gallio or The Tyranny of Science* (Whitefish, Montana: Kessinger Publishing, 2006: A facsimile of the 1927 original), 33-35.

3. David A. Fishbain, Hubert L. Rosomoff , Robert Brian Cutler & Renee Stelle Rosomoff, "Secondary gain concept: A review of the scientific evidence," *The Clinical Journal of Pain,* 11(1), 1995, 16.

4. Sigmund Koch, "The nature and limits of psychological knowledge. Lessons of a century qua "science," *American Psychologist,* 36(3), 1981, 257.

5. Ludwig von Bertalanffy, *General system theory. Foundations, development applications* (New York: George Braziller, 1968), 114.

6. Winkler, K.J. "Questioning the science in social science. Scholars signal a 'Turn to interpretation," *Chronicle of Higher Education,* 1985, 30(17), 1-3; Randall, F. "Why scholars become story tellers." *The New York Times Book Review,* 1984, 31(1); Kenneth Gergen, "The social constructionist movement in modern psychology," *American Psychologist,* 1985, 40(3), 266-275; Lous Heshusius, The Newtonian mechanistic paradigm, special education, and contours of alternative: An overview, *Journal of Learning Disabilities,* 22(10), 1989.

7. Morris Berman, Coming to our senses. Body and spirit in the hidden history of the west (NY: Bantam, 1989), 117.

8. Corradi Fiumara, 20.

9. von Bertalanffy, General System Theory; B. G. Glaser and A. L. Strauss, *The discovery of grounded theory: Strategies for qualitative research* (Chicago: Aldine Publications, 1967).

10. A shortened version of this dissertation is *Meaning in life as experienced by persons labeled retarded: A participant observation study* (Springfield Illinois: Charles C. Thomas, 1981).

11. Nicole K. Y. Tang, Paul M Salkovskis, and Magdi Hanna, "Mental defeat in chronic pain: Initial exploration of the concept," *Clinical Journal of Pain,* 2007, 23(3), 222-232.

12. Nicole Y. Tang & Catherine Crane, "Suicidality in chronic pain: A review of the prevalence, risk factors and psychological links," *Psychological Medicine,* 36, 2006, 575-586.

13. See for instance Carol Jay Levy, *A Pained Life* (Xlibris Corporation, 2003), for a sober account of how she worked herself through the many considerations she brought to bear on whether or not to end her life. See also my memoir, *Inside Chronic Pain,* 116-120.

14. Howard Rome & Jeffrey Rome , "Limbically Augmented Pain Syndrome (LAPS): Kindling, corticolibic sensitization, and the convergence of affective and sensory symptoms in chronic pain disorders." http://onlinelibrary.wiley.com/doi/10.1046/j.1526-4637.2000.99105.x/abstract 25 December, 2001.

15. James Giordano, "Pain, depression, brain-mind, and healing: The potential complementarity of process and purpose," *The Pain Practitioner. Special issue on pain and depression: A Bio-psychosocial model.* 18(2), 2008, 7.

16. Rachel Wurzman, Wayne Jonas, & James Giordano, "Chronic pain and depression: A spectrum disorder?" *The Pain Practitioner. Special issue on pain and depression: A bio-psycho-social model.* 18(2), 2008, 20. Often, using the "Beck Depression Inventory," our depression is "found." This inventory was standardized on psychiatric populations from which those with significant physical illness and disability were excluded. That means I am statistically compared to people who are depressed but do not live with persistent pain and are not disabled – while I am encountering both.

17. http://dictionaryreference.com/browse/morbid

18. http://voices.yahoo.com/depression-serious-side-effect-chronic-pain-1049541.html

19. One of the best explanations of embeddedness and embodiedness can be found in the work of Francisco Varela, biologist, phenomenologist, and neuroscientist. See for instance, Francisco J. Varela, Evan Thompson, and Eleanor Rosch, *The embodied mind. Cognitive science and human experience.* Cambridge, MA: MIT Press, 1991.

20. David Fishbain et al., "Chronic pain-associated depression: Antecedent or consequence of chronic pain? A review," *Clinical Journal of Pain*, 1997, 13(2), 116-137. http://journals.lww.com/clinicalpain/Abstract/1997/06000/Chronic_Pain_Associated_Depression_Antecedent_or.6.aspx, 1-2.

21. Patrick Wall, Pain. *The Science of Suffering* (New York: Columbia University Press, 2000), 63.

22. Lachian A. McWilliams, Kate M. Saldanha, Bruce D. Dick, and Margo C. Watt, "Development and psychometric evaluation of a new measure of pain-related support preferences: The Pain Response Preference Questionnaire," *Pain Research & Management,* 14(6), 2009, 461, 469.

23. Sigmund Koch, "The nature and limits of psychological knowledge. Lessons of a century qua "Science," *American Psychologist,* 1981, 36(3), 258.

24. Sandra Thomas, "A phenomenological study of chronic pain," *Western Journal of Nursing Research*, 22, 2000, 683.

25. Arthur W. Frank, *Letting Stories Breath: A Socio-Narratology* (Chicago: University of Chicago Press, 2010), 42.

26. Kenneth Gergen and Mary M. Gergen, "Explaining human conduct: Form and function." In P. Secord (Ed.), *Explaining human behavior: Consciousness, human action, and social structure* (pp. 127-154), 1982. Beverly Hills: Sage.

27. Carr, "Memoir of a meta-analyst." In Daniel B. Carr, John D. Loeser, and David B. Morris (Eds.), *Narrative, Pain, and Suffering.* Seattle: IASP Press, 2005, 325-350.

28. My comments here are not meant to address the specifics of alternative methodologies and changes in notions of reliability and validity that accompany them. Doing so is beyond the parameters of this essay. There are now many texts addressing these matters available.

29. Scott Fishman, Clinical commentary. In Lous Heshusius, *Inside Chronic Pain* (Ithaca, N.Y.: Cornell University, 2009), 131; Will Rowe, personal communication, 2009.

30. Personal communication, Keith Ballard, 1992.

31. The title of the book by James I. Charlton says it all: *Nothing About Us Without Us. Disability, Oppression, and Empowerment* (Berkeley: University of California Press, 2000).

32. Sara D. Hirst, "An idiographic and phenomenological approach to understanding suicide." Dissertation Abstracts International, 2010, 1341.

33. Carrie Norman, Jacqueline L. Bender, Jaime Macdonald, Marcia Dunn, Scott Dunn, Bo Siu, Sander L. Hitzig, Alejandro R. Jadad, & Judith Hunter. "Questions that individuals with spinal cord injury have regarding their chronic pain: A qualitative study," *Disability and Rehabilitation*, 2010, 32(2), 115.

34. A.L. Dewar, K. Gregg, M.I. White, & J. Lander, "Navigating the health care system: Perceptions of patients with chronic pain." Public Health Agency Canada, 2000, 29(4). www.phac-aspc.gc.ca/publicat/cdic-mcc/29-4/ar_03-eng.php

35. Sandra P. Thomas, A phenomenological study, 686.

36. Amanda Nielsen, "Journeys with chronic pain: Acquiring stigma along the way." In Fernandez J. (Ed.), *Making Sense of Pain. Critical and Interdisciplinary Perspectives* (Oxford, UK: Inter-Disciplinary Press), 2010, 46.

37. Lennard P. Voogt, De ervaringswereld van patienten met chronische pijn: Een Empirisch-Fenomenologisch onderzoek. (The Lifeworld of Patients with Chronic Pain: An Empirical-Phenomenological Study.) (The Netherlands, Den Haag: LEMMA, 2009).

38. Ruth Dubin, "Trajectory of chronic non-cancer pain in six patients: A roller coaster ride." In McKenzie H., Quintner J., & Bendelow, G. At the Edge of Being: The Aporia of Pain, 2012, 47-64.

39. Gemma Corradi-Fiumara, *The Other Side of Language. Philosophy of Listening* (New York: Routledge), 1990

40. Ibid., 2.

41. Ibid., 8.

42. Chronic Pain Australia, "Pain Is Not Invisible Project. Interim report," September 2009.

43. Coralie Wales, Leaders' meeting of the National Pain Summit, ANZCA St. Kilda, Melbourne, September 17, 2009.

44. http://www.painexhibit.com/

45. David Biro, *The Language of Pain. Finding Words, Compassion, and Relief* (New York: Norton, 2010), 174-180.

46. Ibid, 177.

47. Daniel B. Carr, Memoir of a meta-analyst, 335.

48. In Linda Ware, "Worlds remade: inclusion through engagement with disability art," *International Journal of Inclusive Education.* 12(5-6), 2008, 575.

49. Daniel B. Carr, John D. Loeser, and David B. Morris (Eds.), *Narrative, Pain, and Suffering* (Seattle: IASP Press, 2005).

50. One such chapter is by Harald Gundel and Thomas R. Tolle, "How physical pain may interact with psychological pain: Evidence for a mutual neurobiological basis of emotions and pain." In Carr et all., *Narrative Pain, and Suffering.*

51. Peter Watson, "A last poem from Susan," *Pain Research & Management*, 17(1), 2012, 9.

52. For instance, there are three articles in *The Pain Practitioner*, 18(2), 2008, that are not formal research articles. Two are written by artists, and one is personal narrative by a (non-academic) person who lives with pain. All are at the very end of this 66 page issue. All three are, in my opinion, very good, and very informative on lives lived in chronic pain and I am glad they are there. But it is telling that they all were placed at the end of this issue, as if they are only afterthoughts.

53. Peter Kramer, "Why doctors need stories." *The New York Times, The Opinion Pages,* October 18, 2014, 4-6.

54. John Ware, "What and who is the "difficult" patient? Unpublished paper, 2010.

55. John L. Quintner, Milton L. Cohen, David Buchanan, James Katz, & Owen Williamson, "Pain medicine and its models: helping or hindering? *Pain Medicine*, ((7), 2008, 824, 829.

56. James Giordano, "Pain, depression, brain-mind, and healing, 7, 10.

57. Carr, Memoir of a meta-analyst, 343.

58. Arthur Frank, Letting Stories Breath, 90.

12 Anger and pain management: anger's context

1. Sandra M. LeFort & Lisa Cardas, *Chronic Pain Self-Management Program. Workbook,* (LeFort Cardas & Associates), 2008, 8-6, 8-7.

2. Ibid., 13-1.

3. Ibid., 8-7.

4. Ellen Mohr Catalano, & Kimeron N. Hardin. *The Chronic Pain Control Workbook. A Step-by-Step guide for Coping with and Overcoming Pain* (Oakland, CA: new Harbinger Publications), 1996, 88-92.

5. Ibid., 92; Margaret Caudill, *Managing Pain Before It Manages You* (N.Y.: Guilford Press), 2009, 120-122.

6. LeFort & Cardas, 8-7.

7. Tobias Smit, personal communication, November 2012. Mr. Smit insisted I identify him.

8. John W. Burns, Phillip J. Quartana, & Stephen Bruehl, "Anger management style Moderates effects of emotion suppression during initial stress on pain and cardiovascular responses during subsequent pain-induction," *Annals of Behavioral Medicine,* 34 (2), 2007, 154.

9. Ibid., 164.

10. Will Rowe, "It's OK to get mad about your chronic pain." ChronicPainConnection.com July 14, 2008. www.healthcentral.com/chronic -pain/c/3025/33555/shout/pf/

13 Suicide: the end of pain

1. Sharon Kirkey, "Who will end the pain?" Postmedia News, *Vancouver Sun,* October 2, 2011.

2. Mark A. Ilgen, Kara Zivin, Ryan J. McCammon, & Marcia Valenstein, "Pain and suicidal thoughts, plans and attempts in the United States," *General Hospital Psychiatry,* 30 (2008).

3. Carol Jay Levy, *A Pained Life* (Xlibris Corp., 2003), 315.

4. Chronic Pain Australia, "Pain is Not Invisible Project. Interim report," September 2009, 17.

5. In Sandra P. Thomas and Mary Johnson. "A Phenomenological study of chronic pain," *Western Journal of Nursing Research,* 22, 2000, 694.

6. In Thomas and Johnson, 294.

7. In James L. Henry, "The Need for Knowledge Translation in Chronic Pain," *Pain Research and Management,* 3 (6), 2008, 468.

8. Amy Paturel, "Living with pain," *NeurologyNow,* April/May, 2013. www.neurology-now.com

9. Lous Heshusius, *Inside Chronic Pain. An Intimate and Critical Account* (Ithaca, NY: Cornell University Press, 2009), 116-120.

10. Carol Levy, 265.

11. Heshusius, 113-115.

12. Nicole K. Tang and Catherine Crane, "Suicidality in chronic pain: A review of the prevalence risk factors and psychological links," *Psychological Medicine*, 36, 2006.

13. See Tang and Crane, 2006, and Betty Fisher, Jennifer Haythornthwaite, Leslie Hainberg, Michael Clark, and Jeffery Reed, "Suicidal intent in patients with chronic pain," *Pain*, 89(2), 2001, 199-206.

14. Liesl Fulton, personal communication, November 2009.

15. Morris Berman, *Coming to our Senses. Body and spirit in the hidden history of the West* (NY: Bantam Books, 1989), 110-117.

16. Daniel B. Carr, "Memoir of a Meta-Analyst: On the Silent "L" in "Qualntitative." In Daniel B. Carr, John D. Loeser, and David B. Morris (Eds.), *Narrative, Pain, and Suffering* (Seattle: IASP Press, 2005), 335, 337.

17. Sara D. Hirst, An idiographic and phenomenological approach to understanding suicide. Dissertation Abstracts International: Section B: The Sciences and Engineering, 2010, 1341

18. Ilgen et al., 523.

19. Ibid., 525

20. Ilya Prigogine and Isabelle Stengers, *Order Out of Chaos. Man's New Dialogue with Nature* (New York: Bantam Books, 1984). See also David Bohm and David Peat, *Science order, and Creativity* (New York: Routledge, 2000, second edition); S. A. Kauffman, *At Home in the Universe: The Search for the Laws of Self-organization and Complexity* (New York: Oxford University Press, 1995); M. M. Waldrop, *Complexity: The Emerging Science at the Edge of Order and Chaos* (Harmondsworth: Penguin Books, 1992).

21. Carr, memoir of a mega-analyst, 328.

22. "Far from equilibrium" is a construct used throughout Prigogine's and Stenger's work.

23. Tang and Crane, 583.

24. Lous Heshusius, *Inside Chronic Pain,* (Ithaca: Cornell University Press, 2009), 117.

14 The self in pain and others

1. Tobias Smit, personal communication, April 2012, printed with permission.

2. Polly Young Eisendrath, *The Gifts of Suffering* (N.Y.: Addison-Wesley, 1997), 41.

3. Wayne Connell & Sherri Connell, "But you look good! A Guide to understanding and encouraging people living with chronic illness and pain." www.Invisibledisabilities.org

4. Toni Bernard offers a similar list of Do's and Don't's: What those with chronic pain or illness DON'T want to hear, Turning Straw into Gold, blog, Psychology Today, June 27, 2012; What those with chronic pain or illness DO want to hear, Turning Straw into Gold, July 05, 2012; Part 2: What the chronically ill DON'T want to hear, Turning Straw into Gold, August 01, 2012.

5. Mary E. Lynch, "The need for a Canadian pain strategy." Editorial, *Pain Research & Management*, 16(2), 2011, 77.

6. Daniel: Paralyzed after car accident. http://www.painaustralia.org.au/stories/daniel-paralysed-after-car-accident.html

7. UCSF Mini Medical School for the Public, 13074, October 2007.

8. Angela Mailis-Gagnon & David Israelson, *Beyond Pain: Making the Mind-Body Connection* (Toronto: Viking Canada, 2003), 197.

9. Robert W. Teasell, "The denial of chronic pain," *Pain Research and Pain Management*, 1997. http://www.pulsus.com/Pain/02_-2/teas_ed.htm, p.3.

10. Dave: Doctor with pain. Chronic Pain Australia, Stories, webarchive.

11. In Robert Bazell, "Chronic pain frustrates patients, doctors." MSNBC.com 1/16/2006 http://www.msnbc.msn.com/id/10740529/print/1/displaymode/1098/.

12. Scott Fishman, *The War on Pain*, with Lisa Berger (New York: Quill, 2001), 94.

13. In www.psychologytoday.com/blog/turning-straw-gold/201410/i-m-sick-what-is-wrong-with-me

14. Patty Quinn, "Living with pain," *American Pain Monitor*, 2004.

15. In The Chronic Pain Association of Canada Newsletter, 13 (4), 2010, 6.

16. Eric J. Cassell, *The Nature of Suffering and the Goals of Medicine* (New York: Oxford University Press, 1991), 63.

17. Sharon Kirkey, *Who will stop the pain?* Postmedia News, Vancouver Sun, October 2, 2011.

18. Coralie Wales, "National Pain Summit Leaders' Meeting." ANZCA St. Kilda Melbourne. September 17, 2009.

15 Self help pain management programs: helping and hurting

1. Sandra M. LeFort with Lisa Cardas, *Chronic Pain Self-Management Program Workbook.* Lefort Cardas & Associates, 2008.

2. Margaret A. Caudill, *Managing Pain Before It Manages You* (NY: The Guilford Press, 2009).

3. Blake Tearnan, "10 simple solutions to chronic pain." (Oakland CA: New Harbinger Publications, 2007); John E. Sarno, *Healing Back Pain. The Mind-Body Connection. Without drugs, without surgery, without exercise, back pain can be stopped forever* (NY: Warner Books, 1991).

4. In Gillian Woodford, "All it took was an idea. Grassroots pain programs empower patients, ease family doctors' burden," *National Review of Medicine,* 2008 5(3), 1.

5. LeFort with Cardas, 3-2.

6. Ibid., 3-3.

7. Edward Hall, *The Silent Language* (New York: Anchor Books, 1973), 6-7.

8. See my extended description in *Inside Chronic Pain* of this phenomenon of the disappearance of time when in severe pain, pp. 37-40.

9. LeFort with Cardas, 13-1.

10. Marni Jackson, *Pain: The Science and the Culture of Why We Hurt* (Toronto: Vintage Canada, 2002), 144.

11. LeFort with Cardas, Chapter 6.

12. For any reader who thinks I am "catastrophizing," the last pain specialist I saw told me that as people living with pain get older, one third gets better, two thirds stay the same or get worse.

13. LeFort with Cardas, i, 2-1, 14-1.

14. Joanne Dahl & Tobias Lundgren, *Living Beyond Your Pain. Using Acceptance & Commitment Therapy to Ease Chronic Pain* (Oakland: New Harbinger Publications, 2006), 108.

15. Ibid., 128.

16. Ibid., 19.

17. Ibid., 166.

18. See for instance Caudill, 1; LeFort & Cardas, 8-4.

19. Arthur Rosenfeld, *The Truth about Chronic Pain* (New York: Basic Books, 2003); Marni Jackson, *Pain: The Science and the Culture of Why We Hurt* (Toronto: Vintage Canada, 2003); Sharon Kirkey, "Who will stop the pain?" *Postmedia,* Vancouver Sun, October 2, 2011; David Morris, *The Culture of Pain* (Berkeley: University of California Press, 1991); Elaine

Scarry, *The Body in Pain. The Making and Unmaking of the World* (New York: Oxford University Press, 1985); Alphonse Daudet, *In the Land of Pain*, ed. and trans. Julian Barnes (New York: Alfred A. Knopf, 2002); Arthur Frank, *The Wounded Story Teller. Body, Illness, and Ethics* (University of Chicago Press, 1995).

20. From MayoClinic.com, "Chronic pain: Managing your emotions." CNN.com, Health/Library, 2006, 1.

21. Ibid., 3.

22. Ibid., 4.

23. Eric J. Cassell, *The Nature of Suffering and the Goals of Medicine* (NY: Oxford University Press, 1991) 248.

24. Anthony Guarino, "Managing chronic pain through pain diaries and positive thought." In *Disaboom*, October 30, 2009, 3.

25. Ellen Catalano & Kimeron Hardin, *The Chronic Pain Control Workbook. A step-by-step guide for coping with and overcoming pain* (Oakland CA: New Harbinger, 1996), 74-76.

26. Caudill, 94-96.

27. Ibid., 102-103.

28. Ibid., 103-105.

29. Barbara Ehrenreich, *Bright-sided. How Positive Thinking is Undermining America* (N.Y.: Picador, 2010), http://www.barbaraehrenreich.com/brightsided.htm

30. From MayoClinic.com, "Chronic pain: Solidify your social support." CNN.com Health/Library, 2006, 2. http://www.cnn.com/HEALTH/library/PN/00012.html

31. Patty Quinn, "Living with pain," E-news for the Pain Community, American pain Foundation Pain Monitor, 2002.

32. In *The Pain Practitioner*, 2008, 18 (3), 42-43, 39.

33. Hildur Kalman and Naomi Scheman, "Inflecting pain: Expression, acknowledgment and interpersonal space." In Heather McKenzie, John Quintner, & Gillian Bendelow (Eds.), *At The Edge of Being. The Aporia of Pain* (Oxford, UK: Interdisciplinary Press, 2012),40.

34. The Chronic Pain Association of Canada Newsletter, 13(4), 2010, 6.

35. Tobias Smit, personal communication, April, 2012.

36. Female 25-29, in "Pain is Not Invisible Project. One year interim report." Chronic Pain Australia, September 2009, 11.

37. Cassell, 55.

38. See Temple Grandin and Catherine Johnson, *Animals in Translation* (New York: Scribner, 2005), 185-186. See also Heshusius, *Inside Chronic Pain* pp. 15-16.

39. Elaine Scarry, *The Body in Pain: The Making and Remaking of the World* (New York: Oxford University Press, 1985), 33.

40. I read this on a pain blog, but unfortunately misplaced the citation details.

41. Jennifer Schneider http://www.healthcom/health/condition-article/print/0,,20189550,00.html

42. Experiment noted in Andrew Mullins, "Solving the pain puzzle." *McGill News*, Spring/Summer, 2010. 17.

43. In Melinda Back, "Rewiring the brain to ease pain." *The Wall Street Journal, Health Journal*, November 15, 2011, 2.

44. Victor Frankl, *The Doctor and the Soul* (New York: Vintage Books, second edition, 1986), 54.

45. Catalano and Hardin, 91.

46. Ruth Dubin, "The trajectory of chronic pain: Can a community-based exercise/education program soften the ride?" *Pain Research and Management*, 2010, 15 (6), 366.

47. In Jean E. Jackson, "Stigma, liminality, and chronic pain: Mind-body borderlands. *American Ethnologist,* 32(3), 2005, 346.

48. Catalano & Hardin, 79.

49. Ibid., 81.

50. Ibid., 79.

51. Albert Schweitzer, *On the Edge of the Primeval Forest* (London: Adam & Charles Black), 1951, 92, 173.

52. Sandra M. LeFort, Katherine Gray-Donald, Katherine M. Rowat, Mary Ellen Jeans, "Randomized controlled trial of a community-based psychoeducation program for the self-management of chronic pain," *Pain,* 1998, 74, 297.

53. Ibid., 303.

54. Ibid., 302.

55. Ibid., 304.

56. Ibid., 298.

57. In Gillian Woodford, "All it took was an idea." Grassroots pain programs empower patients, ease family doctor's burden," *National Review of Medicine,* 2008, 5(3), 1.

58. LeFort et al., 304.

59. Coralie Wales, "The big Issue: National pain summit." Newsletter, Chronic Pain Australia, March 2010, 2. www.chronicpainaustralia.org

60. The article did not mention how the lack of success was determined in either the Australian or the Scottish model.

16 To take a true measure of our days…

1. David Bohm, *Wholeness and the Implicate Order* (Boston: Routledge &Kegan Paul, 1980), 21-22.

2. Elaine Scarry, *The Body in Pain: The Making and Unmaking of the World* (New York: Oxford University Press, 1985, 12-13.

3. "Jennifer Aniston had the 'hardest day' of her life filming Cake," US Weekly, January 7, 2015, 2.

4. http://www.the guardian.com/film/2014/sep/10/cake-review-jennifer-aniston-toronto-film-festival ; http://variety.com/2014/film/reviews/toronto-film-review.cake-1201301547/

5. Frank Bruni, Putting 'the cloak of Rachel' to rest. Awards season, The New York Times, January 7, 2015, 1-6.

6. Manohla Dargis, The grief spreads across the road to recovery. Movie Review, The New York Times, January 22, 2015, 1-3.

7. The last two characterizations of the film are in the review by Manohla Dargis. Meanings of the word "miasma" include a highly unpleasant or unhealthy smell or vapor; an oppressive or unpleasant atmosphere that emanates from something; poisonous effluvia or germs polluting the atmosphere; a cloud of foul-smelling vapor.

8. Philip Coulter CBC Ideas, *The Culture of Pain,* September 22-26, 2003, 47.